Rousseau

'the best general introduction to Rousseau's life and thought in English
and succeeds brilliantly in conveying Rousseau's ideas in a sympathetic
yet critical manner.'

Christopher Bertram, University of Bristol, UK

'. . . an intelligent and clearly written introduction . . . It will be of great use
to beginners who wish to orient themselves in the corpus of a writer who
produced a large number of works of great diversity. It provides all the
essential background information . . . those familiar with Rousseau will
also read it with profit.'

Christopher Kelly, Boston College, USA

Routledge Philosophers

Edited by Brian Leiter
University of Texas, Austin

Routledge Philosophers is a major series of introductions to the great Western philosophers. Each book places a major philosopher or thinker in historical context, explains and assesses their key arguments, and considers their legacy. Additional features include a chronology of major dates and events, chapter summaries, annotated suggestions for further reading and a glossary of technical terms.

An ideal starting point for those new to philosophy, they are also essential reading for those interested in the subject at any level.

Hobbes	A. P. Martinich
Leibniz	Nicholas Jolley
Locke	E. J. Lowe
Hegel	Frederick Beiser
Rousseau	Nicholas Dent
Schopenhauer	Julian Young
Freud	Jonathan Lear

Forthcoming:

Spinoza	Michael Della Rocca
Hume	Don Garrett
Kant	Paul Guyer
Fichte and Schelling	Sebastian Gardner
Husserl	David Woodruff Smith
Rawls	Samuel Freeman

Nicholas Dent

Rousseau

Routledge
Taylor & Francis Group

LONDON AND NEW YORK

FIRST INDIAN REPRINT 2008

First published 2005
by Routledge
2 Park Square, Milton Park, Abingdon, Oxon OX14 4RN

Simultaneously published in the USA and Canada
by Routledge
270 Madison Ave, New York, NY 10016

Routledge is an imprint of the Taylor & Francis Group

© 2005 Nicholas Dent

Typeset in Joanna MT and Din by RefineCatch Ltd, Bungay, Suffolk
Printed and bound in India by Replika Press Pvt. Ltd.

British Library Cataloguing in Publication Data
A catalogue record for this book is available from the British Library

Library of Congress Cataloging in Publication Data
Dent, N. J. H., 1945-
   Rousseau / by Nicholas Dent.
      p. cm.–(Routledge philosophers)
   Includes bibliographical references and index.
   ISBN 0-415-28349-3 (alk. paper) — ISBN 0-415-28350-7 (pbk. : alk. paper)
   1. Rousseau, Jean-Jacques, 1712–1778. I. Title. II. Series
   B2137.D46 2005
   194—dc22   2004021177

ISBN 0-415-28350-7 (pbk)

I cannot dissimulate from you, sir, that I have a violent aversion to the social classes that dominate others . . . I hate the great, I hate their position, their harshness, their prejudices, their pettiness, and all their vices, and I would hate them much more if I despised them less.

J.-J. Rousseau: Letter to Malesherbes, 28 January 1762 (tr. C.W. Hendel)

By inclination I am an inquirer. I feel a consuming thirst for knowledge, the unrest which goes with desire to progress in it, and satisfaction in every advance of it. There was a time when I believed this constituted the honor of humanity, and I despised the people, who know nothing. Rousseau corrected me in this. This blinding prejudice disappeared and I learned to honor man. I would find myself more useless than the common laborer if I did not believe that this attitude of mine [as an inquirer] can give worth to all others in establishing the rights of man.

Immanuel Kant: Fragments (tr. L.W. Beck)

Preface

Although I have tried in this book to do justice to most aspects of Rousseau's work, I should make it clear – as will no doubt be plain enough anyway from the body of the text – that I am more at home dealing with arguments and evaluating their cogency than I am with the perhaps more complex and subtle techniques of literary criticism and interpretation. I am conscious that this may have led to some imbalance, even though I tried to correct this.

Increasingly many writers on Rousseau argue for a real continuity of vision and intent between what would ordinarily be classified as his central philosophical works, such as the *Discourse on the Origin of Inequality*, *Émile* and *The Social Contract*, and his literary and auto-biographical works, again as ordinarily classified, such as *Julie* (or *La Nouvelle Héloïse*) and *The Confessions*. That there are commonalities of theme and concern is undeniable; it would be more remarkable if this were not so. But for myself I have some difficulty in seeing them as all of a piece as components in one comprehensive edifice. I am inclined to agree with Iris Murdoch, in her essay 'Literature and Philosophy', in thinking that the aims and salient characteristics of philosophy and of literature are markedly different. But whether or not this is right, I must acknowledge the hesitancy I experience in trying to move freely between these modes and in treating the works as being on a par. I have written elsewhere on Rousseau, and have from time to time drawn on this material for this present book. But at no point do I rely on knowledge of this other work.

I have received much valued personal support from Professor

Tim O'Hagan over many years, as well as being influenced by his thinking; I welcome the chance to acknowledge this. I am grateful for the comments of two referees on the manuscript, which have resulted in significant improvements. Especial thanks are owing to Jayne Rowson for word-processing my manuscript, and for much other assistance.

I dedicate this book to Stephanie.

Nicholas Dent
Birmingham, 2004

Acknowledgements

Excerpts from *The Social Contract* and *Discourse on the Origin of Inequality*, translated and introduced by G.D.H. Cole, revised and augmented by J.H. Brumfitt and J.C. Hall, updated by P.D. Jimack (London: Dent Everyman, 1993). Reproduced by permission of the publisher.

Excerpts from *The Confessions*, translated and introduced by J.M. Cohen (Harmondsworth: Penguin, 1953). Copyright © J.M. Cohen, 1953. Reproduced by permission of Penguin Books Ltd.

Excerpts from *Émile, or On Education*, translated and introduced by Allan Bloom. Copyright © 1979 by Basic Books, Inc. Reprinted by permission of Basic Books, a member of Perseus Books, L.L.C.

In the body of the text, I normally refer to Rousseau's works, and to certain key texts, by means of abbreviations, as listed below. Details of these works, and the translations used, are given in the Bibliography at the end of this book.

C	*The Confessions*
Cole et al.	Jean-Jacques Rousseau: *The Social Contract and Discourses*, translated and introduced by G.D.H. Cole; revised and augmented by J.H. Brumfitt and J.C. Hall; updated by P.D. Jimack
DI	*Discourse on the Origin of Inequality*
DPE	*Discourse on Political Economy*
DSA	*Discourse on the Sciences and Arts*
E	*Émile, or On Education*
G	Rousseau: *The Discourses and Other Early Political Writings*; and *The Social Contract and Other Later Political Writings*, edited by Victor Gourevitch
GP	*Considerations on the Government of Poland*
OC	Jean-Jacques Rousseau: *Oeuvres Complètes*, edited by B. Gagnebin and M. Raymond, Five Volumes, I–V
PA	*Politics and the Arts: Letter to M. d'Alembert on the Theatre*, by Jean-Jacques Rousseau, translated and introduced by Allan Bloom
PCC	*Project for a Constitution for Corsica*
RJJ	*Rousseau Judge of Jean-Jacques: Dialogues*
RSW	*The Reveries of the Solitary Walker*
SC	*The Social Contract*

Specific references in the text give the book, chapter and page numbers (as applicable in the translations I have employed), followed by the volume and page numbers in the Gagnebin and Raymond edition of the *Oeuvres Complètes* (OC). I have tried as far as possible to make use of readily available translations of Rousseau's texts even if these are not necessarily the most comprehensive and scholarly.

Rousseau's life can be divided very roughly into three parts. First, the apprentice years (1712–49), in which most of his work is on music, and which ends with the 'illumination' on the way to Vincennes. Second, the years of maturity (1750–64), from which date his greatest works: *Le Devin du Village*, the *Discourses*, *La Nouvelle Héloïse*, *Émile*, *The Social Contract*, and the *Letter to d'Alembert*. Third, the years of decline (1764–78), marked by increasing mental disturbance and great self-absorption. His masterpiece *The Confessions* comes from this period, though much of his writing is prolix and uneven.

1712	28 June: Rousseau born in Geneva
	7 July: His mother dies
1722	His father flees Geneva
	Rousseau is put in the charge of his uncle; lives at Bossey
1725	Apprenticed to an engraver, Ducommun
1728	14 March: shut outside the gates of Geneva; leaves that city
	Meets Madame de Warens
	21 April: Abjures Protestantism, Turin
	Meets Abbé Gaime; steals a ribbon
1729	Trains as a musician; wanderings
1731	Works briefly for the royal surveying office
1733	Sexually initiated by Madame de Warens
1734	Claude Anet (Warens's lover/factotum) dies

	August: Experiences 'illumination' when on his way to visit Diderot at Vincennes
1750	July: *Discourse on the Sciences and Arts* (the First Discourse) wins Dijon Academy prize November: *First Discourse* published
1751	Replies to critics of *First Discourse* June: First volume of the *Encyclopedia* published
1752	Spring: Drafts opera, *Le Devin du Village* 18 October: *Le Devin* performed at Fontainebleau to great acclaim December: *Narcissus* performed at Comédie Française
1753	*Le Devin* published; *Narcissus* published November: *Letter on French Music* published; second Dijon Academy prize-essay topic, on inequality, announced *Essay on the Origin of Languages* begun about this time (never completed; published posthumously)
1754	Writes *Discourse on the Origin of Inequality* (the Second Discourse) Returns to Geneva to be readmitted to the Protestant Church and reclaim his citizenship 10 October: Returns to Paris
1755	June: *Second Discourse* published Article on political economy (future (*Discourse on*) *Political Economy*) published in volume V of the *Encyclopedia* *Letter to M. Philopolis*, critic of the *Second Discourse*
1756	Moves to Hermitage at Montmorency Works on 'Political Institutions'; compiles extracts from works of Abbé de Saint-Pierre (*Projet de Paix Perpétuelle*, published 1761; the rest published posthumously) July/August: *Letter to Voltaire on Providence* (unauthorised publication 1759, Berlin) Autumn: Starts work on *Julie, ou La Nouvelle Héloïse*

1757   Meets Sophie d'Houdetot
             Quarrels with Diderot
             October: D'Alembert's article on Geneva appears in vol.
             VII of the *Encyclopedia*
             December: Leaves the Hermitage; moves to Montlouis
             Winter: *Moral Letters* written for Sophie d'Houdetot
             (published posthumously)

1758   Working on *La Nouvelle Héloïse*; starts work on *Émile*
             September: *Letter to M. d'Alembert on the Theatre* published
             Takes *Vitam impendere vero* as his personal motto
             Finally breaks with Diderot

1759   Voltaire publishes *Candide*; indirect reply to Rousseau's
             letter of 1756

1760   *La Nouvelle Héloïse* completed; *Émile* and *The Social Contract*
             well in hand
             Les Amours de Milord Édouard Bomston drafted

1761   January: *La Nouvelle Héloïse* published
             Asks Madame de Luxembourg to help find his
             abandoned children

1762   January: writes *Letters to Malesherbes* (published
             posthumously)
             April: *The Social Contract* published
             May: *Émile* published
             June: *Émile* denounced and burned; flees Paris; *Le Lévite
             d'Éphraïm* written during his flight
             19 June: *Émile* and *The Social Contract* burnt in Geneva
             July: Settles at Môtiers; Madame de Warens dies
             August: Christophe de Beaumont, Archbishop of
             Paris, publishes a decree against *Creed of a Savoyard
             Vicar*
             Autumn/winter: writes *Émile et Sophie, ou les Solitaires*
             (published posthumously)

1763   March: *Letter to Christophe de Beaumont* published
             May: Renounces Genevan citizenship

Autumn: Publication of J.-R. Tronchin's *Letters Written from the Country*

1764 August: Receives a letter from Buttafoco concerning Corsica

Starts work on *Project for a Constitution for Corsica* (unfinished; published 1861)

December: *Letters Written from the Mountain* published; Boswell visits; Voltaire publishes (anonymously) *The Sentiments of the Citizens*

1765 Work on *Dictionary of Music* largely completed

Stones are thrown at his house in Môtiers; he leaves

Interlude on island of Saint-Pierre

December: Arrives in Paris

1766 4 January: Leaves for England with Hume

Works on *The Confessions* at Wootton

June/July: Quarrels with Hume

In great mental distress

October/November: Hume's *Concise Account*

1767 May: Returns to France; lives near Paris

November: *Dictionary of Music* published

Late in year: Leaves Paris for Switzerland

1768 August: Marries Thérèse in Bourgoin

1770 Returns to Paris via Lyons

Finishes *The Confessions* (published posthumously); gives readings from it to friends

1771 Drafts *Considerations on the Government of Poland* (illicit copies circulated 1772; published posthumously)

1772 Works on *Rousseau Judge of Jean-Jacques: Dialogues* and writings on botanical studies

Writes *Elementary Letters on Botany* (published posthumously)

Starts *Dictionary of Botanical Terms* (unfinished)

1774 Meets Gluck

Works on his last opera, *Daphnis et Chloé* (unfinished)

1776   Completes *Rousseau Judge of Jean-Jacques* (published posthumously)
24 February: Attempts to place the manuscript on the high altar of Notre-Dame
May: Writes pamphlet *To All Frenchmen* . . . .
Autumn: Knocked down by a dog
Begins work on *Reveries of the Solitary Walker* (unfinished; published posthumously)

1778   20 May: Moves to Ermenonville
2 July: Dies; is buried on the Île des Peupliers

1780–9   Moultou and Du Peyrou publish the *Collected Works*, including many otherwise unpublished pieces from Rousseau's last ten years

1794   Rousseau's body is transferred to the Panthéon

See also OC I, CI–CXVIII for a comprehensive chronological table

One

Introduction

THE SUBJECT OF THIS BOOK

This book is about the key ideas of the great eighteenth-century philosopher Jean-Jacques Rousseau. Born in Geneva in 1712, he died at Ermenonville (then just outside Paris but now virtually a suburb) in 1778. Most famous nowadays for his contributions to social and political theory, with *The Social Contract* of 1762, an essay on the fundamental questions of social justice and political legitimacy, being his best-known work in this area and probably overall, he also wrote a best-selling novel, *Julie, or The New Héloïse* (1761); a very important book on educational theory though with a wider intent, *Émile, or On Education* (1762); an extraordinarily original and influential autobiography, *The Confessions*, written between 1764–1770 and published posthumously; other works of self-interpretation and self-defence; essays on language and musical theory, a dictionary of music and a successful opera; works on botany, and a host of other things. This prodigious and wide-ranging output earned him an enormous if controversial reputation at the time, and many of his ideas have continued to have a powerful impact ever since.

The course of his life is also very remarkable. His mother died just a few days after his birth; he left Geneva on an impulse when he was not yet sixteen, converted to Roman Catholicism, was taken in by and became the lover of a woman thirteen years older than himself. That relationship failing after several years, he went to Paris to make his name, had his opera performed at Fontainebleau before

Louis XV and Madame de Pompadour, became an intimate of the leading Enlightenment thinkers of the time, but then withdrew wholly from fashionable society. He was subjected to persecution for his ideas, his books being publicly burnt in Paris and in Geneva, came to England with the great empiricist philosoper and historian David Hume, suffered an acute paranoid breakdown and eventually returned to Paris where, after a further period of severe mental distress, he seems finally to have found some repose of mind and body before his death. All these matters will be considered in more detail in Chapter 2 (and see also the chronological table on pp. xiv–xix). This is far from being the life of a cloistered academic who is troubled only by a misplaced comma!

Clearly this is a body of work – and a man – of formidable interest, and this book aims to go some way towards explaining the nature and significance of his ideas and why his thinking merits our attention.

THE AIMS OF THE BOOK

This book aims to present and assess in a clear and accessible way the arguments and ideas that are, as I believe, central to Rousseau's achievement and make him a writer deserving of our interest. A study of these arguments and ideas is necessarily a study of the works in which they are expressed, so I will look quite closely at a selection of Rousseau's writings, and touch on many of the rest of them. I quote fairly extensively from Rousseau's works so that direct acquaintance with his manner and style can be had – albeit in translation – but also so that the basis of the interpretations I shall be offering can be seen. However, as noted, my principal concern is to understand and assess Rousseau's core arguments and ideas so the treatment overall will be thematic and issue-driven, not just a matter of expository presentation and summary.

I have tried to make the material accessible to those who have little or no previous knowledge of Rousseau's thought, of the concerns that exercised him and the key ideas for which he is celebrated, though I acknowledge that there are some difficult parts. I hope to be able to say enough about his work to demonstrate its importance, why it continues to exert a hold over the imagination of many, and why it justifies sustained reflection and assessment, which I hope some readers will feel sufficiently interested to go on to undertake. However, because of the limited aims of this present account, I shall for the most part avoid involvement in interpretative controversy and scholarly debate and try to offer a treatment that is clear, plain and reasonably definite even if this means being a bit cavalier about some tricky issues. I feel it is better to offer a decided line of account in a fairly uncluttered way rather than get lost in the confusion of a thousand qualifications, whilst accepting that certain complexities will get passed over. The Further Reading section at the end of each chapter will quickly lead one to different approaches and assessments which will supplement and challenge this present one. The idea of any definitive account of Rousseau's thinking is highly implausible. I have tried to present a responsible and cogent assessment without any pretence of finality.

THE PLAN OF THE BOOK

As noted above – and spelt out more fully in Chapter 2 – the range and variety of Rousseau's output is very great and it would be impossible in a book of this kind to try to do justice to all the elements it contains. I have selected for attention those among his works which I consider to be the most significant and enduring, and in assessing these I have picked out the themes that seem to me the most interesting and challenging. For the most part I shall be taking the works I consider in chronological order, but, as I said earlier, my treatment of these will be guided by attention to the key arguments and ideas I am foregrounding.

The works to which I give most attention are:

Discourse on the Sciences and the Arts (1750)
Discourse on the Origin of Inequality (1755)
Discourse on Political Economy (1755/58)
Émile, or On Education (1762)
The Social Contract (1762)
The Confessions (written 1764–70; published posthumously)

However, I shall touch, in more or less detail, on a great many others as well.

The themes in Rousseau's thinking to which I give greatest prominence are these:

- his account and critique of the corruption of man that civilisation brings;
- his concern with power relations between people;
- his celebration of 'natural' man;
- the role of the sentiments of *amour de soi* and *amour-propre*;
- his account of the foundations of political legitimacy and the role of the general will;
- his emphasis on liberty, fraternity and equality in a just and humane society;
- his account of the role of national culture and religion in the lives of individuals and in a just society.

Though much, I fully accept, is put to one side by highlighting these points, they are certainly highly interesting and important matters arising from Rousseau's work and worthy of close attention.

Very roughly, Chapter 3, which treats of the three *Discourses*, concerns the issues of man's corruption and of power relations between people in society. Chapter 4, on *Émile*, considers natural man, and the significance of *amour de soi* and *amour-propre*. Chapter 5, on *The Social Contract*, treats of political legitimacy, the general will, liberty and equality; Chapter 6 looks at fraternity and the role of culture and religion in society. Chapter 7 considers *The Confessions* and, for reasons that will become clear there, returns to the idea of 'natural' man; and, finally, Chapter 8 looks briefly at Rousseau's intellectual legacy and influence. However, much else is also considered as we go along, and the above is only a broad indication of where the themes and the works considered interact. In Chapter 2, I shall be giving a conspectus of Rousseau's life and works.

WHY READ ROUSSEAU?

This book highlights Rousseau's ideas in the areas of individual psychology, social and moral theory and political philosophy. In each of these areas he made highly original contributions which still, in my estimation, have great force and penetration.

Rousseau develops an account of human relationships as very commonly pervaded by an aggressive desire to gain ascendancy over others, to glory in their abjection. This leads, in his view, to the development of a false self, a *persona* (mask) created to try to achieve invidious distinction which alienates people from their own true need and good and makes them cripplingly dependent on the regard and acclaim they solicit from others. Relations between individuals are shot through with deceit and manipulation, and social processes and structures incorporate and consolidate patterns of domination and subordination, mastery and subjection. There is in this the most acute psychological and social observation that is revelatory, in my estimation, not just of what went on in eighteenth century Paris but of a very great deal of what goes on in the lives of individuals and in the dynamics of society today. With these ideas Rousseau anticipates some of the central concerns of both Hegel and Marx, for all that they distance themselves from him (as noted in Chapter 8 below).

To set against this nightmarish vision of man and society, Rousseau argues that human well-being and happiness require relations of mutual respect, equality of status and full participation in the life, and legislative authority that determines the laws, of a society. Only in this way can man's true nature and needs find expression and satisfaction. He stresses the inherent dignity of and regard due to every person, and considers at length the forms of sovereignty, legislative organisation and processes that can best acknowledge this in a just, enduring and prosperous community. He argues for a form of civil authority in which everyone would have an equal voice in determining the declarations of that authority, in so doing setting an agenda for political change, the full ramifications of which we are still struggling with today, or so it seems to me. Although, of course, no one person's influence ever provides the whole story, the fact that today no arguments for political legitimacy can gain any sustained hearing, at least across much of the world, unless they incorporate the enfranchisement of all adult members of a society must in some part be due to the power of Rousseau's ideas.

Rousseau also argues that a great deal of what passes for morality and moral education is little more than coercion and bullying, which so far from improving the individual generates the very vices it purports to restrain. He seeks to put in place of this an ethic based on compassion for the vulnerable and oppressed, responded to with gratitude for help and support received, which involves a reciprocity of regard and care rather than submission to the pressures of moral demands. Finally in this thumbnail sketch, Rousseau's work celebrates simplicity of taste, manners and lifestyle, emphasising a delight in nature and in the development of individual sensibility and genius – so-called 'Romantic' ideas that were to have a massive influence.

Whether the temper of mind I have sketched here is found congenial I am unable to predict. But that we have here an array of ideas that is rich, powerful and striking is hard to deny, and I hope simple curiosity – if nothing else – would make one want to know more. I hope this book will go some way to satisfying that curiosity, but perhaps also convey something of a very distinctive and forceful mind at work.

I turn now to a somewhat fuller account of Rousseau's life, and to giving an overview of the range and variety of his works.

FURTHER READING

Robert Wokler, *Rousseau – A Very Short Introduction*. Oxford: Oxford University Press, 2001. An outstanding overview of Rousseau's work in a brief compass.

Ronald Grimsley, *The Philosophy of Rousseau*. Oxford: Oxford University Press, 1973. Another fine essay looking at all aspects of Rousseau's achievement.

Allan Bloom, 'Jean-Jacques Rousseau' in Leo Strauss and Joseph Cropsey (eds.) *History of Political Philosophy*. Chicago: University of Chicago Press, 1987 (third edition). An illuminating survey essay.

Peter Gay, 'Reading about Rousseau' in Peter Gay, *The Party of Humanity – Studies in the French Enlightenment*. London: Weidenfeld & Nicolson, 1964. A highly interesting essay on how Rousseau has been read over the years.

N.J.H. Dent, *A Rousseau Dictionary*. Oxford: Blackwell, 1992. Covers all of Rousseau's work in a dictionary format.

Colin Jones, *The Great Nation – France from Louis XV to Napoleon 1715–99*. London: Allen Lane, The Penguin Press, 2002. An engaging and accessible history of France during Rousseau's time.

Two

Life and Key Works

In this chapter I will give an account of the principal episodes of Rousseau's life, and offer a picture of its general shape. I will then give an outline of his central works but also of other works not studied closely in this book, so that an overall idea of the totality of his output can be obtained. Finally, I will develop further those key ideas I sketched in the Introduction as providing the dominant themes that give this discussion of Rousseau's work its direction and focus.

ROUSSEAU'S LIFE

Rousseau was born in Geneva on 28 June 1712, the second son of Isaac Rousseau and his higher-status and wealthier wife Suzanne, née Bernard. Jean-Jacques was baptised on 4 July into the Calvinist faith of that city; two days later, his mother died aged forty. Many have seen in this loss of his mother a profoundly formative influence on not only Rousseau's personality but also on what he identified, in his reflective writings, as the best form of human relationship, involving a directness and immediacy he never experienced.

Rousseau's father was a full citizen of Geneva. The city at that time included three orders of inhabitants, and full citizens who enjoyed political rights comprised less than ten per cent of the population. He was a reasonably well-educated man, a watchmaker by trade, with strong literary interests, and Rousseau tells, in The Confessions, of the reading he did with his father at an early age, which included much Plutarch, Rousseau's favourite author at this time:

Plutarch ... was my especial favourite, and the pleasure I took in reading and re-reading him did something to cure me of my passion for novels ... Continuously pre-occupied with Rome and Athens, living as one might say with their great men, myself born the citizen of a republic and the son of a father whose patriotism was his strongest passion, I took fire by his example and pictured myself as a Greek or a Roman.

(C I: 20, OC I: 9)

Isaac Rousseau's fortunes declined, and after a fight he was obliged to flee Geneva in 1722. Jean-Jacques was placed in the care of his maternal uncle and together with his cousin Abraham was sent to live at Bossey, not far away. Here Rousseau spent some idyllic years recalled with great beauty in The Confessions, but also experienced the distresses of injustice and the erotic arousal that pain can bring. (See further, Chapter 7 below.) When he and Abraham returned to Geneva, the differences in their social standing and wealth became apparent. Rousseau was apprenticed to an engraver who was a harsh, imperious master.

In March 1728, Rousseau's life took a dramatic new turn. Returning in the evening from a trip outside the city gates, he found they were locked. He decided to leave, and take his chance in the wider world. After a couple of days' wandering, he was directed to Annecy to meet Françoise-Louise de la Tour, Baronne de Warens, who was paid to seek out and assist potential Catholic converts. Quite soon their lives were to become very closely linked; but first she sent him on to Turin for instruction, and he abjured Protestantism towards the end of April 1728. No solid occupation came his way immediately in Turin, but after some vicissitudes, including episodes of abject love and bizarre exhibitionism, he eventually found a place as a servant in the house of the Comtesse de Vercellis. There took place an event that was to be permanently burned into Rousseau's conscience. He stole a ribbon but falsely accused another servant, Marion, of the theft. He returned to this shameful episode on more than one occasion in his later writings. Finally, in June 1729, he made his way back to the house of Madame de Warens, but she was away in Paris and for the next eighteen months Rousseau's life was very unsettled. He eked out a living giving music lessons for which he was scarcely qualified, and picked up other scraps, but mostly he took part in the heedless adventures of youth. In the autumn of 1731 he eventually settled with Madame de Warens in Chambéry, remaining with her for roughly the next ten years.

Theirs was a strange and remarkable relationship. She called him her *petit*; she was his *maman*. But when he reached twenty-one, she decided to initiate him sexually, an event which appears to have caused him as much confusion and sadness as given him any pleasure. Madame de Warens's factotum, Claude Anet, also lived in this eighteenth-century hippy house and was another of her lovers. When he died, in 1734, Rousseau took his place more completely, not only as a sexual partner but also as a not very effective administrator of her affairs. Rousseau read voraciously during this time, in history, mathematics, musical theory, philosophy and much more; and his own first attempts at writing date from 1737/8. By this time, however, the intimacy and delight he enjoyed with Madame de Warens were beginning to pass away. A preferred lover and assistant, Wintzenried, took Rousseau's place, and another phase of his life was coming to an end.

It was with some keenness, then, that he travelled to Lyons in 1740 to become the tutor to the two sons of Jean Bonnot de Mably, a wealthy nobleman and chief of police. While in that city Rousseau wrote two short essays on education for de Mably, and some poems of no great distinction addressed to Lyonnais friends. In 1741 he returned briefly to Madame de Warens, but there was no further pleasure to be had on either side, and Rousseau determined to set off for Paris to make a career and name for himself. He took with him his *Project for a New Musical Notation* and a draft of his play *Narcissus* (or The Self-Lover), begun some years before. Letters of introduction from the de Mably family gave Rousseau an entrée into cultivated Parisian society, and in August 1742 he was able to present his *Project* to the Academy of Sciences. It received a mixed reception, but he continued to work on it and a modified version was published a year later. Rousseau began to make friends among the rising radical intelligentsia in Paris, most particularly with Denis Diderot, but did not find any settled position or income, and in June 1743 he went to Venice as secretary to the French ambassador. They were soon at odds, however, and Rousseau returned to Paris in the late summer of 1744. Once back, he worked intensively on various musical projects and, in 1745, he began his lifelong liaison with Thérèse Levasseur, an illiterate laundry maid with an interfering mother, who became his mistress, the mother of his five children – all given up to the foundling hospital – and eventually, in 1768, his wife. His relationship with her does appear in many ways strange. Although he often speaks highly of her loyalty and devotion to him, he seems to have directed his own passionate feelings into hopeless romances with high-born women, of which more below.

Still without any really settled path for his life, Rousseau worked for a while as secretary – companion to members of the Dupin family, and continued to see much of Diderot and the emerging *encyclopédiste* circle, that is those involved with the preparation of the famous *Encyclopédie ou Dictionnaire Raisonné des Sciences, des Arts et des Métiers*, edited by Diderot and d'Alembert, the palmary document of 'enlightened' thinking. He himself prepared many articles on music for this *Encyclopedia*. Then, in August 1749, the most fundamental change in Rousseau's life took place. Diderot's 'advanced' views had brought him into conflict with the authorities, and he was imprisoned at Vincennes, just outside Paris. Rousseau went to visit him there, on the way reading the *Mercure de France* in which was announced a prize-essay topic set by the Academy of Dijon asking whether the progress of the sciences and arts had had the effect of purifying morals. Rousseau was transfixed when he saw this; so many ideas and speculations crowded in on him that he felt faint and had to stop for a while. This 'illumination' on the road to Vincennes, he later said, fixed the course of the rest of his life. The first outcome of this new path was his writing the *Discourse on the Sciences and Arts*, often referred to as his *First Discourse*, which won the prize and was then published in late 1750. His thesis, that the advance of science and the arts had in fact corrupted morals, attracted much attention and elicited several replies including one from the King of Poland to which Rousseau, sometimes with care and sometimes somewhat impatiently, replied.

For the next twelve years Rousseau worked with enormous intensity, and his greatest works stem from this period of his life as he tried progressively to articulate everything that he had caught a glimpse of in his moment of illumination. At first, however, musical activities still claimed his attention. In the spring of 1752 he wrote the words and music for *Le Devin du Village* (The Village Soothsayer), his only really enduring musical achievement. This entertainment was performed before Louis XV and Madame de Pompadour at Fontainebleau in October 1752 to great acclaim, and Rousseau had the opportunity to receive a pension from the king. Nonetheless, pleading illness and, later on, republican sentiments, Rousseau returned to Paris, passing up the chance to secure a steady income. *Le Devin* was also put on at the Paris Opéra; and he became further involved in musical affairs when, as the result of the visit of a travelling Italian opera company, *Les Bouffons*, a heated debate arose about the relative merits of French and Italian music. Rousseau threw his weight behind the Italian side, and his *Letter on French Music*, in which he was highly critical of such music and of the fitness of the French language to be set to music, was published in 1753. This caused a great stir and afforded him yet more public attention.

That same year, however, he left these concerns behind. A further prize-essay topic was announced by the Dijon Academy, concerning the origin and justification of inequality, and Rousseau wrote one of his most powerful and important works, the *Discourse on the*

Origin of Inequality, the *Second Discourse*, in response to this question; he did not win the prize on this occasion. At about this time he also began work on his *Essay on the Origin of Languages*, which brings together many of his musical and political preoccupations; but although substantial parts of the *Essay* survive, he never completed it. In the *Second Discourse*, Rousseau argues that modern society incorporates deep and hateful inequalities which lack any justification and cause people to live lives of profound self-estrangement and misery. His views, and also his difficult temperament, placed him now increasingly at odds with many in Parisian society, and in June 1754 he returned to Geneva for a while to be readmitted to the Protestant faith and reclaim his citizen's rights. The *Second Discourse* contains a long and passionate dedication to Geneva, as a city embodying all virtues, a view Rousseau was not to retain all that long even should he have meant it seriously at this time. It was published in August 1755; and a few months later his long entry on political economy appeared in Volume V of the *Encyclopédie*, soon published separately as *A Discourse on Political Economy*, sometimes referred to as the *Third Discourse*.

In April 1756, tired of the artificial life of the salons and the distractions of the city, Rousseau left Paris to live at Montmorency in a cottage, the Hermitage, lent to him by a wealthy friend, Madame d'Épinay, and the five years that followed were the creative climax of his life. He continued work on his large project on political institutions, first conceived when he was in Venice; on preparing extracts from the work of the Abbé de Saint-Pierre, the *Project for Perpetual Peace* and the *Polysynodie*; in rebutting, in his *Letter on Providence*, what he saw as Voltaire's shallow pessimism expressed in his *Poem on the Lisbon Earthquake*; on collecting together, and adding to, the articles on music he had written for the *Encyclopédie* in preparation for a comprehensive *Dictionary of Music*; and in thinking about a treatise on morality and experience, 'La Morale Sensitive, ou le Matérialisme du Sage', which, however, came to nothing.

But what occupied him above all to begin with was something

he had not at all envisaged when he first moved to the country. Walking in the forest of Montmorency, he became entranced by a fantasy world peopled by his amorous visions, and out of this came the plan for his epistolary novel *Julie, ou La Nouvelle Héloïse*. The heroine of this novel took incarnate form when in early 1757 he met Sophie d'Houdetot, Madame d'Épinay's sister-in-law, with whom he fell desperately in love. What Thérèse made of this we do not know. The heady mix of erotic longing and preaching of virtuous restraint that pervades at least the opening episodes of *Julie* is also to some degree seen in the curious love gift of the *Lettres Morales* he wrote for Sophie in the winter of that year. His involvement with her was ill-liked by others of his friends and there was an irrecoverable falling out with Madame d'Épinay by the end of 1757, leading to Rousseau's moving out of the Hermitage to accept support from the Duke and Duchess of Luxembourg. Work on his novel did not proceed without other distractions also. Rousseau's friend, and co-editor with Diderot of the *Encyclopédie*, d'Alembert wrote an article on Geneva for the *Encyclopédie* recommending that a theatre be established there. Rousseau was roused to defend the customs and habits of his native city and wrote in response an extensive and forceful essay, his *Letter to M. d'Alembert on the Theatre* published in 1758.

Julie was finally published in early 1761 and was a runaway best-seller. Yet his triumph did not last long. Sometime in 1758 Rousseau had begun writing *Émile*, which he thought his greatest work, and that was being prepared for publication in 1761. At the same time, the residue of his now abandoned treatise on political institutions was being given its final form as the text of his most famous work, *The Social Contract*. The process of publication of *Émile* did not go smoothly, and Rousseau, who was ill and depressed and feared plots against him, wrote four letters to Malesherbes about himself and his attitude to life. Malesherbes, the director of publications (censor) who regulated what could and could not be published, had long shown a friendly interest in Rousseau and given support

to his work, perhaps in spite of his official role. These letters antici-
pate the great autobiographical works that occupied Rousseau in
the last fifteen or so years of his life, giving, for instance, his first
account of his 'illumination'. But this support was to no avail.
When The Social Contract was published in April 1762, and Émile in
May, the consequences for Rousseau were catastrophic. Primarily
because of a long section in the latter entitled 'The Profession of
Faith (Creed) of the Savoyard Vicar', which was judged to contain
subversive and heretical views, it was condemned by the Catholic
authorities, copies of it were burnt, and Rousseau was to be
arrested.

Warned of this, he fled to Yverdon, Switzerland, on 9 June, but
after the Genevan authorities had also banned and burned Émile
together with The Social Contract he had to move on again, to the
relative safety of Môtiers, under the protection of Frederick II of
Prussia. These frightful events do not at first seem to have unhinged
Rousseau. Even as he was on the road away from Paris he wrote a
short prose poem, The Levite of Ephraïm, which he declared later to be
his 'dearest' work, though it is, in my view, a very odd piece of
writing. In addition, he set to work to rebut the condemnation of
his work. He wrote a strong essay, defending Émile and himself
against the charges laid by the Archbishop of Paris, the Letter to
Christophe de Beaumont published in 1763, which also usefully summarises what Rousseau saw as key pervasive ideas running through
all his work. In July 1762, Madame de Warens died, an event which
seems to have left Rousseau unmoved at the time, though he later
made some amends in his last work, The Reveries of the Solitary Walker,
in the 'Tenth Walk'; the chapters of this are called 'Walks', being
represented as the record of reflections and recollections he had as
he walked alone in and around Paris.

Angered by the treatment of his books by the Genevan authorities, Rousseau renounced his citizenship in May 1763. But matters
of contention did not end with this. Jean-Robert Tronchin, the
Genevan attorney general, wrote in justification of the actions taken

against Rousseau an essay called *Letters Written from the Country*.
Rousseau replied at length in his complementary *Letters Written from
the Mountain* published December 1764, detailing many abuses of
power then rife in that city as well as defending himself against the
particular accusations made against him. Around this time he
acquired a serious interest in botany, which stayed with him for the
rest of his life, of which more below. Despite his dislike of interrup-
tions, his fame brought him many unsought visitors, ranging from
Johnson's biographer-to-be James Boswell, then on the Grand Tour,
to representatives of the Corsican rebels who approached him
because of the complimentary remarks he made about their island
in *The Social Contract*, in Book II Chapter 10: 'The valour and persist-
ency with which that brave people has regained and defended its
liberty well deserve that some wise man should teach it how to
preserve what it has won' (OC III: 391). Rousseau's essay *Project for a
Constitution for Corsica* was begun at this time, though he never completed it and the fragments we have were not published until 1861.

However, there was no secure repose for Rousseau. Voltaire
published in late 1764 a pamphlet anonymously revealing to
everyone that Rousseau had abandoned his children, and Rousseau
was hugely distressed by this exposure; once again, we are told
nothing of how Thérèse may have felt. At the same time he fell out
with the religious authorities in Môtiers, and in September 1765
his house was stoned and he had to flee once more. After a brief
idyllic stay on the island of Saint-Pierre in the Lake of Bienne near
Bern in Switzerland, he made his way eventually back to Paris, from
where he travelled to supposed safety in England in the company
and under the protection of his then admirer David Hume, the great
Scottish philosopher and historian. Yet they soon became deeply
estranged; differences in their temperaments and ease in society,
and the behaviour of some of Hume's worldly friends, defeated
Hume's attempts to make Rousseau comfortable and welcome, and
he became agitated and distressed. Hume wrote about their quarrel
in *The Concise Account*, published in October 1766. By now Rousseau

was suffering acute mental anguish, delusions of persecution and general physical debilitation, and after a period when he lived in Staffordshire and worked on the first part of *The Confessions* he left England in haste and disarray in May 1767. Later that year his finally completed *Dictionary of Music* appeared; and after yet another unsettled period during which he finally made Thérèse his wife (in August 1768) he finally returned, in June 1770, to Paris, where he was to remain on sufferance, because his arrest warrant had never been revoked, for the rest of his life.

In Paris he earned his living mostly by copying music, though his publications also brought him in some steady income and his long-time publisher, Marc-Michel Rey, based in Amsterdam, sensibly made pension arrangements for Thérèse in the event that she might outlive him, which she did by twenty-two years. He arranged private readings of extracts from *The Confessions* to groups of friends, but these were soon banned under pressure from Madame d'Épinay, his former confidante and supporter. He continued his botanising activities but also began work on his extraordinary work of self-defence and self-explanation, *Rousseau Judge of Jean-Jacques: Dialogues*, between 1771 and 1776. In an ecstasy of despair and mental torment he tried, in February 1776, to place a copy of this on the high altar of Notre-Dame, only to find the gates closed. Still believing himself to be the hunted object of secret malign plotting, he wandered the streets with a leaflet entitled *To All Frenchmen Who Still Love Justice and Truth*, handing this to passers-by, who must have thought they were being accosted by a lunatic. In October 1776, a strange accident took place in which Rousseau was knocked down by a large dog – a Great Dane – and quite badly hurt. For some unaccountable reason this episode seems to have eased his mind and spirit, and in his last years he worked on his collection of brief essays, *Reveries of the Solitary Walker*, left unfinished at his death and to which I alluded earlier.

Although, as indicated, many of the years from 1770 were marked by severe mental disturbance and distress, Rousseau did also during this time prepare a strikingly interesting political work, *Considerations on the Government of Poland*, after being approached by members of the Confederation of Bar, a group opposed to the Russian domination of that country. He also wrote some short works on botany, which are available in a beautiful edition with illustrations by the famous painter of roses, Redouté.

In May 1778, Rousseau moved to Ermenonville, near central Paris, where he died suddenly on 2 July and was buried there on the Île des Peupliers, his grave becoming a place of pilgrimage for many Parisians and others. In October 1794 his remains were transferred to the Panthéon in Paris amid great celebrations. The outstanding autobiographical works of his last decade were not published in his lifetime. Two of his most enduring Genevan friends, Moultou and du Peyrou, put in hand a collected edition of all his works in which these first appeared, though as noted above in connection with his essay on Corsica further material continued to be found, and even today important bibliographical discoveries are still being made as, for instance, discussed in the Introduction to Grace Roosevelt's *Reading Rousseau in the Nuclear Age* concerning her reconstruction of Rousseau's manuscripts on 'The State of War'.

To take an overview of Rousseau's life, one could say that it falls into roughly three parts: his 'apprentice' years, 1712–1749, in which most of his work is on music, and which ends with his 'illumination' on his way to Vincennes; his years of maturity, 1750–1764 from which date his greatest works, the three *Discourses*, *La Nouvelle Héloïse*, *Émile*, *The Social Contract*, the *Letter to d'Alembert*; and the years of decline, 1764–1778, marked by periods of acute mental disturbance and great self-absorption. His wonderful *The Confessions* comes from this period, but much of his writing is prolix and uneven. J.H. Broome, in his *Rousseau – A Study of His Thought*, marks five divisions: Rousseau's childhood up to 1725; the years of adventure to 1741; the years of ambition to 1750; the years of achievement to 1762; and the years of atonement to his death in 1778. There is, evidently, nothing definitive about any such framework, but these divisions are helpful in giving a readily comprehensible shape to the great variety of events and works that made up Rousseau's life.

Such an account as I have just given of this great variety of events and works gives, of course, little or no real idea of what manner of man Rousseau was, what he must have been like to be with, to engage with. We know that he aroused very strong reactions in people, some admiring him to the point of besottedness, some hating him with an almost physical loathing. It is difficult with anyone to say what they are 'really' like – whatever exactly that might mean – and, given the forceful impact Rousseau made and still makes on people, we are scarcely likely to find dispassionate accounts, least of all from Rousseau himself, despite his very frequent attempts to present himself to us truly and justly. Nonetheless, we get what I personally believe to be something of the flavour of the man from these remarks by Kingsley Martin:

Rousseau was first received [in Paris] as a neophyte of the Encyclopaedists, an interesting novelty, whom Diderot and Madame d'Épinay had adopted. Few things require so much social experience, so much poise and self-reliance, as to enter a clique of clever people who share a common experience, laugh at the same things, know each other just well enough and suspect the newcomer of being a bore or a disturbance. Rousseau had none of the necessary qualifications . . . Vain and sensitive, earnest and sentimental, with no sense of proportion and no capacity for trifling, devoid of wit and contemptuous of a smooth society which did not recognise his latent genius, the goodness of his heart and the purity of his intentions, he could do nothing right. Retarded by a morbid inferiority, he was the more eager to be recognised as the central figure; jealous of his independence, but furious at every hint of patronage; every word of encouragement led him to assert himself and every slighting glance led him to withdraw precipitately . . . Like other men whose puritanism is reinforced by a sense of their own private sensuality he could not tolerate licentiousness in others. He

was genuinely religious, convinced by emotional experiences, not by
arguments, and altogether unable to let the scoffer go without
rebuke . . . he desired desperately to produce some special
impression – usually that of an affectionate and natural person who
was too independent to mind what others thought of him . . . It was
his fate to pass his life in rushing into intimacy with those who were
merely prepared for amicable relations . . . Humour or wit might
have saved him, but he had none.

(Martin: 110–12)

Many, I would think, will see something of themselves in this, but
Rousseau is unique in making of his predicament works of great
depth and enduring value. Martin, some pages later, goes on to say:

in truth Rousseau was a genius whose real influence cannot be
traced with precision because it pervaded all the thought that
followed him . . . Men will always be sharply divided about
Rousseau; for he released imagination as well as sentimentalism;
he increased men's desire for justice as well as confusing their
minds, and he gave the poor hope even though the rich could make
use of his arguments. In one direction at least Rousseau's influence
was a steady one: he discredited force as a basis for the State,
convinced men that authority was legitimate only when founded on
rational consent and that no arguments from passing expediency
could justify a government in disregarding individual freedom or in
failing to promote social equality.

(Martin: 219, see also pp.195 ff.)

ROUSSEAU'S WORKS OUTLINED

The purpose of this section is to give a thumbnail sketch of most of
Rousseau's works so that an overall picture of his output may be
obtained. I shall be brief throughout but give slightly more attention here to works not returned to for fuller examination in later
chapters, for obvious reasons. I shall not touch on quite everything;
some material is very much the province of the Rousseau specialist.

With some awkwardness of fit, Rousseau's works can be sorted into nine groups as follows:

(1) works on social and political themes – for which he is best known;
(2) works on education;
(3) polemical works;
(4) autobiographical works and other works of self-explanation and disclosure;
(5) writings on music and language;
(6) his novel, La Nouvelle Héloïse, and miscellaneous prose and poetry;
(7) musical works;
(8) writings on botany;
(9) correspondence; and writings on religion and war.

I shall look at these in order.

Works on social and political themes

The principal works under this head areing the three Discourses, The Social Contract and the Constitutional Project for Corsica and Considerations on the Government of Poland. All these will be examined closely in later chapters, so the outline given here will be very brief.

In the First Discourse, the Discourse on the Sciences and Arts, Rousseau argues that the restoration of the arts and sciences has not had a purifying effect on morals. Sciences and arts flourish where there is idleness and luxury, and these encourage ostentatious self-display, diverting people from moral decency and loyalty to others. Whilst a limited number of gifted individuals can be said to possess real genius, the majority do better for themselves and for others by devoting their lives to deeds of unassuming honesty. Rousseau here gives voice to preoccupations with the human desire for invidious distinction, the desire for private riches being valued above loyalty to one's fellow men and other concerns that receive a fuller and more developed treatment in his brilliant Second Discourse, the Discourse on the Origin of Inequality. Here, Rousseau argues that natural man has become corrupted and unhappy through social interactions that are pervaded by the wish to dominate others, to glory in their despite. Government and law, he goes on to say, often do no more than reinforce the privileges of the rich and the abjection of the poor, and this is quite contrary to justice and the respect for human dignity to which everyone is entitled.

The Third Discourse, the Discourse on Political Economy, is in many respects an interim presentation of some of the ideas Rousseau was working on for The Social Contract. He argues that the authority of the state must be founded on convention, and that civil authority stems from the general will 'which tends always to the preservation and welfare of the whole and of every part, and is the source of the laws' (DPE: 132, OC III: 245). In the second part of the essay, Rousseau concentrates primarily on the best principles to be employed for raising revenue so as to avoid entrenching inequalities between people living within a state.

In The Social Contract, standardly regarded as his most important work and as one of the classic texts of political philosophy, we find a much more fully developed, though not necessarily more transparent, account of the general will, its role as the source of civil authority, and of the principles of liberty, equality and fraternity which, he believes, are essential to any just and humane political community. Rousseau assigns an important role to a quasi-divine 'legislator' who helps to create the conditions in which people are able to come together on a just and equitable footing; and he insists on a strong distinction between sovereignty, the fount of political authority and legitimacy, and government, a function and body with delegated powers applying the law to particular individuals and particular cases. The Social Contract also contains a detailed account of the place of religious belief and practice in a good society, with Rousseau arguing for the principles of a civil religion.

As noted earlier, Rousseau in Book II Chapter 10 of The Social Contract makes favourable mention of Corsica, and in 1764 a representative of the rebel forces contacted him asking him to prepare a new system of legislation and government for post-revolutionary life on the island. This essay was never completed, but along with *Considerations on the Government of Poland* written in 1770–1 it gives us some idea how Rousseau envisaged the working out of the abstract principles of right and justice set out in *The Social Contract* in concrete circumstances, conditioned by accidents of time and place. We find in both essays – though much more fully in the work on Poland – a strong emphasis on the need to cultivate national character and customs, to inspire people with an overriding loyalty to their country and their fellow citizens. But also, and interestingly, despite the paramount value he places on equal liberty and standing for all, he argues for only a gradual liberation of the serfs of Poland since, after years of brutalisation, they will see in this only an opportunity to continue the same practices but with themselves now in charge.

Works on education

Rousseau's first essays on educational objectives and techniques, dating from 1740–1, the *Mémoire Présenté à M. de Mably* and the *Projet pour l'Éducation de M. de Sainte-Marie*, written while he was in Lyons, are slight works. Rousseau argues in them that education should be more than dry book-learning but should form the heart, judgement and spirit, sentiments with which it is both hard to disagree and to get excited. His claim to be an educational theorist of the first rank derives from the ideas he presents in *Émile*, which is subtitled: 'On Education'. In this Rousseau favours what he calls 'negative education', where the child is not controlled, directed, admonished at every turn but instead provided with an environment and resources in which the naturally healthy and ordered course of development of their body, feelings and understanding is allowed to unfold at its own pace in accordance with its own proper dynamic and they are able to grow to maturity whole and happy. The child's own emerging interests should be supported and enriched, not be subjected to impositions and requirements. It is in this work too that Rousseau presents the 'Creed of the Savoyard Vicar' defending a form of natural religion and explaining his hostility to established religious groups and reliance on revelation; this will be looked at again below in Chapter 4. And, in Book V, Rousseau treats at some length of relations between men and women – a discussion generally regarded as highly sexist – before going on to give what is a brief summary of the key ideas of The Social Contract purportedly as a necessary part of Émile's political education as a mature adult.

It is in Émile that Rousseau most fully explains and defines his well-known view that man is by nature good but corrupted by society. He himself said that the work was not really a practical treatise on education but a work of philosophy, but his ideas have very plainly influenced many practitioners of 'progressive education' and stand in sharp contrast to those who see in the child the germs of wickedness that require chastening and repression. He regarded Émile as his greatest work; and I believe that in it we find very many of his key ideas developed with exceptional depth and subtlety. Rousseau wrote, probably in late 1762, a short sequel, Émile and Sophie, in which the fortunes of his pupil and wife as they move to Paris are described. All falls into ruin: Sophie is unfaithful, while Émile leaves France but is captured by pirates and eventually ends up as a valued adviser to a powerful ruler. Some have seen in this Rousseau's acknowledgement that despite every effort to prevent it humans will ruin themselves and one another.

Rousseau's Moral Letters of 1757–8 – written for Sophie d'Houdetot, not the imagined Sophie who is Émile's wife – may also be considered as educational works, loosely defined, for although not truly intended as sources of guidance and instruction they have a didactic tone and do echo many of the key themes of Émile. In them Rousseau lays strong emphasis on the importance of heeding one's conscience, an innate principle directing us to love virtue and order, a view which runs parallel to ideas propounded in the Creed.

The publication of his *First Discourse* elicited a number of replies, and Rousseau responded to these sometimes with care and courtesy, sometimes with irritation and scorn. But his most substantial disputatious pieces came later. Among these we could number his *Letter to Voltaire on Providence*, written in 1756 in response to that writer's 'Poem on the Lisbon Earthquake'. In that, Voltaire dismissed the idea of a beneficent deity who could allow hundreds to die in an earthquake, and scorned the shallow optimism of a belief in providence. Rousseau wrote to controvert this view, arguing that adding up the goods and ills of life always omits the fundamental thing, the sweet sentiment of existence itself; and also that a conviction of providential order stems from deep feeling rather than ratiocination. Not long after this appeared another work in which Rousseau saw Voltaire's malign influence, namely d'Alembert's article on Geneva, written for the *Encyclopedia*, in which he proposed, among other things, establishing a theatre in that city. Voltaire at that time lived just outside that city and had put on theatrical performances at his home; Rousseau suspected he sought a larger stage.

This provoked one of Rousseau's strongest controversial pieces, the *Letter to M. d'Alembert on the Theatre*. In this he contends that attendance at the theatre takes people away from participation in the public, communal celebrations necessary to sustain a true republican spirit and commitment to social justice. Instead, they are shut away in the dark, showing off their finery and feeding on synthetic emotions designed only to amaze or excite without any moral responsibility. Here Rousseau is exploring, as in so many of his works, the attitudes and allegiances necessary to sustain a just and humane community in which the least is valued as much as the mightiest. It is perhaps hard to believe that attendance at the theatre could be seen as such a powerful agent of social dissolution, though parallel arguments concerning television viewing are familiar today; but in any event, we learn clearly from this exchange how much Rousseau valued public festivals in which people gather to celebrate events which have significance for them as part of their civic and cultural inheritance, a point he stressed also in his essays on Poland and Corsica.

After the condemnation of *The Social Contract* in 1762, the Archbishop of Paris, Christophe de Beaumont, wrote later in the year a pastoral letter setting out the reasons for that condemnation. This provoked a very powerful riposte from Rousseau defending his work and questioning the justification for the judgement. In the *Letter to Christophe de Beaumont*, published in 1763, he argues that he has always put forward the same basic principles throughout his works, most particularly that man is naturally good but corrupted by society, so it is incomprehensible why it is only now that what he says is subject to censure. He goes on to make a point-by-point rebuttal of the Archbishop's criticisms, showing up their confusions but insisting anyway that if he has erred he has done so openly and sincerely and that this is not a crime. In addition, he stresses – as he also does in the *Creed* – the need to separate Christian belief and conviction from subservience to priests or subscription to one particular church. These latter give rise to tyranny and murderous conflicts; at the heart of the former is a commitment to charity and forgiveness.

Rousseau's last disputatious work was published a year later, in 1764, in response to Jean-Robert Tronchin's *Letters Written from the Country*, which defended the actions of the Genevan authorities in banning and burning Rousseau's books. The nine letters (chapters) of Rousseau's *Letters Written from the Mountain* fall into two parts. In the first, he defends his ideas and challenges the justice of the actions taken against him; in the second, he argues that the political structures and processes of Geneva have departed a great deal from the basic principles contained in the city's constitution. Sovereignty and control have become vested in a small patrician clique and the ordinary citizen has been denied their liberty and role in legislative action. Rousseau writes here with particular pointedness and penetration, but even those among his friends who wanted to use the case of his ill-treatment as a ground for remonstrance against abuses of power in Geneva found the work too inflammatory to be helpful. Although this is, I believe, a fine piece of self-defence and scourging of his antagonists, its overall significance for understanding Rousseau's thinking is quite limited because it is so closely tied to the particularities of this conflict. This is in contrast, in my judgement, to the responses to d'Alembert and to the Archbishop, in which important points of a wider import are also made.

Autobiographical works

Particularly during the last fifteen years of his life, Rousseau wrote some very substantial works of self-accounting, self-explanation and defence, including one unquestionable masterpiece, *The Confessions*. As early as 1761, Rousseau's Amsterdam publisher Marc-Michel Rey urged him to write his autobiography. At first, this suggestion failed to take root, but then he began to make notes, assemble copies of letters and so on. Indeed, his first autobiographical writing of any import comes from this period also, though its genesis seems to have been independent of Rey's suggestion to Rousseau. As noted earlier, Rousseau was becoming very distressed at what he believed were plots and conspiracies blocking the publication of *Émile*. Eventually, Lamoignon de Malesherbes, official director of the book trade and a supporter of Rousseau and his work, was contacted and was able to put Rousseau's mind at rest. A few months later, in January 1762, Rousseau addressed to him four letters, not originally intended for publication, expressing his gratitude and attempting to explain his character and conduct and describe some of the principal formative episodes of his life. In the first of these, Rousseau explains why he turned his back on city and salon life and why he prefers the country and solitude; only there can he express himself freely and avoid the falsity that artificial manners and the requirements of *politesse* demand. In the second letter, we find Rousseau's first account of his 'illumination' on the way to Vincennes, and of the myriad ideas that flooded his mind then. The third letter treats of his present state of mind, speaking of the simple pleasures of his daily life and of his freedom to realise his dreamy nature.

Finally, in the last letter, he indicates how, in his own view, the meaning and value of his life should be understood. He had sought in all his writings to be of benefit to all men; he treats all humanity as his equals and that is why he avoids the bickering and quarrels that living in society always seems to engender. These are attractively written pieces and touch on many issues and concerns that receive a fuller account in later writings.

Just as these *Letters to Malesherbes* were not published during Rousseau's life, neither were the three much bigger autobiographical works that followed. Rousseau began working at *The Confessions* off and on from 1764 onwards, and Part 1, which takes us up to 1741/2 when Rousseau came to Paris hoping to make his name, was pretty well complete by the end of 1767. Part 2, which is more sombre in character and less fully realised, brings the story up to 1765 and was completed by mid-1770. I will discuss this work at some length in Chapter 7 below and will only make the briefest comment on it here. It presents one of the most vivid stories of the formation, sensibility and adventures of an individual ever written. Often with painful openness, Rousseau recounts episodes of shame and humiliation, but also presents moments of great beauty and joy. His first meeting with Madame de Warens, his sexual adventures in Venice, his triumph with his opera, his hopeless love for Sophie d'Houdetot and many other matters are written of with great intensity and life. It is a deeply arresting work, the paradigmatic Romantic autobiography of the genesis and journey of an individual's genius.

More consciously and intentionally written in self-defence is Rousseau's extraordinary *Rousseau Judge of Jean-Jacques: Dialogues*, written between 1772 and 1776. Here, Rousseau constructs three dialogues between 'Rousseau' and 'a Frenchman' concerning the character, conduct and works of Jean-Jacques (Rousseau himself), in an attempt to show how he has been misunderstood and vilified in innumerable ways by men and women whose awareness of their own defects has been rendered intolerable to them because of Jean-Jacques' integrity and simplicity. Although prolix and repetitive, and betraying decided signs of paranoid delusions, the work has undeniable force and contains important comments on, for instance, the role and character of *amour-propre*, on natural goodness, and about Rousseau's own estimates of the value of his works. Whether or not it is agreed that this work itself shows marks of delusional states of mind, it is clear as noted earlier that Rousseau was in great distress when he had completed it. His abortive attempt to place it on the high altar in Notre-Dame was followed by some days of acute breakdown.

Rousseau's final work of self-revelation is the *Reveries of the Solitary Walker*, written between 1776–8 but unfinished at his death. Here too Rousseau adopts a highly original literary form – the work being divided into ten sections entitled *Promenades* or *Walks*, being as it were the record of what he recalled or mulled over as he wandered in and around Paris. Within this frame, he offers a collection of miscellaneous reflections, records of his life and opinions, resulting in a work that is often lyrical despite containing a good deal of acute observation regarding the malignancies of human beings and society. Rousseau talks of his recent accident in which he was knocked down by a Great Dane but recovered his stability of mind; of his continuing piercing shame over the episode of the stolen ribbon and his false accusation of Marion; of his right to use the motto *Vitam impendere vero*, 'Dedicate life to truth', as his own; of his trance-like absorption in the rhythms of nature, and much more. The work breaks off after Rousseau reflects once more on his meeting and time with Madame de Warens, probably the most important time of his whole life. As with *The Confessions* this is a particularly accessible work of Rousseau's – though some have found extraordinary depths of meaning in it – and it deserves to be more widely known.

It is, at times, easy to become impatient with Rousseau's seemingly never ending self-examination and self-justification, but overall this is a very powerful body of work which is as central to his total achievement as is his 'philosophical' work more narrowly conceived.

Writings on music and language

The linkage of music and language may seem incongruous, but Rousseau saw profound connections between the two. In his *Essay on the Origin of the Languages* begun around 1753, added to and modified over a number of years but never completed, Rousseau argues that the first human speech was full of rhythm, accent and melody expressing and arousing passion. Melody in music, he says, imitates passion; but harmony imposes patterns and structures that constrain passionate utterance. In making this contrast Rousseau was attacking the dominance of Rameau's work in France, and defending his preference for Italian music where, he believed, the melodic impulse was dominant. I shall return to this point in a moment. Words bearing a fixed, literal meaning only emerge later on as languages become shared more widely and are used less for expressive purposes. Ideas of reason replace sentiments of the heart, and accentuation is replaced by monotony. These changes, according to Rousseau, take place more quickly and are more pronounced in inhospitable northern climes, where man's primary need is for help not for love, reversing the priorities of the warm, lush south. Speech becomes harsh, abrupt and demanding, and language becomes more precise in order to convey needs and impose requirements with exactness. Many themes central to Rousseau's mature work are in play here: the primacy given to feeling, the claim that precision and complexity are signs not of superior development but of degeneration and increased distance from what is natural to and good for us.

The primacy given to melody, noted earlier, is present also in Rousseau's most important writing on music, the *Letter on French*

Music of 1753, contemporaneous with his first efforts on the *Essay*. Rousseau's contribution to the quarrel over the respective merits of French and Italian music was typically forceful. The Italian language is, he says, flowing, full of resonance, clearly accented and as such perfect for the melodic unfolding which all beautiful and expressive music excels in. The French language, on the other hand, is harsh, thin, monotonous, devoid of colour and incapable of lending itself to melody; hence the dominance of harmonic intricacy in French music. Rousseau concludes somewhat contradictorily: 'The French have no music and cannot have; or, should they ever have, that would be so much the worse for them' (OC V: 328). As may be imagined this did little to mollify the supporters of French music, and so great was the furore that followed the publication of the *Letter* that, or so Rousseau claimed (C 8: 358, OC I: 384), it diverted attention away from an incipient rebellion over Louis XV's decision to dissolve the Paris *parlement*.

Going back in Rousseau's career, it is worth noticing his *Project for a New Musical Notation*, which he presented to the Academy of Sciences in Paris in August 1752, soon after his arrival in the capital. In this, Rousseau proposes replacing standard musical notation with a linear numerical arrangement. He claimed to have successfully instructed pupils in the use of it, and although it has attracted the occasional admirer it never made any serious impact, being much less easily surveyable. In addition, Rousseau's many entries on musical topics for Diderot and d'Alembert's *Encyclopedia*, covering a wide range, began to be written from around 1748, and much later he collected these together, with additions, to make up his *Dictionary of Music*, published in 1767. This enjoyed considerable success, and brought him in a steady income during the last years of his life.

Rousseau's novel and miscellaneous prose and poetry

Rousseau's greatest popular success arose from the publication of his novel *Julie, ou la Nouvelle Héloïse*, which appeared in January 1761. It caused a sensation, with over seventy editions appearing in French before 1800, and around thirty in English translation. People were so keen to read it that parts were passed from hand to hand and everyone claimed to be, or to know someone who was, the model for one or another of his characters. The circumstances surrounding Rousseau's writing of it were considered earlier, and I shall not touch on them again.

The novel is epistolary in form, comprising exchanges of letters between the principal characters, Julie the heroine, Saint-Preux her tutor and lover, Claire her cousin and friend, and in due course the man Julie marries, Baron de Wolmar. It opens with a crisis. Saint-Preux, whom Julie's father has employed as her tutor, confesses his love for her. At first she is appalled, but soon becomes complicit in the effort of admonishing him to be virtuous and restrained. She is unable to treat his attachment lightly, and is drawn into greater intimacy with Saint-Preux whilst dissuading him from his foolish passion. Hurrying over a thousand details, the plot may be summarised as follows. Saint-Preux and Julie consummate their love, and she becomes pregnant. When her father finds out he is outraged and strikes her, and she miscarries. Julie's mother, too, is deeply shocked and falls mortally ill, and Julie is stricken with feelings of guilt. She too falls ill with smallpox and is disfigured. Saint-Preux has gone away with Lord Edward Bomston and sails with Anson's expedition, seemingly lost to Julie for ever. She, now recovered and repentant, marries the Baron de Wolmar, the husband her father originally intended her for. They establish a model estate, Clarens, where they live with their two sons and with Claire, now a widow, and her daughter.

Saint-Preux, however, then returns. Wolmar, who is presented as a somewhat aloof, impassive, all-seeing and all-knowing presiding figure in the lives of everyone on the estate, decides to employ him as tutor to their children even though he knows of his previous relationship with Julie. They live together amicably for some time, but when Wolmar goes away for a while, Julie and Saint-Preux go boating on Lake Geneva and are trapped at the very spot where, years before, Saint-Preux had lain in a torment of desperate love yearning for Julie. She, however, resists his renewed declaration and seems to have overcome the intemperate passions of her youth. Yet having contracted pneumonia after saving one of her children from drowning, she confesses in her dying moments to having never ceased to love him. The novel ends with Saint-Preux, Wolmar and Claire living on the estate together united in memory of the incomparable soul of Julie.

Debate has raged over how this work should be interpreted. Some see it as disjointed, the first four books being given over to a tale of illicit passion of considerable intensity, with the reality and significance of the feeling depicted there being denied in the last two books as Julie devotes herself in purity to life with Wolmar. Others see in it, especially in the over-controlled and manipulated human environment of Clarens presided over by Wolmar, a recognition on Rousseau's part that unbridled passion and unregulated relationships cannot form either a proper basis for human happiness or an enduring human bond. In any event, despite what strikes us a stilted idiom and melodramatic plot, there are passages of real erotic intensity and it is not impossible to understand something of the excitement that greeted its first appearance.

No others of Rousseau's literary writings approaches *Julie* in scale and importance. There are a number of short poems and some plays of interest only to the specialist scholar (and indeed, of little interest to them), but two other pieces merit notice. The first relates to Rousseau's play *Narcissus*, not for itself (it is very slight) but for the 'Preface' Rousseau wrote to it after its publication in 1753. In this he defends himself against the charge that, having condemned the arts as inimical to good morals in his *First Discourse* published just the year before, how can he possibly bring this work forward now? He argues, first, that he did not always think as he now does; this was a work of his youth. But more importantly he says, second, that where contemporary morals are already so corrupt, for instance as in big cities like Paris, it is better to divert people with frivolous plays to reduce the possibility of their otherwise doing serious harm to others. Rousseau's longest discussion of the influence of the theatre is in his *Letter to M. d'Alembert* referred to earlier and considered further in Chapter 6. In any event, he goes on, whether his play succeeds or fails is nothing to him; his spirit has never been corrupted by the craving for invidious distinction which really lies at the heart of the moral perversions brought on by excessive esteem being given to artistic achievement. Finally, there is the curious prose poem *The Levite of Ephraïm*, which Rousseau wrote as he fled Paris in June 1762. He retells the macabre tale of the murder of the Levite's companion/wife set out in *Judges* 19–21, which leads to the massacre of 26,000 men from the tribe of Benjamin. One can perhaps imagine that Rousseau saw in this indescribably brutal story some image of the kind of vengeance that should be his for the wrongs he had suffered. Yet why this was his 'dearest work' is, to me, almost incomprehensible.

Musical works

As well as his writings on music, considered above, Rousseau wrote a considerable amount of music including the highly successful opera *Le Devin du Village*. This, being written in French but full of charming pastoral melody, gives the lie to Rousseau's strictures on the French language's suitability for being set to music. Music was, in fact, Rousseau's first great passion, although or perhaps because he was almost wholly self-taught. *Le Devin* was preceded by some earlier operas with a very different manner and idiom, including *Les Muses Galantes* (1743–5), and *Les Fêtes de Ramire* of 1748, which was also performed before the king. This latter was an adaptation of a work by Voltaire and Rameau. But it was *Le Devin* that was his only real success, taken up by the Opéra after its triumph at Fontainebleau. It concerns the vicissitudes of the love the shepherdess Colette feels for the shepherd Colin. Colin has turned his longing looks on the lady of the manor, and Colette seeks the aid of the village soothsayer to make Colin believe that she too has another love. He is overcome by jealousy, realises that she is his true love, and returns to her arms. Rousseau's music is delicate, simple and melodious, free from elaborate decorations and musical ornamentation of the kind that he consistently disparaged. Madame de Pompadour was so smitten with it that she herself took the part of Colin at a private performance held at her country house, Belle-Vue, in 1753. Of such things is the imagined world of Boucher and Fragonard made.

Writings on botany

A very small – but particularly attractive – part of Rousseau's output comprises his writings on botany. We saw earlier how much he enjoyed collecting and cataloguing plants, and he used also to pre-pare displays of specimens for his friends. He continued to do this into his old age, taking walks out from the centre of Paris into the fields and woods. His interest first burgeoned when he was living in Switzerland having fled Paris in 1762, and he planned to write a *Dictionary of Botanical Terms* of which fragments survive. Even when at his most distressed in England, he would often collect ferns and mosses from around the house he was living in in Staffordshire. It was on his final return to Paris that he started to write on botanical topics again, writing in 1771/2 eight *Elementary Letters on Botany* for the child of a friend. In these he recommended the study of plants as a way of learning to see the world around you clearly and accur-ately, to appreciate the miracles of nature and to still the cravings of the greedy self. He writes 'It is a study of pure curiosity, one that has no real utility except what a thinking, sensitive human being can draw from observing nature and the marvels of the universe' (Seventh Letter, OC IV: 1188). Neither of these works was pub-lished until after Rousseau's death, but in 1805 the painter Redouté, universally known for his paintings of roses, came across them and prepared illustrations for a lovely edition. Although this is only a tiny part of Rousseau's work, his joy in plants is one of his most engaging attributes.

Correspondence; and writings on religion and war

I noted at the start that Rousseau's works do not automatically slot into pre-prepared categories. In this final grouping, I shall note three further bodies of work that merit mention but without pretending that they form a coherent category of work.

First, there is Rousseau's correspondence. Quite aside from those polemical works noted above that were given the form of open letters, such as the *Letter to Christophe de Beaumont*, and the *Letters Written from the Mountain*, and putting aside other pieces in which he makes major declarations about his ideas or himself, such as the *Letter to Voltaire on Providence* or the *Letters to Malesherbes*, there remains Rousseau's enormous day-to-day correspondence with friends, inquirers, publishers, well- or ill-wishers, and so on. Rousseau was an indefatigable correspondent, and very many of his letters have survived and been collected and edited – in one of the greatest achievements of modern scholarship – by R.A Leigh, making up the *Correspondance Complète de Jean Jacques Rousseau*. From these one acquires what is in many respects a more rounded and faithful impression of Rousseau's life and personality than one does from the carefully prepared works of self-apology and self-disclosure considered above. Rousseau drew extensively on his letters in *The Confessions*; 31 August 1757 is sometimes known as the day of the five letters and Rousseau reproduces in the text the letters of hurt, complaint, plea, despair, reconciliation, affront and so on that passed between him and Madame d'Épinay as their relations reached a crisis point (C9: 419–21, OC I: 450–3). Another work, published in Rousseau's lifetime, that contains some of Rousseau's letters is David Hume's *Exposé Succinct* (*Concise Account*) of their quarrel, published in 1766 and alluded to before. Drawing on correspondence from Rousseau, Hume sets out the supposed grounds of grievance against him and rebuts these. There can be no doubt Hume was overall in the right, and some of Rousseau's letters are quite painful to read because of the disclosure of distress in them.

Second, it is helpful to draw together Rousseau's writings on religion, although there is no separate work on this theme in which he set out his ideas at length and in detail. The nearest we come to this is the long section in Book IV of *Émile*, the *Profession of Faith (Creed) of the Savoyard Vicar* where Rousseau considers the basis for and character of individual religious conviction. Additionally, in Chapter 8 of Book IV of *The Social Contract* Rousseau discusses the place and role of religious beliefs and institutions in a stable and humane civil society. And I have already noted his *Letter to Voltaire on Providence* of 1756, where Rousseau sets out his ideas concerning God's providential governance of mankind and the world.

In the *Creed*, Rousseau presents, through the voice of an imagined priest from Savoy (a figure probably based on two priests whom Rousseau had known earlier in his life), his ideas about the basis of religious belief, the nature of God, God's relation to his creation, and about the relations between religious belief and morality. As mentioned several times already, it was this section of *Émile* that was principally responsible for the book's condemnation and all that then ensued for Rousseau since he outlines in it a form of natural religion and mounts a scathing attack on the established churches, criticising them for harshness and the damning of unbelievers in contradiction of Christ's message, which speaks directly to the heart of each individual, and is one of love and forgiveness.

In the chapter on 'civil religion' in *The Social Contract* (Book IV Chapter 8), Rousseau also maintains that whilst, in his view, all citizens should subscribe to a 'civil profession of faith', the principal tenet of that faith should be the prohibition of religious intolerance and other forms of intolerance also. Rousseau agrees that religious allegiance is one of the great spurs to action and thus it needs to be considered how it can be accommodated within a just polity, indeed harnessed to the survival and prosperity of that polity. In essence, his concern is that no man can serve two masters, and if religion establishes a separate source of authority in conflict with the civil powers then at the very least a believer may be only half-hearted in their commitment to the civil order, or at worst may think they have just cause to flout or overturn the requirements of state law. In holding this Rousseau is unquestionably correct. I shall consider these matters further in Chapter 6, and the material of the *Creed* in Chapter 4.

Third and finally, another topic to which Rousseau returned from time to time is the nature and justification of war, and his ideas, though limited in scope, have had a small but enduring influence. Rousseau denies that the natural condition of man is a 'war of all against all', in Hobbes' famous words. In his view, human beings are by nature timorous and peaceful. But even should they fall to combat, it would not be proper to call this a war since war does not involve individuals as such but persons as representatives of states. War is a relation between state and state in which 'individuals are enemies only accidentally, not as men, nor even as citizens, but as soldiers' (SC 1: 4, OC III: 357). The encounter of those who have combat status does not mean the abolition of all other aspects of their humanity and moral relationship, nor does it extend to all members of the state with which another state may be in conflict. Several of Rousseau's ideas about the condition of war defied clear interpretation until very recently when, as indicated earlier, the noted American scholar Dr Grace Roosevelt worked out the proper order of the primary material.

This concludes this hasty overview of what is almost the whole range of Rousseau's output. In concluding this chapter, I will take up again the principal themes identified in the Introduction that will provide the direction and analytical focus for the more detailed discussions of the works selected here for fuller attention in the coming chapters.

KEY THEMES AND IDEAS

I stressed in the Introduction that there can be no serious question of there being a 'definitive' account of Rousseau's thinking. However, the themes to which I give prominence do, I believe, contain much of what is deepest and most enduring in his work, and that is why I have selected them for sustained attention. I here enlarge on the sketch I gave in Chapter 1 in order to give a solid general orientation in relation to these before proceeding the closer discussions of the coming chapters, in the course of which it might be easy to lose one's overall bearings. I identify five general themes here before moving on to show in more detail how Rousseau articulates these and how they pervade his arguments and intent. I begin with what is very overt in his earliest mature works, particularly DSA and DI, namely his account of the evils of civilisation.

The critique of civilised man

Rousseau came to abhor the form of society and the conditions of life that he found around him in Paris and in the France of his time generally, even though such a society was widely viewed – and not just by the French themselves – as the finest, most advanced and civilised that mankind had been able to rise to. However, the basis of his criticisms do not pertain to just one time and place; they provide grounds for criticism of many societies, including our own, and offer a critical perspective of considerable power.

Rousseau detested above all the vast inequalities of many kinds that pervaded society: those of wealth, status, power, esteem, influence and so on. Everywhere he saw habits of contempt for inferiors, people forced into destitution, marginalised and disregarded, denied any recognition of their humanity and left dependent on the vagaries of capricious patronage or the flukes of fortune for their survival. For all that they are alike members of one nation, millions of individuals received no acknowledgement as fellow creatures let alone fellow citizens. How and why could a society grow up that contained such inhumanity? For Rousseau, the key factor here is the demands of man's *amour-propre*. There is considerable debate about what exactly we should understand by Rousseau's use of this term, but I interpret *amour-propre* as, in its essence, a desire or need to secure recognition from others, for an acknowledgement of oneself in their eyes and actions. This desire very readily takes on, in Rousseau's view, an aggressive and competitive character, whereby individuals come to feel that they have received their due acknowledgment only if they are preferred above others, have precedence or superiority over others in whose ignominy and abjection they rejoice as a sign that they themselves are better people who count for more, are a 'better class of person'. Inequalities arise and are elaborated and maintained, on this account, in order to afford people a sense of their own significance in society that they crave. Domination and subservience become the key marks of social structures and relations between groups and individuals. We shall see later that *amour-propre* can have a positive and constructive character too, but in his early writings Rousseau concentrates on its damaging forms.

Rousseau does not merely try to reveal and explain the sources of such inequalities; he goes on to argue that this demand for precedence exacts a terrible toll. That it does on those who are despised, disregarded or deprived is self-evident; but what of those who appear to prosper, to stand on the pinnacle of fortune and bask in widespread esteem and acclaim? He holds that they have in effect handed over the meaning and value of their lives and themselves to the judgement of others, and whilst seeming to have command they are in fact ruled by the verdict of others upon them. They are not the self-possessors of the significance and worth of what they are and do; that is rather determined by the assessment others make of them, and in that way they are in thrall to other people, subject to their disposal. The rise and fall of celebrities illustrates this situation pretty clearly.

At the heart of Rousseau's thinking on these issues lies his concern with power relations in society of which he was a sharp diagnostician. Inequalities in power between individuals were, I should say, almost his constant preoccupation, both in terms of trying to understand and explain their causes and consequences but also of attempting to work out how individuals and societies could come into existence for whom instead equality and mutuality of regard and esteem would be the leading concerns and interests. This is apparent in his constructive social and political theorising, but before turning to this I shall look at the apparently obvious complement to his criticism of civilisation, namely his positive evaluation of 'natural' man and 'natural' goodness.

Natural man and natural goodness

If civilisation corrupts and deforms human beings, making them delight in others' despite and alienating them from themselves, what seemingly more obvious solution to this than withdrawal from society and an attempt to recapture, or to model life on, the character and circumstances of pre-social man, natural man in the state of nature? Rousseau has certainly been widely understood as a champion of such a redirection. The life of the simple Indian, a 'noble savage' (though this is not a term Rousseau himself used), self-reliant and self-sufficient, living independently of other people and untroubled by competition for precedence, unconcerned for the future, living a life of primitive innocence and plainness – such seems to be the kind of figure and kind of life held up as the saving alternative. There can be no doubt that Rousseau saw a great deal to value in such a person and their way of life, certainly when set in contrast with the oppression and misery experienced by civilised peoples. But it is, I feel sure, a mistake to think that he held this up as the 'solution' to the discontents of civilisation, as if it were possible and desirable to go backwards and divest oneself of one's human qualities and become a creature only half awakened, half realised. The issue for Rousseau is, rather, one of finding a basis for human relations in society that does not deform and stifle man's desire for fullness of life and recognition from others but conduces to that for each and all alike. He did not, in fact, hold that where society is nature is no more. For him, what is 'natural' to us is not that which is untouched by human artifice but rather that which conduces to our well-being and the completion of our lives. It is only because so often, in his view, human intervention results in harmful interference that it seems proper to equate what is natural with what is unaffected by human artifice. But this is not a necessity of the case.

Related points apply to Rousseau's account of man's 'natural' goodness. Rousseau is very well known for saying, in various slightly different ways, that men are by nature good but corrupted by society. I have just warned against reading the latter half of this epigram in terms that imply that he meant that all forms of society whatsoever will be corrupting. But how should we understand the claim about man's natural goodness? Here it is common for critics to say that Rousseau very naively thought that if people were not oppressed by others they would all be nice, kind and well disposed. But hard-headed people claim to know that this is far from the truth and that thinking in these terms prevents individuals from taking responsibility for their own evil inclinations and actions since the blame is always someone else's.

Yet this is not his position at all. First, he argues rigorously and in detail that the origin of malign dispositions lies in outside influences on an individual. This is not some ungrounded assumption that he is making but the upshot of careful analysis. Second, under the general heading of man's natural goodness, he treats of a number of different concerns. He draws, for instance, important contrasts between spontaneous and unreflective feelings of affection and generosity on the one hand and the conscious, deliberate commitment to these as values to be adhered to and objectives to be sought on the other. Also, he writes with great discernment about the limits of a morality that focuses dominantly on obligation, duty and requirement. The coercive character of such regulation produces the very evils it purports to correct. Instead, he lays emphasis on compassion as the mainspring for a more humane and productive basis for moral union between people. So although concern with what is natural to man, and man's natural dispositions, is very central to Rousseau's thinking at all points, it is necessary to be cautious in interpreting his meaning and to avoid too formulaic an account.

I have suggested in both these sections that the key issue for Rousseau is not whether one will live, work and have one's being at all with fellow humans in society but rather with the question of on what footing one shall do this, what character the terms and conditions of one's human union will be. Concern with this comes wholly to the fore in his key political writings.

Foundations of political legitimacy and the general will

One of the most obvious centres of power in society lies with the agencies of the state, through the creation and enforcement of law. Rousseau was therefore profoundly interested in the question of how the possession and exercise of political power could be made legitimate and employed for the benefit of all citizens in a state and not just a privileged few. His fundamental thought regarding this is perhaps best captured in the remark: 'The people, being subject to the laws, ought to be their author.' (SC II: 6, 212, OC III: 380), though the precise meaning of this needs some discussion; see below Chapter 5.

For Rousseau, the sovereign body, that is the body in the state with which lies final authority beyond which there is no appeal, makes the fundamental laws of the community, and it should comprise all adult members of the community on a footing of perfect equality with regard to its primary processes and functions. By this, all citizens alike achieve equal standing and an equal role in the legislative arrangements of the community, and gross inequalities of status and power in society are excluded at the start. Indeed, every member of the society is, to use Rousseau's own words, an 'indivisible part of the whole' (SC I: 6, OC III: 361) and as such receives recognition and support as an equal participant in the social enterprise. This sovereign body declares its fundamental rules for all in the community through the exercise of its will, the 'general will' of the whole body. The idea of the general will is a complex one, and controversy over its meaning is still widespread, but in broad terms the general will is directed towards securing what is in the common interest and legislates to achieve that. Rousseau makes a strict distinction between sovereignty and government as a function and body. Government is concerned with the administration of the laws, and their application to particular situations and people. He recognises that members of the government as a group will come to possess a good deal of effective power, and may comprise a sectional interest at odds with the common interest. He therefore tried to introduce arrangements that will reduce the likelihood of this, emphasising at all times that government is a subordinate function with delegated powers. Possibly surprisingly, Rousseau is not at all keen on a directly democratic form for government, largely for practical reasons, but favours a kind of elective aristocracy of which so-called 'representative' democracy may be seen as a form. However, the objective throughout remains the same: that each and every citizen shall enjoy a basic equality of status, dignity and material support, this being the objective that in his view any just and humane society must set for itself. Only by this will the fundamental human worth of every individual receive its proper acknowledgement and realisation in the life of the civil community. Such equality of recognition and status requires also, in Rousseau's view, the enjoyment of liberty by, and also the existence of bonds of common loyalty between, citizens. How these seemingly disparate elements come together in his thinking will be sketched in the next section.

Liberty, fraternity, equality

For Rousseau, the enjoyment of liberty is one of the defining marks of man. 'To renounce liberty is to renounce being a man' (SC I, 4: 170, OC III: 356). But it is very easy to jump to conclusions about what he means by saying this, and care needs to be taken to grasp his thinking here. One might, for instance, assume that the enjoyment of complete liberty signifies the capacity and opportunity to do exactly what you like when and as you like, without reference to anyone else at all. And if this is perfect liberty, then how it could co-exist with submission to law that requires acknowledgement of the rights of others and restrictions on what one can decide for oneself is hard to see. However, for Rousseau, liberty understood as such wholly unfettered scope is not what lies at the heart of his thinking. In his view, liberty conceived of in these terms leads only to the competition for dominance, the desire to outdo or do down other people, which we have noted above. And, as also noted, the use of liberty in this way leads in the end to modes of enslavement, to direct or indirect forms of control by others. Instead of this, submission to law relieves one of dependence on others and enables one to enjoy a secured freedom that is compatible with a like freedom being enjoyed by others. So the requirement to acknowledge the needs and rights of others, which properly grounded law imposes, is better seen as a condition for individual freedom and escape from entrapment in invidious competition rather than as a diminution or restraint on liberty.

Rousseau recognises that what he at one point calls the 'austere laws' of liberty (GP VI: 196, OC III: 974) do not so easily appeal to people as does the more straightforward-seeming if delusive idea of unfettered liberty. Only if there is a bond of union with those with whom one is in society, so that their well-being matters to you as some part of your own well-being, will acceptance of the restraints of law not really be felt as a restraint but rather as the proper principle of one's own goal and volition. This idea is often captured in terms of a spirit of fraternity binding together those in society, though this is not a phrase Rousseau uses; it is best known from the rhetoric of the French Revolution. Rousseau develops the idea in a number of ways. Perhaps most problematically, he talks of a quasi-divine 'legislator' who will remake people and lift them out of their narrow, atomised egoism into a union of reciprocal regard with their fellows. Less spectacularly, he elsewhere lays emphasis on the bonds generated by shared pride in country and nation, a sense of common history and shared destiny. I turn now to an outline of some of his thinking on this.

Culture and religion

As just noted, it is Rousseau's view that a sense of common life with those others with whom one lives in one society is necessary if good laws beneficial to all are to be experienced as the principle of one's own will rather than as a restraint curbing a liberty that accepts no limit. Where does such a sense of common life come from, and how is it to be fostered and sustained? Rousseau frequently addresses this issue, giving paramount place to patriotism, a sense of belonging to a distinctive nation with a special history, this yielding a footing of shared cause and commitment for individuals of otherwise diverse interests and passions. We are apt to look askance at this, being aware of the massive conflicts and huge loss of life that have come out of national ambitions and the desire to oppress other peoples and cultures. However, on the one side it should be stressed that Rousseau had no interest at all in promoting national self-assertion of this kind. He believed that individual nations would do well to make themselves as self-sufficient and independent of one another as they could precisely to avoid the conflicts that arise from dependency. On the other side, Rousseau's close attention to this cluster of matters shows his awareness that adherence to law is not something that is well sustained by intellectual assent or threat of sanction alone, but requires education and the development of appropriate dispositions. Faced with a group of people from whom I feel estranged or who are nothing to me, I will find it hard to accept that I should be required to act in ways that will be for their benefit as they will in regard to mine. Only if the idea that they are my 'fellows' is more than an empty term will I see and feel the value in doing this; and for that idea to have life and vitality the cultivation of social sentiments, the upholding of customs where our shared life is at the fore, must be important.

In practice we know that in many societies the sense of common fellowship is very limited and that sectional interests seek ascendancy, disregarding or exploiting other groups. The sense in which we have in such instances common membership of one community is very attenuated; rather, some are simply in servitude to others. Rousseau was vividly aware of this, as we saw above. His point is that if there is to be community in nature not just in name, a bond of union, carried in shared customs and mutual loyalty, is required.

It is this same concern with a bond of union between members of a society that informs his reflections on the role of religion in society. Rousseau knew how strongly religious attachments shaped people's lives, often, in his estimation, leading to the most violent and bloody conflicts. Consistently with his general approach, he argues that religious attachments, where they impinge on public conduct, should be harnessed to upholding and sustaining the fundamental laws of a society which respect the rights of all. Private worship is a matter for the individual, providing that no one thinks that their own particular form of religious adherence places them above the law and the sovereign. Though such views are, evidently, far from uncontroversial, Rousseau's guiding intent to sustain the unity of a society under laws addressed to the common good is surely a proper one.

CONCLUSION AND PROSPECT

The preceding section as a whole has attempted to provide a general orientation in regard to some of Rousseau's dominant concerns, and to indicate some aspects of his thinking about these. In the chapters that follow, I shall elaborate and enrich the discussion of these matters so that, by the end, a fairly full and balanced appreciation of his position on these and related matters may be obtained. I begin by looking at the three *Discourses*, on the *Sciences and Arts*, on the *Origins of Inequality* and on *Political Economy*, in which – particularly the first two – we find Rousseau's most detailed discussions of the corruptions of civilisation but also the beginnings of a search for a remedy for these ills.

FURTHER READING

Maurice Cranston, *Jean-Jacques: The Early Life and Work of Jean-Jacques Rousseau, 1712–1754*. London: Allen Lane, 1983.

Maurice Cranston, *The Noble Savage: Jean-Jacques Rousseau, 1754–1762*. London: Allen Lane, 1991.

Maurice Cranston, *The Solitary Self: Jean-Jacques Rousseau in Exile and Adversity*. London: Allen Lane, 1997, completed by Sanford Lakoff. These three volumes make up the most interesting and important biography of Rousseau.

Jean Guéhenno, *Jean-Jacques Rousseau*, tr. J. and D. Weightman, 2 vols. London: Routledge, 1966. An engaging biography making good use of his letters.

L.G. Crocker, *Jean-Jacques Rousseau: The Quest (1712–58)*. New York: Macmillan, 1968.

L.G. Crocker, *Jean-Jacques Rousseau: The Prophetic Voice (1758–78)*. New York: Macmillan, 1973. Another comprehensive, if somewhat hostile, biography.

James Miller, *Rousseau – Dreamer of Democracy*. New Haven: Yale University Press, 1984. Combines a study of the life and works.

C.W. Hendel, *Jean-Jacques Rousseau: Moralist*, 2 vols. New York: Bobbs-Merrill, 1934. A full and scrupulous account of the life and works.

Timothy O'Hagan, *Rousseau*. London: Routledge, 1999. A comprehensive and subtle account of full range of Rousseau's work.

Helena Rosenblatt, *Rousseau and Geneva*. Cambridge: Cambridge University Press, 1997. An account of Geneva in Rousseau's time.

Three

The Three *Discourses*

THE PURPOSE OF THIS CHAPTER

The purpose of this chapter is to present and assess the ideas Rousseau broaches and explores in his three *Discourses*, the *Discourse on the Sciences and Arts* (DSA) commonly known as the *First Discourse*, of 1750; the *Discourse on the Origin of Inequality* (DI), the *Second Discourse*, of 1755; and the *Discourse on Political Economy* (DPE), the *Third Discourse*, which first appeared as an article in Diderot and d'Alembert's *Encyclopedia* in 1755 but was published separately in 1758. As well as bringing forward the core arguments of these works I shall highlight the presence of certain of the salient themes which I identified in the preceding chapter since these are plainly central to Rousseau's thinking in these *Discourses*. The *First Discourse*, for example, explores the corruptions of civilised man, as does the *Second Discourse* with great brilliance, and we find in that too extensive discussion of natural man and natural goodness. In the *Third Discourse* there is a sketch of Rousseau's thinking about the grounds of political legitimacy, and a considerable treatment of the role of culture and patriotism in creating citizens. Through the treatment given here we will be in a position to understand more fully the character and force of Rousseau's thinking about these matters and to begin to form a view about the cogency of his approach. Of course, more remains to be considered in the following chapters as well, but these *Discourses* lead us very quickly to much that is right at the heart of Rousseau's thinking.

THE *FIRST DISCOURSE*

The *Discourse on the Sciences and Arts* is a short work, of only around 12,000 words, but contains both much argument interesting in itself as well as the germs of many ideas which were only to come to fruition in Rousseau's later works. The title makes reference to the question set by the Dijon Academy to which Rousseau was responding: Has the restoration of the arts and sciences had a purifying effect upon morals? His essay falls into two parts. The First Part considers whether sophisticated developments in the arts and sciences, and much interest and value being attached to high achievement in these, are generally found to be co-present with moral excellence in a society, and Rousseau concludes that they are not. The Second Part tries to explain how and why the advancement of the sciences and arts brings with it moral deterioration, thus sketching an explanation for the conjunctions he noted in the First. This at any rate is the surface structure of Rousseau's argument; we shall see in a moment that there are more complex patterns of thinking running through it.

He begins by arguing that the moral temper of his own day is, despite appearances and conventional estimates, corrupt and hypocritical:

> there prevails in modern manners a servile and deceptive conformity . . . Politeness requires this thing; decorum that; ceremony has its forms, and fashion its laws, and these we must always follow, never the promptings of our own nature.
>
> (DSA 6, OC III: 8)

Because of this polished surface that society and manners require we never know, Rousseau continues, what men are really like, what their true character and dispositions may be:

> Sincere friendship, real esteem and perfect confidence are banished from among men. Jealousy, suspicion, fear, coldness, reserve, hate and fraud lie constantly concealed under that uniform

and deceitful veil of politeness; that boasted candour and urbanity,
for which we are indebted to the enlightened spirit of this age.

(DSA 7, OC III: 8–9)

To set in contrast to this deceptive urbane smoothness, Rousseau
locates true virtue and the moral excellence of a society in 'liberty,
disinterestedness and obedience to law' (DSA 12, OC III: 14).

This false refinement of morals, Rousseau says, runs along with,
to make no stronger claim as yet, cultivation of taste and increase in
knowledge, or at least alongside increase in esteem given to the
display of taste and show of knowledge. He writes, very early in
the *Discourse* and without clear explanation: 'Arts, literature, and the
sciences . . . stifle in men's breasts that sense of original liberty, for
which they seem to have been born; cause them to love their own
slavery, and so make of them what is called a civilised people.'
(DSA: 4–5; OC III: 7). Nor, he proceeds, is this unique to the France
of this time; with perhaps more panache than accuracy, he cites as
other examples Egypt, Greece, Rome, Asia Minor and China, writing
of the last-mentioned:

If the sciences improved our morals, if they inspired us with courage
and taught us to lay down our lives for the good of our country, the
Chinese should be wise, free and invincible . . . But . . . What
advantage has that country reaped from the honours bestowed on
its learned men? Can it be that of being peopled with a race of
scoundrels and slaves?

(DSA 9, OC III: 11)

We should note from this passage that it is not scientific knowledge
and artistic excellence as such that Rousseau is hostile to, but the
high esteem attached and time devoted to them, which is taken
away from concern with honesty, integrity and service of the
common good and does not bring other moral improvements.
Also, as we shall see in a moment, he will further argue that the
practitioners of the arts and sciences are corrupted by the esteem

given to their productions and are thus led to pursue pseudo-science and the affectation of artistic creativity.

To note a conjunction is not yet to have found a casual connection; we do not know from it alone whether refinement of arts etc. actually produces degeneracy of morals, or whether this conjunction is just a coincidence, or the upshot of other buried causes. In Part Two, Rousseau turns to this question. He considers advancement in the sciences and arts as a complex individual and social phenomenon to which various motives and interests contribute and which in turn contributes to diverse social processes and outcomes. He does not take the image of the scientific inquirer as a disinterested seeker after truth at face value, but seeks to demystify and unmask the questionable interests that find expression and satisfaction in seeking high achievement in the field. Where learning is honoured and esteemed, individuals use the academic life as a path to personal prestige and celebrity. They will argue for a view or promote a position just because it will capture attention and bring acclaim, however meretricious, irresponsible or glib the thing may be:

> We do not ask whether a book is useful, but whether it is well written. Rewards are lavished on wit and ingenuity, while virtue is left unhonoured. There are a thousand prizes for fine discourses, and none for good actions.
>
> (DSA 24, OC III: 25)

Or again:

> these vain and futile declaimers go forth on all sides, armed with their fatal paradoxes, to sap the foundations of our faith, and nullify virtue . . . What extravagances will not the rage of singularity induce men to commit!
>
> (DSA 17, OC III: 19)

Despite this being how things stand generally, in Rousseau's estimate, leading many who have neither the disposition nor the ability for higher learning to give themselves over to it and be no good to themselves nor to others, there are a few – Rousseau names Bacon, Descartes and Newton – whose genius is genuine and whose achievements are 'monuments to the glory of the human understanding' (DSA 28, OC III: 29). However, he argues, these individuals would have achieved their great works without lavish praise or prestige being attached to their calling; theirs is a true gift that, if anything, thrives on obstacles. It is thus patent that Rousseau does not devalue learning and the enlargement of the human mind as such, but more the deceptive show of these where personal distinction and desire for acclaim are the real motive and dictate the character of the work done.

What underlies the growth and dominance of this deceptive show is luxury and idleness combined with the craving for personal ascendancy and the admiration of others on the part of producers and *soi-disant* connoisseurs alike, or so Rousseau maintains. So in fact it is not that the advancement of learning and taste by itself causes degeneracy of morals, but rather that both are manifestations of the deleterious effects of the pursuit of wealth, the value attached to adornment and ostentation, and the diversion of energy and esteem away from the achievement of real goods. (See, for instance, DSA 15, 17, OC III: 17, 19.)

This view of Rousseau's requires more explanation. It is natural that most people, setting aside the few of true genius referred to above, will choose to devote their time and effort to a mode of life that promises to yield to them things they will value, enjoy, take pride in. Rousseau is arguing that in very many cases what people value and enjoy is prestigious distinction, standing out from and above the crowd who can be looked down on as common, coarse and ignorant. The life of learning and artistic achievement will yield such prestige only if wit and ingenuity elicit differential esteem and acclaim; and they will do so only if people have the leisure to indulge in the business of distributing their favour or scorn on others depending on their productions in these arenas. But there is more. So powerful is the 'rage of singularity' in Rousseau's estimation that differentiations of quality and merit are created and insisted upon merely in order to establish a pecking order, merely to enable one person, group or 'school' to think the better of itself and to scorn and denigrate others. These differentiations have no other basis or role than that, to provide a way of creating sheep and discarding goats, to make social divisions between the estimable and contemptible possible in order to keep the game of those who are 'in' and those who are 'out' going. What any particular achievement may in actual fact be like is immaterial; all that is needed for it to count as meritorious is that it should catch favour and enable acclaim to go one way and contempt and scorn go the other. Such are the diversions of the idle rich, those at the top of the social pile.

Rousseau in different places calls these pseudo-excellences caprice, artificial, fashionable, prestige or mere 'opinion' merits or excellences, and the idea of them and their opposite, the true, real and genuine thing has a central role in all his thinking. In the First Discourse we see really only the outline of a set of notions that he progressively refines and extends and applies widely in his more developed works. This notion of prestige-based pseudo-excellences has an important corollary. Since their function is that of drawing esteem and regard to oneself and away from others, it follows that anyone aspiring to such excellences must be ever guided by what others think of him. The meaning and rewards of an individual's life are at others' disposal; if other people's favour finds another target, that person's own sense of the good in their life and in themself vanishes. People who base their activities on such 'merits' lose custody of their own lives; their success or failure hangs on the vagrant esteem of others and the possible emergence of a newer, more interesting diversion. This also is a point Rousseau greatly enlarges on in his later writings and of which we gain only a hint in this essay.

One more point should be added at this stage. The craving for distinction is, in Rousseau's view, not confined to just a limited number of individuals but is very pervasive indeed. However, by its very nature, distinction can only be enjoyed by a few, and logically it requires the deference of many and the ignominy of more. Its achievement is apt to be unstable and perilous, for those in ignominy will not be content but consumed by envious hatred of those who enjoy the preference and precedence they seek for themselves. There will then be a perpetual effort to deflect favour and regard away from those who presently enjoy it, using whatever resources come to hand – perhaps innuendo, slander and other forms of denigration. Thus social relations come to be marked by malice, spite and vindictiveness (recall the quotation given earlier), though these must be veiled in case the biter gets bitten.

In sum, Rousseau is arguing, as yet without any great explanatory depth and richness, that the desire for invidious distinction has, in most instances, motivated so-called advances in the sciences and arts. This being so, the upshot is that the actual value of these advances, estimated roughly in terms of the benefit they bring to mankind, becomes largely irrelevant to what is going on. All that matters is that they should draw acclaim onto the practitioner and away from others, leading to the result that the success or failure, value or worthlessness of a person and their life lies at the disposal of others' judgements. Finally, from this issues a pattern of relations pervaded by mutual competition, spite and the desire to humiliate and the fear of humiliation born of the need to have precedence.

This is a sombre, even nightmarish vision of human life and society. But, in my opinion, it is a profoundly perceptive one even though we are as yet only seeing its initial outline. A brief reflection on the worlds of fashion, film, popular music, television and writing that exist today will, I believe, suggest how penetrating Rousseau's assessment is of what is going on. Rousseau does say, however, that we can escape these perversions of value and from handing over our lives to the verdict of others, though how we are to do this is scarcely touched on in the *First Discourse*. What we need to take from his account thus far is the importance of this issue, and we shall see in due course how he thinks we can set about it and what different mode of life it is better to seek.

Rousseau's essay won the Dijon Academy's prize, and secured him considerable popular esteem of the very kind he had so exhaustively criticised. A number of replies to his arguments were published, Rousseau responding to some of these, and I shall pick up one or two helpful points from these exchanges. I shall also draw on some aspects of the Preface to his play *Narcissus*, referred to in Chapter 2 above, which have an immediate bearing on the arguments of the *First Discourse* and their reception.

Two points recur in Rousseau's responses to his critics. First, that he is not saying that the esteem coming to be attached to the sciences and arts is the sole cause of degeneracy in morals, so that if we were to revert to ignorance we should at once become virtuous again. He has held all along, he says, that there are many contributory causes of moral decay:

> There are a thousand sources of corruption among men and
> although the sciences may be most profuse and swiftest in their
> effect, they are far from being the only one.
> (Preface: G96 note; OC II: 964 note; see also G55, OC III: 63)

Neither is it the case that ignorance by itself could engender virtue; at best it is a necessary but in no way a sufficient condition for that. Also, Rousseau argues that moral probity having been lost, it is no easy task to recover it; and this leads on to the second point I want to attend to.

As might have been anticipated, the charge was levelled against Rousseau that whilst he disparages the arts he himself writes plays, music and operas. Is he not, therefore, a hypocrite, exhibiting the very vices he denounces? He replies that once a people has become corrupt it is better that they are amused and diverted by artistic productions since, first, this deflects them from doing more harm elsewhere and, second, the polish and refinement, however hypocritical, that cultivation of the arts in the quest for personal distinction requires produces 'a certain mildness of morals which sometimes compensates for their lack of purity, a certain appearance of order which averts terrible confusion' (Preface: G103–4 note; OC II: 971–2 note). It is possible to feel that these ripostes do not cut very deep.

Let us draw together the key elements in Rousseau's First Discourse. In it we find a not yet fully developed presentation of several crucial ideas that he develops in much of his mature writing. They are that contemporary society and morality are deeply corrupt, despite the appearances of civility and courtesy; that little or no honour is accorded men and deeds of true virtue but is rather given to attributes and achievements which solicit invidious acclaim and celebrity; that idleness and luxury work together with a craving for distinction to cause men to glory in one another's despite; that seeking such distinction places the meaning and value of one's person and life at the disposal of others' opinion of you; that the achievements that crown a life are very usually no more than pseudo-merits which have only the significance of making it possible to have the famous and the unknown; and that, beneath the appearance of civility, social and personal relations are pervaded by hostility, envy, contempt and malice as each individual tries to do down others.

A more comprehensive diagnosis of the ills of men and society in a short space is seldom to be found, and whilst it was, and is, quite easy to see the essay as an exercise in the mischievous ingenuity which it decries, it is clear that Rousseau was bringing forward issues he took very seriously indeed. Many of these are found again in the Second Discourse, his most brilliant essay, to which I now turn.

THE *SECOND DISCOURSE*

The Second Discourse, like the First, was written in response to a prize essay question set by the Academy of Dijon, though this time Rousseau did not win the prize. It contains some of Rousseau's

most penetrating and forceful writing and is one of his masterpieces.
Cranston has written:

> In less than a hundred pages, Rousseau outlined a theory of the
> evolution of the human race, which prefigures the discoveries of
> Darwin; he revolutionised the study of anthropology and linguistics,
> and he made a seminal contribution to political and social thought.
> Even if his argument was seldom fully understood by his readers, it
> altered people's way of thinking about themselves and their world;
> it even changed their ways of feeling.
>
> (Cranston, Introduction: 29)

The question set was 'What is the origin of inequality among
men, and is it authorised by natural law?' He completed his essay
in June 1754, and wrote a long dedicatory note to the Republic of
Geneva, to which he returned for a period at this time to reclaim
his citizen's rights by renouncing the Catholic faith his espousal of
which had led, in 1728, to the forfeit of those rights. It was finally
published in 1755 by Marc-Michel Rey, who was to become
Rousseau's long-term publisher, friend and support. The *Second
Discourse* was greeted once again with considerable acclaim, but
Rousseau did not much engage in the subsequent debate. As well as
deepening and extending several of the ideas adumbrated in the
First *Discourse*, the *Second Discourse* brings to the fore one of the conceptions for which Rousseau is best known, that of natural man in
his character as a 'noble savage' albeit that, as I believe, what
Rousseau intended in this idea is often ill understood. And we are
given a detailed account of the transmutation of this figure into
the corrupt and civilised man who peoples cities and dominates
society.

Rousseau opens his argument in the Preface to the *Discourse*. He
says that to know the sources of inequality among men we must

> begin by knowing mankind . . . and how shall man hope to see
> himself as nature made him, across all the changes which the

succession of place and time must have produced in his original constitution? How can he distinguish what is fundamental in his nature from the changes and additions which his circumstances and the advances he has made have introduced to modify his primitive condition?

(DI 43, OC III: 122)

He continues, in one of his most eloquent passages:

Like the statue of Glaucus, which was so disfigured by time, seas, and tempests, that it looked more like a wild beast than a god, the human soul, altered in society by a thousand causes perpetually recurring, by the acquisition of a multitude of truths and errors, by the changes happening to the constitution of the body, and by the continual jarring of the passions, has, so to speak, changed in appearance, so as to be hardly recognizable.

(Ibid.)

Rousseau is here at once broaching a profound theme. Whereas many philosophers are apt to suppose man's powers and dispositions are relatively fixed but simply reveal themselves differently if circumstances are different, Rousseau is suggesting that the whole character of man's self-understanding, the footing of an individual's engagements with other people, that individual's mode of apprehension of the world, can and do undergo fundamental changes during human history. Hence Cranston's remark that Rousseau outlined a theory of the evolution of the human race. Rousseau proceeds by arguing that most philosophers have erred by reading into man's natural character and circumstances capacities of understanding, inclinations, attitudes etc. that could only be drawn from society: 'in speaking of the savage, they described the social man' (DI 50, OC III: 132). He acknowledges that it is no easy task to strip away all these accretions in order to know what truly belongs to natural human beings in their natural circumstances. Rousseau suggests that his own ideas should 'not be considered as historical truths, but only as mere conditional and hypothetical reasonings, rather calculated to explain the nature of things, than to ascertain their actual origin' (DI 50, OC III: 133), though it has to be said that he shows little interest in considering and evaluating any alternative explanations that might prove more economical or comprehensive.

Taking this as his approach, Rousseau says that he finds as the most basic and simple dispositions of human beings 'two principles prior to reason, one of them deeply interesting us in our own welfare and preservation, and the other exciting a natural repugnance at seeing any other sensible being, and particularly any of our own species, suffer pain or death' (DI 47, OC III: 126). Being 'prior to reason', these are not principles consciously formulated and deliberately adhered to; rather they are the basic, inherent dispositions that belong to human beings, on Rousseau's conjectures. From the combination of these two dispositions, he goes on, all the duties of a person towards themself and others can be derived. These opening remarks establish the basic frame of the whole essay – the contrast between natural man in his natural setting, and artificial, social, civilised man in developed society, the former being inclined to peaceableness and gentleness, the latter to cruelty and malice. How has natural man, what is natural in and to man, become displaced or corrupted? And how does inequality between humans stand in relation to the law, rules, that best fit the original constitution of human beings?

Rousseau distinguishes two kinds of inequality. One he calls 'natural or physical', which consists in a 'difference of age, health, bodily strength, and the qualities of the mind or of the soul'; and the other 'moral or political', which depends on a 'kind of convention' and consists in 'the different privileges which some men enjoy to the prejudice of others; such as that of being more rich, more honoured, more powerful, or even in a position to exact obedience' (DI 49, OC III: 131). The origin of the former inequalities is, he says, self-evident and calls for no investigation; it is the origin of the latter we need to understand. How have they come into existence, and do they have any legitimacy?

At this point, Rousseau begins his argument proper, by offering an account of the character, dispositions and capacities that are original to man and a description of his natural environment. Natural man's concern for his own welfare (see the quotation regarding the 'principles prior to reason' given above) — his *amour de soi* — first expresses itself without significant forethought or self-awareness:

> His imagination paints no pictures; his heart makes no demands on him. His few wants are so readily supplied, and he is so far from having the knowledge which is needful to make him want more, that he can have neither foresight nor curiosity . . . His soul, which nothing disturbs, is wholly wrapped up in the feeling of its present existence, without any idea of the future, however near at hand; while his projects, as limited as his views, hardly extend to the close of day.
>
> (DI 62, OC III: 144)

Not inclined to be combative, natural man is fearful of the strange and unknown, and spends much of his time asleep (DI 58, OC III: 140). But he is not entirely a creature of impulse and rigid instincts; he has the capacity to regulate the immediate impulse of appetite, a rudimentary form of free will, and also the capacity to learn about his environment and to acquire new skills to enable him the better to make use of it for his own benefit which Rousseau calls man's 'perfectibility'. However, to begin with there is little occasion for these capabilities actually to be employed.

Reflecting on 'the distance between pure sensation and the most simple knowledge' (DI 62, OC III: 144), Rousseau spends some pages considering the origin of languages and general concepts, a matter he treated elsewhere in the *Essay on the Origin of Languages*, which he began work on at the same time but never completed. Picking up the main theme again, Rousseau stresses the separateness and independence of original man from his fellows in his natural setting. Such contact between humans as there may be is fleeting and inconsequential and, in this connection, he makes some slightly sardonic comments on the 'physical and moral ingredients in the feeling of love':

> The physical part of love is that general desire which urges the sexes to union with each other. The moral part is that which determines and fixes this desire exclusively upon one particular object . . . It is easy to see that the moral part of love is a factitious feeling, born of social usage, and enhanced by the women with much care and cleverness, to establish their empire.
>
> (DI 77, OC III: 157–8)

Whilst some encounters between men may be violent they do not lead to protracted quarrel, bitterness and vendettas:

> each man, regarding his fellows almost as he regarded animals of different species, might seize the prey of a weaker or yield up his own to a stronger, and yet consider these acts of violence as mere natural occurrences, without the slightest emotion of insolence or despite, or any other feeling than the joy or grief of success or failure.
>
> (DI 73 note 2, OC III note XV: 219–20; see also DI 76, OC III: 157)

What, then, can have brought it about, in Rousseau's conjectural history, that this condition was left behind, that men's dispositions changed, and that natural differences were overtaken by artificial inequalities? In Part Two of the *Second Discourse*, Rousseau turns to his hypotheses about this. He begins with some remarks about the institution of private property which have suggested to some that a proto-Marxist account is being sketched of man's loss of primitive integrity and simplicity and of his becoming self-estranged and aggressively competitive towards others. However, Rousseau himself says that 'the idea of property depends on many prior ideas . . . and cannot have been formed all at once in the human mind . . . Let us then go farther back' (DI 84, OC III: 164). If, following him, we do so, we find him suggesting that the root causes of the changes in man's nature and relationships lie elsewhere.

Material hardship and increase in numbers gradually caused people to associate together in a more settled and stable way, and to acquire the skills needed to assure their future needs, and thus the potential for 'perfectibility' comes into employment. Rousseau highlights two settings that bring new forms of self-understanding and encounter with others. First is sexual feeling; no longer does this prompt simply a brief coupling, but it generates a jealous exclusive claim on the loved object provoking competition for the unique enjoyment of favours (see DI 89–90, OC III: 169). Second, and more importantly, increased leisure made possible occasions of shared amusement, and:

> They accustomed themselves to assemble before their huts round a large tree; singing and dancing, the true offspring of love and leisure, became the amusement, or rather the occupation, of men and women thus assembled together with nothing else to do. Each one began to consider the rest, and to wish to be considered in turn; and thus a value came to be attached to public esteem. Whoever sang or danced best, whoever was the handsomest, the strongest, the most dextrous, or the most eloquent, came to be of most consideration; and this was the first step towards inequality, and at the same time towards vice. From these first distinctions arose on the one side vanity and contempt and on the other shame and envy: and the fermentation caused by these new leavens ended by producing combinations fatal to innocence and happiness.
>
> (DI 90, OC III: 169–70)

This important and vivid passage merits some reflection. Key is Rousseau's idea that we each want for ourselves a position with and acknowledgement from others; we demand 'consideration'. By this, we are coming to see ourselves in a new way in our engagement with others, as someone entitled to regard and esteem from them, and this means that a wholly new kind of significance comes to attach to our relations with other people. Enjoying the high regard – indeed paramount regard – of others becomes a matter of great importance and its presence or absence can make or mar the value to us of ourselves and our lives. We assume a 'being-for-others', to use an idiom more familiar from the work of Jean-Paul Sartre, though this is a phrase Rousseau occasionally uses too. We are no longer simply going about our practical affairs independently and separately, with occasional encounters or sometimes lending our energy to a joint enterprise, but have acquired a conception of ourselves as assessed and esteemed or despised by other people just as we in turn assess and appraise them. In this, quite plainly, there is a very far-reaching transformation in forms of self and other understanding and in the modes of interrelation associated with these.

It is striking that Rousseau does not think that this 'newborn' state of society straightaway produces those combinations 'fatal to innocence and happiness'. Indeed he writes:

> Thus, though men had become less patient, and their natural compassion had already suffered some diminution, this period of expansion of the human faculties, keeping a just mean between the indolence of the primitive state and the petulant activity of our *amour-propre*, must have been the happiest and most stable epochs.
>
> (DI 91, OC III: 171)

Indeed he goes on to call it 'the real youth of the world' (ibid.). However, things seldom stand still.

Further alterations in material conditions extend these first changes, in Rousseau's account. Metallurgy and agriculture extended men's powers and their needs, and it is at this point that ownership and property begin to assume their importance. For it is not the accumulation of property as a means to self-preservation, in its instrumental significance, that plays the central role, but conspicuous consumption as a mark of privilege and distinction, in its symbolic significance, that is key, and monopoly ownership as

a way of enforcing dependency and servitude on inferiors, that
drives the changes that follow.

> Insatiable ambition, the thirst of raising their respective fortunes,
> not so much from real want as from the desire to surpass others,
> inspired all men with a vile propensity to injure one another, and
> with a secret jealousy, which is the more dangerous, as it puts on
> the mask of benevolence, to carry its point with greater security . . .
> The wealthy . . . had no sooner begun to taste the pleasure of
> command, than they disdained all others, using their old slaves to
> acquire new, thought of nothing but subduing and enslaving their
> neighbours; like ravenous wolves, which, having once tasted human
> flesh, despise every other food and thenceforth seek only men to
> devour.
> (DI 96, OC III: 175; Rousseau makes like points at several places)

This is Rousseau writing in full flood; the picture he paints is very
familiar to those who live in 'advanced' Western societies.

Before long the pervasiveness of conflict, competition and
exploitation made any continuation of settled co-existence almost
impossible. Rousseau then envisages a 'trick' being played by the
rich and powerful on the indigent and weak. The rich emphasise
the need for law and punishments to bring stability to society and
reduce disorder. But this 'false social contract', as it is sometimes
called, does nothing except give new powers to the rich and
impose yet further burdens on the poor:

> All ran headlong to their chains, in hopes of securing their liberty;
> for they had just wit enough to perceive the advantages of political
> institutions, without experience enough to enable them to foresee
> the dangers. The most capable of foreseeing the dangers were the
> very persons who expected to benefit by them; and even the most
> prudent judged it not inexpedient to sacrifice one part of their
> freedom to ensure the rest . . . Such was, or may well have been, the
> origin of society and law, which bound new fetters on the poor, and

gave new powers to the rich; which irretrievably destroyed natural liberty, eternally fixed the law of property and inequality, converted clever usurpation into unalterable right, and, for the advantage of a few ambitious individuals, subjected all mankind to perpetual labour, slavery, and wretchedness.

(DI 99, OC III: 177–8)

On this basis, Rousseau criticises virtually all forms of established rule and government as nothing more than the enforcement of unjust and oppressive inequalities in power, riches and domination. So far from all in a state having an obligation to obey laws, most are simply in servitude to a superior force whose claim to legitimacy is wholly spurious. It may be retorted that whilst this is true for the majority of people in a society, there are a few 'on the pinnacle of fortune and grandeur' (DI 112, OC III: 189) who do very well out of it. But Rousseau, extending a line of argument we already glimpsed in the *First Discourse*, argues that even such people are made 'happy and satisfied with themselves rather on the testimony of other people than on their own' (DI 116, OC III: 193). Summarising the distance between 'moving, sweating, toiling' civilised man and the 'indolent savage', Rousseau writes:

In reality, the source of all these differences is, that the savage lives within himself, while the social man lives constantly outside himself, and only knows how to live in the opinion of others, so that he seems to receive the consciousness of his own existence merely from the judgement of others concerning him . . . in short . . . always asking others what we are, and never daring to ask ourselves, in the midst of so much philosophy, humanity, and civilization, and of such sublime codes of morality, we have nothing to show for ourselves but a frivolous and deceitful appearance, honour without virtue, reason without wisdom, and pleasure without happiness.

(DI 116, OC III: 193)

Rousseau, in winding up his discussion, does not spend more than a few lines on considering, as the original question asked, whether these 'moral' inequalities are or are not authorised by natural law. His answer is contained in the final words of the *Discourse*:

> it follows that moral inequality . . . clashes with natural right, whenever it is not proportionate to physical inequality – a distinction which sufficiently determines what we ought to think of that species of inequality which prevails in all civilised countries; since it is plainly contrary to the law of nature, however defined, that children should command old men, fools wise men, and that the privileged few should gorge themselves with superfluities, while the starving multitude are in want of the bare necessities of life.
>
> (DI 117, OC III: 194)

Now that we have seen what is at the centre of Rousseau's attention in the main body of the *Discourse* we can briefly return to the dedicatory note to Geneva with an understanding of why he highlights what he does in that, however remote from the actualities of social and political life in Geneva what he says actually is. Thus he emphasises right at the start that 'the equality which nature has ordained between men, and the inequality they have introduced' have been 'in this State happily combined and made to coincide, in the manner most in conformity with natural law, and most favourable to society' (DI 32, OC III: 111). And he goes on to highlight that no one is, in Geneva, above the law, and that whilst it is good and proper that there should be rulers, they are repositories of the trust of the people with whom the ultimate right of legislation reposes. Plainly, Rousseau is here stressing the contrasts with the inequalities and the false social contract which he has in the main body of the *Discourse*, as we have seen, identified as the situation prevailing in most modern states. It is striking also how many of the points he foregrounds in this Dedication are ones of which he gives a much fuller and theoretically supported account in the text of *The Social Contract*, as we shall see in Chapter 5 below. It is evident, as will also emerge when the Third Discourse is considered in a moment, that Rousseau's thinking about the best form for a just and prosperous state was well advanced at this time even though the text of The Social Contract was not completed for another five or six years.

ANALYSIS OF THE *SECOND DISCOURSE*

Analysis of and commentary on the Second Discourse could productively fill a book on its own, as has been done; it is one of Rousseau's most powerful and challenging works. I shall concentrate here however just on two points: first, Rousseau's treatment of *amour-propre*, which I haven't as yet spoken of explicitly; and secondly, and more briefly, on the significance he attaches to pity, one of the 'principles prior to reason' in the human soul noted earlier which excites 'a natural repugnance to seeing any other sensible being, and particularly any of our own species, suffer pain or death' (DI 47, OC III: 125–6). Attention to the first point will deepen our understanding of the 'rage of singularity' to which Rousseau gave such a central place in Discourse on the Science and Arts, but without a great deal of explanation. But additionally, it will lead into the further treatment Rousseau gives of *amour-propre* in Émile, where he provides his most subtle and sophisticated account of it (to be considered in the next chapter), just as he also gives there a much fuller account of the nature and role of pity as a foundation for constructive and creative human relationships to take the place of those destructive and malign relationships he has diagnosed in Discourse on the Origin of Inequality. It is in preparation for that that I here also attend to what he says about pity in the Second Discourse.

I begin with Rousseau's treatment of *amour-propre*, which, it may be recalled, I roughly explained previously (in Chapter 2) in terms of its being a need or desire to secure recognition and acknowledgement for one's person from others, as others have a like need for recognition from one. We can see this at work in the story Rousseau gives about people assembling before their huts, singing and dancing. He says, as cited before:

Each one began to consider the rest, and to wish to be considered in
turn; and thus a value came to be attached to public esteem.
Whoever sang or danced best, whoever was the handsomest, the
strongest, the most dextrous, or the most eloquent, came to be of
most consideration; and this was the first step towards inequality,
and at the same time towards vice. From these first distinctions
arose on the one side vanity and contempt and on the other shame
and envy.

(DI 90, OC III: 169)

The passage continues:

As soon as men began to value one another, and the idea of
consideration had got a footing in the mind, every one put in his
claim to it, and it became impossible to refuse it to any with
impunity. Hence arose the first obligations of civility even among
savages; and every intended hurt became an affront; because,
besides the hurt which might result from it, the party injured was
certain to find in it contempt for his person, which was often more
insupportable than the hurt itself.

(Ibid.)

What Rousseau is presenting here is the emergence of quite new
forms of self-understanding and terms of relationships between
people. Previously, as discussed, people lived independent lives,
scarcely aware of one another, at most coming together for brief
sexual couplings or for occasional concerted acts. But now, each
person comes to feel they merit 'consideration', that is some kind of
regard or respect from other people, the failure to receive which
provokes a sense of affrontedness, of having been improperly treated
or insulted. The idea of oneself as someone who is deserving of
proper regard being paid to one's person, a sense if you will of one's
having a right to deference, comes into play and radically alters the
footing on which people treat one another, what they expect from
one another, what kind of 'presence' they have to one another.

It is in this sort of context that the notion of *amour-propre* has its place. It is *amour-propre* that makes one mindful that one receives one's due esteem and deference, is properly regarded and treated with ample attention being paid to one's status and importance. In his only explicit discussion of it in *Discourse on the Origin of Inequality*, Rousseau writes:

> *Amour-propre* is a purely relative and factitious feeling, which arises in the state of society, leads each individual to make more of himself than of any other, causes all the mutual damage men inflict on one another, and is the real source of the 'sense of honour'. This being understood, I maintain that, in our primitive condition, in the true state of nature, *amour-propre* did not exist; for as each man regarded himself as the only observer of his actions, the only being in the universe who took any interest in him, and the sole judge of his deserts, no feeling arising from comparisons he could not be led to make could take root in his soul; and for the same reason, he could know neither hatred nor the desire for revenge, since these passions can spring only from a sense of injury.
>
> (DI: 73 Note 2, OC III Note XV: 219)

Here Rousseau is contrasting *amour-propre* with *amour de soi*, 'love of self'. Of the latter, he says it 'is a natural feeling which leads every animal to look to its own preservation' (ibid.); like pity, it is a principle 'prior to reason'.

As Rousseau presents the character of *amour-propre* here it appears to be inherently competitive and combative, leading people to make more of themselves than of others and hence at once leading to the demands for precedence, for dominance over others and for those others to accept an inferior and deferential position. And since a more settled and stable social existence brings *amour-propre* into play, at least in Rousseau's account, it seems to follow that social life will automatically assume the character that Rousseau attributes to it in the argument of *Discourse of the Origin of Inequality* — it will be driven by competition for precedence, by malice, by patterns of domination and servitude, and so on as described above. It seems that at the very moment we take on a human presence for each other our relationships inevitably take on a combative and aggressive character.

There is undoubtedly much in the argument of DI which fits this pattern, with benign *amour de soi* on the one side and corrupt *amour-propre* on the other; primitive innocence and independence on the one side and perverted civilisation and crippling dependency on the other; with happiness and well-being on the one side and misery and abjection on the other; and so on. And many assessments of Rousseau's thinking take this to be his definitive view of the nature and implications of *amour-propre*. However, two considerations should give us pause in accepting such assessments.

First, if this is how he views the immediate implications of people living together in settled societies, then the prospects for any just and humane society ever to emerge are slight or nonexistent. Yet Rousseau himself, of course, seeks to explain the character of such a society in the argument of The Social Contract. So either his thinking is deeply confused – a conclusion many have not long hesitated to reach – or else it is perhaps not the case that *amour-propre* necessarily assumes this competitive and aggressive expression. This thought can be reinforced by reflecting, second, that wishing to receive 'consideration' from others does not necessarily involve wishing more consideration to be given to oneself than to anyone else, wishing to be fawned upon whilst everyone else is ignored, although we are very familiar with suchlike cases. To wish to be considered may entail desiring no more than that one's voice, one's needs and one's ideas are heard and heeded not just because someone is kind enough to do this but because this is one's right and due as a human being, and/or as a member of society. To have a sense of what is due to one does not automatically mean that one is demanding flunkeys and a red carpet; it may only mean that one is entitled to be treated with dignity and respect as a person of intrinsic worth. If one's *amour-propre* demands that from others, this is not a competitive desire nor is securing such treatment bought at the cost of denying it to others. Basic equality of status and regard granted to all by all as of right may be sufficient to meet the requirements of the *amour-propre* of every person, without anyone being done down so that another can be at the top of the heap.

I have said that we do not find such lines of thought much followed up in *Discourse on the Origin of Inequality*; the argument of that is pretty much cast up in the black-and-white terms I indicated above: benign or corrupt; primitive innocence or perverted civilisation, and so on. But I do suggest that we should be wary of taking what we find here as the whole story. In the next chapter I shall try to show that such caution will be repaid, and a more complex and interesting account of *amour-propre* will be uncovered which is wholly consistent with Rousseau's other principal guiding ideas.

As my second point to note, I shall look briefly at what Rousseau says about pity or compassion in *Discourse on the Origins of Inequality*. As remarked, pity, along with *amour de soi*, is in his view a principle prior to reason, by which he means that the capacity to feel compassion is innate and that it does not require reflection or calculation for a compassionate response to another's suffering to be evoked:

> I think I need not fear contradiction in holding man to be possessed of the only natural virtue, which could not be denied him by the most violent detractor of human virtue. I am speaking of compassion, which is a disposition suitable to creatures so weak and subject to so many evils as we are: by so much the more universal and useful to mankind, as it comes before any kind of reflection; and at the same time so natural, that the very brutes themselves sometimes give evident proofs of it.
>
> (DI 73, OC III: 154)

Rousseau goes on to say that from compassion flow all the social virtues, and that through compassion we identify with the suffering person and directly wish, as they do for themselves that they are relieved of 'pain and uneasiness' and we are moved to try to procure this. Such compassionate responses are however, in his view, easily silenced by the demands of excessive *amour-propre* or other forms of self-absorption and hence social virtues do not generally flourish.

His treatment of this theme is quite slight in *Discourse on the Origins of Inequality*; its importance for our purposes is twofold. First, it readies us for an altogether more comprehensive and thorough treatment given to the significance of pity in the argument of *Émile*, in which it has a really central place. But also it provides us with a glimpse of the possibility – which, however, Rousseau does not develop further here – that human beings may have a footing in one another's lives on terms other than competing for precedence. As someone who suffers, helped by another person out of compassion for my predicament, I have been recognised and treated with decency and care, not scorned or derided by someone who wishes to do me down. This provides us with another reason for thinking that it may be possible, in Rousseau's way of thinking, for human beings to relate to one another on a non-competitive, non-aggressive footing so that settled life in society may not inevitably be driven by malice and misery. But, as I say, this line of thought is not followed up in *Discourse on the Origins of Inequality*; we need to wait for the discussion in *Émile* to see this idea given full development (see below Chapter 4, in the section on *Émile and the 'moral order'*).

It is worth noting too that in the *Essay on the Origin of Languages* which was begun around the same time as the *Second Discourse* Rousseau provides a strikingly different account of compassion, stressing the place of reflection and knowledge as a precondition for feeling pity; see Chapter 9 of the *Essay*. Interestingly, in the same chapter he also locates 'the golden age' at an earlier stage than that of the 'real youth of the world' we looked at a moment ago. But, as discussed before, the *Essay* was never completed, so we can only conjecture whether these remarks would have remained in a published version, to the detriment of the consistency of Rousseau's thought.

There is, of course, a great deal else in the *Second Discourse* that merits close attention and analysis, but these two elements in it are particularly significant in relation to the overall shape and direction of Rousseau's thinking. I shall, therefore, at this point move on to considering the *Third Discourse* on political economy.

THE *THIRD DISCOURSE*

The *Third Discourse* was not, as noted before, originally designed as an independent essay but was written for inclusion in Diderot and d'Alembert's *Encylopedia*, where it appeared in Volume V in 1755. It was first published on its own in 1758, in Geneva.

I shall hope to show, particularly in Chapter 5, that the *Second Discourse* especially provides key background ideas for understanding Rousseau's political project in *The Social Contract*. In the case of the *Discourse on Political Economy* this is quite plainly and explicitly addressed to issues central to the argument of SC and may helpfully be regarded as providing a preliminary study of elements in that work. Indeed, DPE begins by distinguishing political authority and the obligation of obedience that citizens in a just an legitimate state lie under from the authority of a father over the members of his family, a topic that Rousseau considers again almost at the very start of SC in Book I Chapter 2. We are perhaps apt to find the idea that political authority could be understood on such an analogy, or be conceived of as actually an instance of the same kind of obligation, almost inconceivable, but Locke, just as much as Rousseau, felt it necessary to argue against this conception. (See, for instance, Locke, *Second Treatise on Civil Government*, Chapter VI.)

The *Third Discourse* continues with Rousseau bringing forward certain notions that will be deployed more extensively in SC. He distinguishes the supreme authority in a society, the sovereign, from government both as a body and function; only the former has the right to legislate, to determine law. He goes on:

> The body politic ... is ... a corporate being possessed of a will; and
> this general will, which tends always to the preservation and
> welfare of the whole and of every part, and is the source of the laws,
> constitutes for all the members of the State, in their relations to one
> another and to it, the rule of what is just or unjust.
>
> (DPE: 132, OC III: 245)

In contrast to this general or public will which is the will of the whole body of the citizenry, there are also particular wills of individuals and the corporate wills of smaller associations, such as the will of priests or of senators, which may stand in conflict with the general will. All these ideas require further elucidation, which they will receive when we see them put to more developed use in the argument of *The Social Contract*. But it is already plain what great significance Rousseau attaches to the 'general will', his crucial notion for explaining the basis of legitimate authority and just law, albeit that in DPE there is a want of full explanation of its source and character.

For the rest, Rousseau concentrates on what he holds to be the primary responsibilities of government, and in three short sections he identifies what these are. First, it is 'the most pressing interest of the ruler [that is, the head of government] ... to watch over the observation of the laws of which he is the minister, and on which his whole authority is founded' (DPE: 136, OC III: 249). In no case must he suppose he is above or exempt from the requirements of law, and his chief task must be to inspire love of the law in all citizens. Rousseau emphasises that securing obedience by the imposition of penalties is very much a second best, leading to resentment and a desire to evade the law, viewed as an enforced constraint. This is an assessment from which he never departed, and we shall find it returning in different contexts in later chapters (see especially Chapter 6 below). The second section continues this theme. He writes:

If you would have the general will accomplished, bring all the
particular wills into conformity with it; in other words, as virtue is
nothing more than this conformity of the particular wills with the
general will, establish the reign of virtue.

(DPE: 140, OC III: 252)

As noted earlier, much of what Rousseau says in this *Discourse* is
taken up again and developed further in *The Social Contract*, and I
will be looking at these matters again when I discuss that. However, it is useful to try to deflect certain misunderstandings even at
this point. It might, for instance, be possible to read what Rousseau
is saying here as meaning that no one should have any interests and
concerns apart from their role in and contribution to the body
politic as a whole, almost as if they were ants in a colony where the
preservation and continuity of that is each and every ant's entire
life. But I do not believe this is Rousseau's position at all. Rather, he
is concerned that private and sectional interests are so apt to dominate, or displace, concern with the requirements of the general
will (the law) that he wishes to provide additional supports for the
claim and influence of the latter not to argue for the abolition of
other concerns altogether as if that were even conceivable. Thus he
gives prominence to the need to engender patriotic feelings in citizens, not out of some form of mindless jingoism but out of a desire
to ensure that the well-being of our fellow citizens comes to be
vivid and precious to us and we will not countenance their hurt and
deprivation even should our own narrow private interests have to be
circumscribed. Without this fairly low-key identification with our
country's men and women, limiting our private interests is very
likely to be experienced as an imposition, a demand only reluctantly
acceded to for the sake of an end, the good of someone else in the
same society, that is merely cerebrally acknowledged but not keenly
embraced and warmly sought. When Rousseau said, as cited before,
that the 'general will . . . tends always to the preservation and welfare of the whole and of every part' he takes the preservation and

welfare of 'every part' altogether as seriously as that of the whole, and is thoroughly hard-headed about the conditions necessary to ensure that this is attended to. In some of his most exalted writing, he puts the matter thus:

> The security of individuals is so intimately connected with the public confederation that . . . that convention would in point of right be dissolved, if in the State a single citizen who might have been relieved were allowed to perish, or if one were wrongfully confined in prison, or if in one case an obviously unjust sentence were given . . .
>
> In fact, does not the undertaking entered into by the whole body of the nation bind it to provide for the security of the least of its members with as much care as for that of all the rest? Is the welfare of a single citizen any less the common cause than that of the whole State? It may be said that it is good that one should perish for all. . . . if we are to understand by it, that it is lawful for the government to sacrifice an innocent man for the good of the multitude, I look upon it as one of the most execrable rules tyranny ever invented, the greatest falsehood that can be advanced . . . and a direct contradiction of the fundamental laws of society.
>
> (DPE: 144, OC III: 256–7)

And more to the same effect. The root of his concern is with how to create and sustain the attachments and dispositions that make these principles an actuality. Those who disparage Rousseau's attention to customs, sentiments, patriotism rather seldom, in my estimation, squarely face the issues he is looking at. In many contemporary societies we see that in effect very many people who live within a certain boundary and under a body of law are not really regarded as members of the state; their living or dying is by no means the 'common cause' and the affirmation of principles unaccompanied by changes of disposition will not alter this. These points will come to the fore again when we look at the role of the 'Legislator' in Rousseau's argument in The Social Contract in Chapter 5.

Finally, in the Third Section, Rousseau turns to issues of public finance, taxation and the generation of revenue for the state's disposal. There is a good deal of detail here, which need not detain us; his leading thoughts are plain and fully in accord with the central directions he has indicated in the first and second sections. Raising revenue must reduce the differences between the rich and poor, otherwise the rich will attach no importance to their shared membership of the state and have no concern at all for the poor. We plainly see this in many countries still. Taxes on luxury goods, where there is a choice to purchase or not, are to be preferred to those that fall on producers of necessities and on those necessities themselves. 'As long as there are rich people in the world, they will be desirous of distinguishing themselves from the poor, nor can the State devise a revenue less burdensome or more certain than what arises from this distinction' (DPE: 166, OC III: 277).

The Discourse on Political Economy is overall a slighter essay than the Second Discourse and has generally been less discussed, although there are some powerful passages in it and some key ideas are introduced. It is, I believe, best read in direct conjunction with The Social Contract where, in some instances, it usefully supplements elements of the argument in that, for example, concerning the importance of the development of fellow feeling, and where in other instances we find ideas sketched out in the Third Discourse receiving a fuller and more systematic working-out, such as those concerning the general will, sovereignty and so on.

SUMMARY AND PROSPECT

This concludes my scrutiny of Rousseau's three Discourses. In these, particularly in the first two, Discourse on the Sciences and Arts and Discourse on the Origin of Inequality, we have seen his assessment of the evils and miseries of civilised societies and his attempt to diagnose the sources of these. In the third, Discourse on Political Economy, we see the beginnings of his constructive thinking about the basis for and character of a just and humane society, but with a great deal as yet only sketched out at this point.

In the account I have given I have laid particular emphasis on the 'rage of distinction', the competitive desire to gain ascendancy over others and to rejoice in their subjection. This leads, in Rousseau's view, to merely fashionable, factitious achievements being esteemed instead of genuinely beneficial virtues, and to the worth of people and their lives being handed over to the verdict others pass on them. Human beings become alienated from their own true good, and relations between them are pervaded by malice, aggression and deception.

In contrast to this, Rousseau emphasises the happiness and peaceableness of natural man in the state of nature, who seeks his own preservation with little or no involvement with other people. At times, Rousseau appears to suggest that as soon as we leave this state of near-paradisal innocence and live with others in settled communities we fall inevitably into a corrupted condition, seeking invidious precedence motivated by the demands of our *amour-propre*. However, I have suggested that this contrast is too stark; Rousseau does in fact believe that there are ways in which we may live in society with others without corrupt inequalities dominating everything. We see the germs of this possibility in his account of compassion in the *Discourse on the Origin of Inequality*; and in the *Discourse on Political Economy* we also see that he believes social virtue and individual happiness may be brought to coincide.

With these primary points in mind it is possible to outline an 'agenda' for Rousseau's further work, which will address the key elements in the problematic situation he has described – not that I am suggesting he himself thought in these terms. He will need above all to consider whether and if so how it is possible for human beings to live together in stable societies without bringing down deformation and desolation on themselves. How can the demands of *amour-propre* be met without some triumphing and others being discarded? Is it possible for rule and law to deal with all citizens justly as opposed to being merely a codification of the power and privileges of dominant individuals or small groups? Can the human capacity for compassion provide a basis for a more harmonious and beneficial form of human intercourse? These questions will all be addressed in the coming chapters; whether or not Rousseau saw himself as working in quite this way, it does in fact make quite a lot of sense to see his thought as moving progressively from the diagnosis of human and social ills to an attempt to find their remedy. I turn now to an account of *Émile*, which will provide us with an ample view of Rousseau engaging with the issues he has brought to the fore in these earlier essays.

FURTHER READING

Timothy O'Hagan, *Rousseau*, chapter II. London: Routledge, 1999. A penetrating discussion of the *Second Discourse*.

Roger D. Masters, *The Political Philosophy of Rousseau*, chapters III–IV. Princeton: Princeton University Press, 1976. A full and subtle account of the *First* and *Second Discourses*.

M.F. Plattner, *Rousseau's State of Nature*: DeKalb, IL: Northern Illinois University Press, 1979. A book-length treatment of the *Second Discourse*.

Robert Wokler, 'The *Discourse sur les sciences et les arts* and its Offspring' in S. Harvey, M. Hobson, D.J. Kelley, S.S.B. Taylor (eds.), *Reappraisals of Rousseau*. Manchester: Manchester University Press, 1980. A detailed account of the *First Discourse* and its reception.

A.O. Lovejoy, 'Rousseau's supposed primitivism' in A.O. Lovejoy, *Essays on the History of Ideas*. Baltimore, MD: Johns Hopkins Press, 1948). A classic essay on the *Second Discourse*.

Four

Émile

Rousseau considered *Émile* to be his most penetrating and foundational work (RJJ 211; OC I, 933). Its subtitle is 'On Education', but although the work is cast as the narrative of the education of Émile from infancy to adulthood, and although it includes a great deal about the processes and objectives of an appropriate education (as well as many vividly depicted episodes of educative intent), Rousseau denied that it was a 'real treatise on education'. Rather:

> It is a quite philosophical work on the principle advanced by the author in other writings, *that man is naturally good*. To reconcile this principle with the other truth, no less certain, that men are bad, it would be necessary to show in the history of the human heart the origin of all the vices . . . In that sea of passions which submerges us, before one seeks to clear the way, one must begin by finding it.
>
> (Letter to Philibert Cramer, 13 October 1764, tr. Hendel: 296, also cited in Masters: 3)

Although I shall note some of Rousseau's pedagogic strategies and tactics in passing, my approach to the work is guided by what he says here: one must find the way first, and how then to clear it comes after. This being so, I think it is reasonable to see Rousseau, in *Émile*, as attempting to show what it would be like for an individual to have a whole and intact life and possess his own soul despite the almost overwhelming tendencies towards deformation and self-alienation that ordinarily befall us, according to the accounts that we have been examining in the previous chapter. Rousseau's project can then, I suggest, be seen as part of his response to the 'Agenda' I identified at the end of Chapter 3 focusing closely on the life of an individual, as equally we can see *The Social Contract* as a response to that agenda at the level of the design of political principles and procedures.

Rousseau probably began work on Émile in early 1759, when he was living at Montlouis, near Montmorency, just outside central Paris. It has been suggested that it was the wish on his part to meet the requests of some of his women friends for advice on how best to bring up their children that induced him to formulate his educational ideas in book form; he dispensed much advice in letters also. But this idea does not really explain why they turned to him for advice in the first place, especially as he had brought up no children. However, and as discussed just above, his dominant concern is not really child-rearing techniques but rather the means by which a person may come to live the best life for himself, maintaining his personal integrity both as an independent being but also while living with others in society and the state. The manuscript was more or less ready for publication by July 1761; there exist parts of an earlier draft also, about one-third the length of the final version, the MS Favre. It eventually appeared in May 1762, a month after the publication of *The Social Contract*. I have given, in Chapter 2, a more detailed account of the circumstances of its publication, and the aftermath of that – its being banned, Rousseau fleeing Paris and so on. Rousseau cannot have imagined that publishing this book would turn him into a hunted and stateless fugitive. But for all that the work was so firmly condemned by the public authorities – or perhaps because of this – it sold well and won him many individual admirers.

I noted at the start Rousseau's own estimate of this work, as the one which cut deepest and revealed the foundations of his thinking; this is an estimate of it that I share. The book has the form of a

narrative account of the development of an imaginary, but supposedly representative, male child, Émile, from his birth until he is
around twenty-five, under the guidance of his tutor and constant
companion Jean-Jacques who obviously bears some likenesses to
Rousseau himself. In the MS Favre, alluded to above, Rousseau
divides the developmental stages into four: the age of nature, up to
twelve years old, treated in Books I and II in the final version; the
age of reason, practical, applied intelligence, from twelve to fifteen,
treated in Book III; the age of 'force', energy, vitality of life, including the awakening of sexual interest in adolescence, from fifteen to
twenty, the topic of Book IV; finally the age of wisdom, from
twenty to twenty-five, covered in Book V (see OC IV: 60). The table
Rousseau gives there continues, rather optimistically: 'The age of
happiness and well-being – all the rest of life'. But this is not
discussed. What Rousseau is concerned with at each stage is a
whole constellation of capabilities, dispositions, forms of self-
understanding and forms of relationship with the material world,
with the human world of other people especially, and with the
divine that go make up the identity and characteristics of the
human being at that particular time. It is central to his argument
that the constitution of the self and the forms of self and other
understanding undergo radical transformations during the life of
an individual. In saying this, there are clear echoes of his arguments in the *Discourse on the Origin of Inequality*. I believe that no crucial
significance attaches to the particular chronology Rousseau gives
for the emergence of each of these different self-constituting
constellations; it is rather the description of their character and
implications that is key. At the same time, Rousseau throughout
warns of deformations that may occur in relation to each of these
configurations, and makes many proposals about how to avoid
these; this is in fact the principal educational burden of the work.
Some of these proposals strike me as very interesting and plausible;
others as much less so. But here, too, I suggest that it is the character
and implications of the distorted forms that is the principal

object of concern, not whether this or that practical pedagogic tip is likely to be effective or not. To repeat Rousseau's own metaphor: identifying the correct path must precede suggesting methods for clearing it.

He sets out the principal intent of the work in the opening pages, to determine whether it is possible for a man to be good both for himself and for others. It may seem surprising that I say this is the principal intent because, at first sight, Rousseau seems to indicate that this is quite impossible. Men are, he says, naturally interested in their own well-being: 'natural man is entirely for himself' (E I 39, OC IV: 249). On the other hand, the good citizen is 'denatured':

> Good social institutions are those that best know how to denature man, to take his absolute existence from him in order to give him a relative one and transport the / into the common unity, with the result that each individual believes himself no longer one but a part of the unity and no longer feels except within the whole. A citizen of Rome was neither Caius nor Lucius; he was a Roman.
>
> (E I 40, OC IV: 249)

And he goes on, just a line or two later:

> He who in the civil order wants to preserve the primacy of the sentiments of nature does not know what he wants. Always in contradiction with himself, always floating between his inclinations and his duties, he will never be either man or citizen. He will be good neither for himself nor for others. He will be one of these men of our days: a Frenchman, and Englishman, a bourgeois. He will be nothing.
>
> (Ibid.)

Many interpreters take these passages as definitive, attracted perhaps by the simple either/or that they present: man is either natural or denatured; good for himself or for others; has an absolute existence or a relative one – and so on. However, it is very clear that

Rousseau's view is that someone raised for himself may still find an effective rôle and footing with others. The key passage is this:

> what will a man raised uniquely for himself become for others? If perchance the double object we set for ourselves could be joined in a single one by removing the contradictions of man, a great obstacle to his happiness would be removed. In order to judge of this, he would have to be seen wholly formed: his inclinations would have to have been observed, his progress seen, his development followed. In a word, the natural man would have to be known. I believe that one will have made a few steps in these researches when one has read this writing.
>
> (E I: 41, OC IV: 251)

It thus appears that Rousseau is anxious to show that these are not exclusive alternatives, but that it is possible to find a basis for and form of engagement with others in society and the state that will preserve man's nature and goodness intact and hold out the prospect of enduring happiness and completion of life for the individual. If this is possible, then in thinking about how Rousseau construes the forms of relationship between the individual and society we are faced with four possibilities not just the usually suggested three. First, one could preserve oneself whole and entire by withdrawal or separation from society, to achieve a condition approximating to the condition of man in the state of nature as described in DI, or one might confine oneself to a small circle of family and friends bound by ties of warm affection. Or, second, one might become deformed and self-estranged because of the deleterious effects of aggression and the desire for dominance in society. Third, one might yield one's absolute existence and become 'neither Caius nor Lucius ... [but] a Roman'. But then, fourth, one could find a footing for oneself with others in society that is appropriate to one's needs and nature as an individual and which will be conducive to one's personal happiness and self-actualisation. To show the substance of this fourth possibility is, as I take it, the primary burden of *Émile*, and my assessment of the work will be guided by this idea.

ÉMILE: BOOKS I–III

Books I and II of *Émile* consider Émile in his infancy and early childhood, up to around twelve years old, as noted earlier. In early infancy, Émile's sense of self and self-understanding is very limited: 'He has no sentiment, no idea; hardly does he have sensations. He does not even sense his own existence' (E I: 74, OC IV: 298; see also E I: 42, 61; OC IV: 253, 279). Rousseau dispenses a good deal of practical advice about the best way to treat infants. He warns against swaddling, and coddling, them and urges that they should be breastfed by their mother rather than by a wet nurse, all of which comments had significant influence. But of more importance are Rousseau's reflections on the significance of a child's cries and the way these are responded to by those around them, most especially in instances where the child is reacting to failing to have their desires satisfied or to finding their actions impeded. He finds a great deal in these episodes, and his comments merit careful reflection. Thus he writes:

> A child cries at birth; the first part of his childhood is spent crying. At one time we bustle about, we caress him in order to pacify him; at another, we threaten him, we strike him in order to make him keep quiet. Either we do what pleases him, or we exact from him what pleases us. Either we submit to his whims, or we submit him to ours. No middle ground; he must give orders or receive them. Thus his first ideas are those of domination and servitude. Before knowing how to speak, he commands; before being able to act, he obeys . . . It is thus that we fill up his young heart at the outset with the passions which later we impute to nature and that, after having taken efforts to make him wicked, we complain about finding him so.
>
> (E I: 48, OC IV: 261)

Or again:

> The first tears of children are prayers. If one is not careful, they soon
> become orders. Children begin by getting themselves assisted; they
> end up getting themselves served. Thus, from their own weakness,
> which is in the first place the source of the feeling of their
> dependence, is subsequently born the idea of empire and
> domination. But since this idea is excited less by their needs than by
> our services, at this point moral effects whose immediate cause is
> not in nature begin to make their appearance; and one sees already
> why it is important from the earliest age to disentangle the secret
> intention which dictates the gesture or the scream.
>
> (E I: 66, OC IV: 287)

There is much else to the point as well (see especially E II: 87–8, OC
IV: 314–5).

What Rousseau is suggesting here is that the innate reactions that
a child has which enable them to lay hold on life and preserve
themself are susceptible to different pathways of development and
consolidation depending on how they finds their environment is
affected by those reactions. I use the colourless term 'environment'
for reasons that will become plain below; it is meant to cover
human reactions, its social environment, as well as inanimate
surroundings. Two points stand out. First, if the child learns that
they have only to cry to be fussed over, comforted, anxiously
attended to, they will soon learn, in Rousseau's marvellous words,
'how pleasant it is to act with the hands of others and to need only
to stir one's tongue to make the universe move' (E I: 68, OC IV:
289; see also E II: 88, OC IV: 314). But then, second, when – as will
inevitably happen – their desires, already ludicrously enlarged by
the delusive idea afforded to it of its scope and power, are not
satisfied, they will become enraged at this. Rousseau sees in this
rage a considerable degree of complexity, albeit plainly not consciously and explicitly present in the child's awareness. In rage and
anger is the idea that one's dissatisfaction is the upshot of the

thwarting interference, or hurtful negligence, of another person taken to be malign whether or not they truly are. The enraged child finds themself in a world permeated by believed ill intent and thus begins to attack or defend themself, if only out of a desire for self-preservation in the first instance:

> the child who has only to want in order to get believes himself to be the owner of the universe; he regards all men as his slaves. When one is finally forced to refuse him something, he, believing that at his command everything is possible, takes this refusal for an act of rebellion. All reasons given him at an age when he is incapable of reasoning are to his mind only pretexts. He sees ill will everywhere. The feeling of an alleged injustice souring his nature, he develops hatred towards everyone; and, without ever being grateful for helpfulness, he is indignant at every opposition.
>
> (E II: 87, OC IV: 314)

Of course – and this is part of Rousseau's point – such a mindset is not confined to the young; it is every bit as familiar among those who are chronologically adult but psychologically not yet so.

Rousseau's discussion of a child's wilfulness interestingly echoes several aspects of John Locke's treatment of this in his *Some Thoughts Concerning Education*. Thus Locke writes:

> We see Children (as soon almost as they are born, I am sure long before they can speak) cry, grow peevish, sullen and out of humour, for nothing but to have their *Wills*. They would have their Desires submitted to by others; they contend for a ready compliance from all about them; especially from those that stand near, or beneath them in Age or Degree, as soon as they come to consider others with those distinctions.
>
> (Some Thoughts, Para. 104)

And Locke, just as Rousseau, makes many subtle observations on the meaning of a child's cries and how to respond to these (see *Some Thoughts*, Para. 111 ff). Rousseau refers quite extensively in the text of Émile to Locke's work and often favourably, though their general approach to the purposes of education is very different; for Locke, its dominant end is the development of virtue. On some occasions where Rousseau is critical of Locke his points do not seem entirely justified. Rousseau, for instance, writes: 'To reason with children was Locke's great maxim . . . I see nothing more stupid than these children who have been reasoned with so much' (E II: 89, OC IV: 316). But Locke is careful to explain what he means:

> But when I talk of *Reasoning*, I do not intend any other, but such as is suited to the Child's Capacity and Apprehension. No Body can think a Boy of Three, or Seven Years old, should be argued with, as a grown Man . . . When I say, therefore that they must be *treated as Rational Creatures*, I mean, that you should make them sensible by the Mildness of your Carriage, and the Composure even in your Correction of them, that what you do is reasonable in you, and useful and necessary for them: And that it is not out of *Capricio*, Passion, or Fancy, that you command or forbid them any Thing.
>
> (*Some Thoughts*, Para. 81)

There is much in this from which Rousseau would not in fact dissent.

Returning now to the progress of Rousseau's discussion, he argues that the contest of wills has now begun and that it must be controlled and contained very firmly if it is not to become the child's predominant way of engaging with the world and the people in it – either the child wins or you do, there is no middle ground, nor other terms of encounter, or so it will seem. Rousseau makes this point very clearly in the later *Dialogues*:

> The primitive passions, which all tend directly toward our happiness, focus us only on objects that relate to it, and having only the love of self (*amour de soi*) as a principle, are all loving and gentle in their essence. But when they are deflected from their object by obstacles, they are focused on removing the obstacle rather than

reaching the object; then they change nature and become irascible and hateful.

(RJJ 9–10, OC I: 688–9)

Why is this pattern of response, with its incorporated interpretations of people and the world, of such interest to Rousseau? There are a variety of reasons. First, he holds that trying to make your way in life on these terms will make any child very unhappy. The passage cited above about the child's soured nature continues thus:

How could I conceive that a child thus dominated by anger and devoured by the most irascible passions might ever be happy? . . . With their desires exacerbated by the ease of getting, they were obstinate about impossible things and found everywhere only contradiction, obstacles, efforts, pains. Always grumbling, always rebellious, always furious, they spent their days in screaming, in complaining. Were those fortunate beings? Weakness and domination joined engender only folly and misery.

(E II: 87–8, OC IV: 314–5)

Second, Rousseau sees in these patterns the first seeds of the development of combative *amour-propre*:

In growing, one gains strength, becomes less restless, less fidgety, withdraws more into oneself. Soul and body find, so to speak, an equilibrium, and nature asks no more of us than the movement necessary to our preservation. But the desire to command is not extinguished by the need that gave birth to it. Dominion awakens and flatters *amour-propre*, and habit strengthens it. Thus, whim succeeds need; thus, prejudices and opinion take their first roots.

(E I 68, OC IV: 289)

This point is both important in itself, in view of the significance Rousseau attaches to the role of *amour-propre* as we have already seen in the argument of DI and will examine further here. But also it enables him to avoid a potentially serious theoretical problem.

Rousseau, as we have seen several times, maintains that man is by nature good but corrupted by society. Exactly how this view is to be understood requires close attention, but not in order to make the present point; see further below. In DI, it seems that *amour-propre* with all its deleterious effects emerges from human nature during the processes of socialisation. Does it not therefore follow that at least the germ of this damaging form of self-concern must be present in our nature, even should it not germinate until we come together with others in society? But that is not enough for Rousseau to say that men are by nature good; the propensity to the malignities of *amour-propre* appears to be inbuilt.

The main argument of E is more subtle, however. Patterns of domination and subservience, of mastery and enslavement, are shown not to be the ineluctable upshot of innate propensities, but emerge because of the ways in which a child's tears, angry reactions to frustration and so on are responded to and handled by those around them. Thus Rousseau can consistently say that 'the first movements of nature are always right. There is no original perversity in the human heart. There is not a single vice to be found in it of which it cannot be said how and whence it entered' (E II: 92, OC IV: 322). This has the corollary that the primitive forms of a child's self-assertion, of their efforts to establish their presence in the world, that are shown in tears and outbursts of anger need not take on the character of combat for ascendancy over others. Recognition by and acceptance from others may perhaps be acquired on other terms, and human relationships take on a more benign character. I shall be looking at Rousseau's account of how this might go in a while.

A third reason for interest in tendency for human engagement to become a contest of wills lies in its helping to make sense of one of Rousseau's pedagogic recommendations that is widely found to be at best strange and at worst frightful. He urges that Émile's environment up to the age of twelve and perhaps beyond be 'stage managed' in such a way as to make it appear that any disappointment of his desires or failure of his actions is the upshot of an inhospitable and unaccommodating inanimate world and not of the decisions and choices of other people even if the latter be true. Émile, that is to say, will have his engaged encounters with other people reduced to a minimum. And this, naturally enough, sounds like a dreadful way to bring up a child. But Rousseau has a very serious point here. As discussed earlier, a child's angry response to frustration posits an opposing will that is thwarting him. The consequences of having that posit confirmed are very damaging, as we have seen. Therefore, Rousseau concludes, everything possible must be done to undermine this postulate, by presenting to the child a world that is stable, orderly, predictable and quite unaffected by the imperious or petulant flailings of the child's little will:

> Treat your pupil according to his age. At the outset put him in his place, and hold him there so well that he no longer tries to leave it. Then, before knowing what wisdom is, he will practice its most important lesson . . . Let him know only that he is weak and you are strong, that by his condition and yours he is necessarily at your mercy . . . Let him see this necessity in things, never in the caprice of men . . . It is thus that you will make him patient, steady, resigned, calm even when he has not got what he wanted, for it is in the nature of man to endure patiently the necessity of things but not the ill will of others.
>
> (E II: 91, OC IV: 320; see also E II: 85, OC IV: 311)

What Rousseau says here may seem harsh and strange, but it is not so very distant from the talk of 'boundary setting' which one still hears much of in child-rearing books and, indeed, in organisational management books too.

It is in connection with this that we can usefully note some of Rousseau's very striking thoughts about the role of morality in regulating a child's behaviour, and human behaviour generally. He writes:

the words *obey* and *command* will be proscribed from his lexicon, and even more so *duty* and *obligation*. But *strength, necessity, impotence* and *constraint* should play a great role in it.

(E II: 89, OC IV: 316)

What is Rousseau's thinking here? It is that almost always things identified as duties and obligations are disagreeable to undertake and just as often the point of doing them is opaque to the agent, especially if a child. How, then, do requirements of obligation appear? As arbitrary impositions inflicted by an imperious authority, which provoke resentment and the desire to avoid them or to dissemble:

He who is aware of the need he has of others' help, and who never fails to experience their benevolence, has no interest in deceiving them; on the contrary, he has a palpable interest in their seeing things as they are, for fear that they might make a mistake prejudicial to him. It is, therefore, clear that the de facto lie is not natural to children. But it is the law of obedience which produces the necessity of lying, because since obedience is irksome, it is secretly dispensed with as much as possible and the present interest in avoiding punishment or reproach wins out over the distant interest of revealing the truth.

(E II: 101, OC IV: 335)

For all that Rousseau's examples relate to the upbringing of a child, his point is a perfectly general one – that to attempt to regulate human conduct by means of appeals to moral obligation where there is no palpable sense otherwise in doing that thing is to engender more evils than were intended to be eradicated. In the *Letter to Christophe de Beaumont* he writes:

despite the most sound and most virtuous principles of education; despite the most magnificent promises and most terrible threats of religion, the errors (perversities) of youth are still only too frequent, only too numerous . . . I have proved that these errors of youth of

which you complain cannot be restrained by these means, in that
they are the very handiwork of them.

(OC IV: 943, my translation)

Moral coercion produces the evils to which it purports to provide
the remedy.

I believe these ideas of Rousseau's are still much under-
appreciated. The propensity of individuals and governments to use
moral appeals to provide a basis for measures that are increasingly
repressive – and by this produce exactly the 'delinquent' behaviour
Rousseau predicts – seems unstoppable. But how, then, should one
direct people's behaviour; or – to return to the narrative development of Émile – how should one guide a child's behaviour? By
engaging their interest and showing them the evident utility in their
own terms of what is in view, by allowing them to explore, develop
and enlarge their powers and capabilities by practical engagement
with their world. Much of Books II and III of E is devoted to giving an
account of how to do this. Rousseau constantly encourages Émile's
enrichment of his competencies, strengthening his self-reliance,
testing his hardihood so that he becomes a thoroughly proficient
and effective person in terms of looking after himself and providing
for his needs. Rousseau stresses the need to remain perpetually
vigilant against the re-emergence of the contestation for dominance, and there are some brilliantly described episodes where this is
checked. Summarising his condition at age fifteen, Rousseau writes:

Émile has little knowledge, but what he has is truly his own . . . Émile
has a mind that is universal not by its learning but by its faculty to
acquire learning; a mind that is open, intelligent, ready for everything,
and, as Montaigne says, if not instructed, at least able to be
instructed.

(E III: 207, OC IV: 487)

And new forms of self-awareness and understanding have been
achieved also:

Now our child, ready to stop being a child, has become aware of himself as an individual. Now he senses more than ever the necessity which attaches him to things . . . We have made an active and thinking being. It remains for us, in order to complete the man, only to make a loving and feeling being – that is to say, to perfect reason by sentiment.

(E III: 203, OC IV: 481)

And, a few pages later:

He considers himself without regard to others and finds it good that others do not think of him. He demands nothing of anyone and believes he owes nothing to anyone. He is alone in human society; he counts on himself alone.

(E III: 208, OC IV: 488)

This, then, is Rousseau's alternative configuration for the human self, to stand in contrast to the combative will in endless contention with others which, as he has argued, so often becomes the form our selves and lives take. And if it were truly Rousseau's view that only keeping oneself apart from others save for occasional practical engagements driven by utility held out any prospect for human happiness and wholeness, we might expect Émile's story to end here and anything further to be simply an account of misery and disintegration, of paradise lost. But nothing could be further from the truth; indeed, it is clear from the second of the three quotations just given that more is needed 'to complete the man', and in Book IV of E Rousseau takes the argument through some very significant further steps.

ÉMILE: BOOK IV

This, the longest book in the work overall, finds Rousseau writing at his most brilliant and intense as he describes how Émile forms, first, ties of mutual feeling and concern with others, and then, second, enters into relations of reciprocal moral right and responsibility with them, enters, as Rousseau puts it, 'the moral order' (E IV: 235, OC IV: 522). In so doing, and this is the key point, Rousseau holds that we can still follow the path of nature, keep faith with man's nature, not dislocate or deform this. Thus he says:

> But consider, in the first place, that although I want to form the man of nature, the object is not, for all that, to make him a savage and to relegate him to the depths of the woods. It suffices that, enclosed in a social whirlpool, he not let himself get carried away by either the passions or the opinions of men.
>
> (E IV: 255, OC IV: 551)

This understanding of Rousseau's intent, though it is well borne out, goes against many presumptions about the form of his thinking and for this reason I shall, in a moment, discuss his notion of man's nature explicitly before returning to the main argument of E. Before doing this, it merits repeating that what is in view at this point in Rousseau's argument, as throughout, is not so much a particular chronology of a child's life, but new and importantly different forms and structures of self-understanding, footings for relationships with other people, forms of self and other assessment and so on. These configurations can in fact emerge at quite different times in people's lives; Rousseau himself holds that, in some cases, their emergence should be held back, thereby making it quite plain that he is not really inquiring into child development in any detail as we saw before. It is the prospects for human happiness and completion that each of these complex patterns of self and modes of being holds out that is the dominant issue throughout.

Rousseau's account of 'nature'

What, then, does Rousseau understand by 'nature' and the 'natural'? Scarcely any notion has been given a wider and more diverse significance, nor more held to be dependent upon it, than the notion of 'nature', of what is 'in accordance with nature' and so on. And it is clearly a very key idea in Rousseau's thinking. I will not attempt anything like an exhaustive account of his deployment of this idea, which would require a book to itself, but will try to highlight aspects of it and his use of it that have a direct bearing on justly understanding and assessing key arguments in Émile.

One idea of what's natural is of that which is untouched by human hand, not shaped or formed (or deformed) by human design and artifice. It is perfectly clear this is not a key notion for Rousseau in E since the tutor's omnipresent planning and action are everywhere shown to be necessary to enable Émile to develop in accordance with nature. Admittedly, much of the tutor's role is preventative, concerned with stopping the impact of events and influences that might distort Émile's natural development, as it were creating a space in which his nature can unfold without impediment. But there is also more to his role than this; he checks nascent tendencies and introduces experiences, learning opportunities and so on that are intended to foster Émile's natural development. The haphazardness of truly untended nature is quite absent here.

So what else could be in view? There are two key aspects to Rousseau's thinking about nature in E. The first concerns what naturally pertains to human beings, to their condition, circumstances, capabilities. The second concerns what the dispositions, desires and attitudes are that are natural to humans. I shall look at this second issue first. On this, Rousseau adopts what is basically an Aristotelian position, according to which, roughly speaking, something is natural to human beings, part of their nature, if it relates to the realisation of a human being's potential, contributes to its conservation and the actualisation of its proper character (see, for example, K.F. Roche's, *Rousseau: Stoic and Romantic*, p.3 ff). Thus Rousseau identifies our 'natural' passions in the following way: 'Our natural passions are very limited. They are the instruments of our freedom; they tend to preserve us' (E IV: 212, OC IV: 491).

What he says here regarding our passions can be extended to cover desires, attitudes, dispositions; among these the natural ones are those that tend to our preservation, conduce to our final actualisation. This is, if you will, Rousseau's definition of one aspect of the significance of the idea of the natural. So conversely, something is unnatural, contrary, repugnant to our nature, if it tends to destroy or damage us, to diminish or harm the fullness of our life. And Rousseau further argues that anything unnatural in us will have grown up because of external influences, because things or people have worked upon us to our detriment though not necessarily on purpose:

> The source of our passions, the origin and the principle of all the others, the only one born with man and which never leaves him so long as he lives is self-love (*amour de soi*) – a primitive, innate passion, which is anterior to every other, and of which all others are in a sense only modifications. In this sense, if you wish, all passions are natural. But most of these modifications have alien causes without which they would never have come to pass, and these same modifications, far from being advantageous for us, are harmful. They alter the primary goal and are at odds with their own principle. It is then that man finds himself outside of nature and sets himself in contradiction with himself.
>
> (E IV: 212–3, OC IV: 491)

This claim, that those among our passions which are harmful to us are unnatural, have alien causes, is not just something Rousseau assumes but something he argues intensively for; recall the letter to Cramer cited at the start of this chapter. We have seen the beginning of this argument in his account of how the tears and rage of the infant can become consolidated into imperious petulance and capricious domination by the way they are treated by those around it. But, as we have also seen, they can be treated differently, and if so the child is less likely to be 'dominated by anger and devoured by the most irascible passions' (E II: 87, OC IV: 314) and in that way has a much better chance of happiness.

This pattern of argument is closely related to Rousseau's discussions of man's natural goodness. The image this conjures up, of people being naturally disposed towards gentleness, generosity, kindness and affection, is apt to be treated with scorn as revealing a want of hard-headed awareness of human depravity, as being sentimental and weak-minded. If one adds to this the claim Rousseau so often makes, in one form or another, 'that man is naturally good ... But ... society depraves and perverts men' (E IV: 237, OC IV: 525) it is easy to reach the conclusion that we have here the self-exculpating theory of someone who is unwilling or unable to acknowledge their own responsibility for any evil intentions or actions, placing the blame on others for making one do things one never really wanted to. But however Rousseau may have conducted his personal life, his theoretical arguments are a good deal more robust. His thought is that those dispositions which are good in a perfectly conventional sense, such as benevolence, compassion, patience, generosity and so on, are at the same time dispositions that conduce to our own well-being and fullness of life let alone that of those around us, and are thus 'natural' in the primary significance we have identified. And those dispositions that are in an equally conventional sense 'evil' – malevolence, spite, imperiousness, meanness, etc. – contribute to our own misery and impoverishment let alone that of those around us. They are, thus, unnatural or contrary to nature, and by the arguments Rousseau has canvassed may be seen to have come to be our dispositions, if they are, through the effect upon us of how others treat us. Of course one may want to take issue with his arguments, but there is no question of Rousseau's just making emotionally influenced assumptions about this.

I turn now to the question of what naturally pertains to humans to their condition, circumstances and so on, according to Rousseau. Two brief quotations will best convey what I have in view here. Rousseau writes, for example:

Men are not naturally kings, or lords, or courtiers, or rich men. All are born naked and poor; all are subject to the miseries of life, to sorrows, ills, needs, and pains of every kind. Finally, all are condemned to death. This is what truly belongs to man. This is what no mortal is exempt from.

(E IV: 222, OC IV: 504)

Again:

> In the natural order, since men are all equal, their common calling is man's estate, and whoever is well raised for that calling cannot fail to fulfil those callings related to it . . . On leaving my hands, he (Émile) will, I admit be neither magistrate nor soldier nor priest. He will, in the first place, be a man. All that a man should be, he will in case of need know how to be as well as anyone; and fortune may try as it may to make him change place, he will always be in his own place . . . Our true study is that of the human condition. He among us who best knows how to bear the goods and ills of this life is to my taste the best raised.
>
> (E I: 41–2, OC IV: 251–2)

Central to Rousseau's thinking here is that we too seldom acknowledge our true circumstances and adjust our expectations and behaviour accordingly; we are beings of finite power, limited endurance and lifespan occupying limited positions in a large world. Delusions of grandeur, of unlimited potency, of mortality held at bay, fuel our dreams and waking life and in so doing, or so Rousseau argues, bring down misery and ruin on us. See, for example, the 'Maxims' discussed at E IV: 224–6, OC IV: 507–9. In this, we find one further link in Rousseau's tightly integrated thinking. These delusions of grandeur, which deny the finitude of one's person and circumstances and imagine exemption from the ordinary burdens of life, are part and parcel of that exaggerated sense of self-importance that the mishandling of a child's tears gives rise to, as considered earlier. And that same mishandling gives rise to the vices, as also considered. So a full realisation of the reality of one's personal limits and the vicissitudes of one's circumstances, a true appreciation of what naturally belongs to man, leads to the same point as does the cultivation of those dispositions that are natural to man. When Rousseau writes:

> This is, then, the summary of the whole of human wisdom in the use of the passions: (1) To have a sense of the true relations of man, with respect to the species as well as the individual. (2) To order all the affections of the soul according to these relations.
>
> (E IV: 219, OC IV: 501)

this is not a vague general statement of a programme, but an exact assessment of how error and delusion in understanding one's scope and circumstances fuels sentiments and dispositions that are harmful to oneself as well as to others, which he has examined and analysed at length.

Rousseau's account of pity

I return now to the point where Émile is about to enter 'the moral order', to become enclosed in the 'social whirlpool', to determine what transformations of the understanding of self and other this brings, and how these can – with the elucidation given – be seen to be in accord with, or contrary to, nature now that we are disabused of the idea that it is automatic that once Émile (any individual) enters society they are bound to deform their nature or adopt an artificial persona. As noted earlier, Rousseau considers the onset of adolescent sexuality as the key 'trigger' that opens Émile fully to personal encounter and engagement with others. Rousseau writes:

> The study suitable for man is that of his relations. So long as he knows himself only in his physical being, he ought to study himself in his relations with things. This is the job of his childhood. When he begins to sense his moral being, he ought to study his relations with men. This is the job of his whole life, beginning from the point we have now reached.
>
> As soon as man has need of a companion, he is no longer an isolated being. His heart is no longer alone. All his relations with his

species, all the affections of his soul, are born with this one. His first
passion soon makes the others ferment.
(E IV: 214, OC IV: 493; Bloom's note to this passage is very helpful.)

However, Rousseau argues that the yearning for love and com-
panionship should not be given priority; rather friendship is the
'first sentiment of which a carefully raised young man is capable'
(E IV: 220, OC IV: 502). This sows 'in the adolescent's heart
the first seeds of humanity'; he is drawn 'toward the tender and
affectionate passions' (ibid.) commiserating with his fellows,
anxious not to cause hurt, generous and kind, whereas the first
impulses of love readily give rise to jealousy and rivalry.

Rousseau builds on this a very important discussion of the role
of pity or compassion in establishing a bond between people and
creating a footing for them in one another's lives which will not be
corrupting and have ill effects. We noted the importance of pity in
DI, but the discussion here goes much deeper. In compassion, we
respond to another's hurt or distress as if it were our own, that is to
say, without any intermediate reflection on e.g. a trade-off for
services rendered, or appeal to a moral principle of helping those in
need. This 'identification' with others in such instances is facilitated
by three things. First, Émile himself will have had experience of
suffering, and so will well understand how it is with others when
they suffer when he first 'begins to feel himself in his fellows'
(E IV: 222, OC IV: 504). Second, vulnerability to suffering is one
of the things that 'truly belongs to man', as was discussed a
moment ago. Thus, the capacity for compassionate response opens
one to all sorts and conditions of human beings and is not confined
to one particular subclass of individuals. Third, and a key point in
Rousseau's larger designs, in those circumstances where compassion is evoked the person who suffers stands in need of us, does not
threaten or stand over us. So it is that we are not apt to be provoked
into an aggressive contention for dominance when encountering
them, of the kind considered earlier. A footing of amity and equality

in the face of the common lot of humanity can begin to be established, giving us a position in others' lives and them a position in ours that does not necessarily involve the aggressive drive for invidious precedence and the doing down of one another. Rousseau warns that Émile must, however, never be tempted to think that he is exempt from the ills that beset those for whom he feels compassion; nor think that it is somehow to his credit, or proof of his superiority, if he is fit and well, for the time being. Such ideas will feed and foster the impulse to dominate and an idea of supremacy which will only return us to the mutually damaging competitive relationships that we seek a way out of (see for example E IV: 229, 251, OC IV: 514, 545).

The human relationship established in compassion is not all 'one-way', so to speak, from the compassionate person to the one who suffers. Compassion, spontaneously shown and not used to trap, control or patronise, elicits gratitude as its natural response and by that the compassionate person is thanked and cherished by the one they have helped. A union of mutual regard and esteem is established, created by these interconnections of feeling and concern. Thus it is that another can have a place in our life but without at once being experienced as presenting a challenge and confrontation. Yet this is only a first step:

> So long as his (Émile's) sensibility remains limited to his own individuality, there is nothing moral in his actions. It is only when it begins to extend outside of himself that it takes on, first, the sentiments and, then, the notions of good and evil which truly constitute him as a man and an integral part of his species.
>
> (E IV: 219–20, OC IV: 501)

The sentiments we have looked at; but now we must consider the 'notions of good and evil' and how these shape Émile's thinking and the terms of his understanding of himself and others.

Émile and the 'moral order'

Once more, controlling or avoiding the resurgence of the desire for domination of others is a key part of Émile's apprehension and internalisation of moral ideas:

> Since my Émile has until now looked only at himself, the first glance he casts on his fellows leads him to compare himself with them. And the first sentiment aroused in him by this comparison is the desire to be in the first position. This is the point where love of self (*amour de soi*) turns into *amour-propre* and where begin to arise all the passions which depend on this one.
>
> (E IV: 235, OC IV: 523)

But, as Rousseau at once stresses, *amour-propre*, which demands a position, a standing, for oneself with regard to others does not necessarily result in aggression, cruelty and malignancy. The passage just cited continues:

> But to decide whether among these passions the dominant ones in his character will be humane and gentle or cruel and malignant, whether they will be passions of beneficence and commiseration or of envy and covetousness, we must know what position he will feel he has among men, and what kinds of obstacles he may believe he has to overcome to reach the position he wants to occupy.
>
> (Ibid.)

So the key issue is for Émile to understand what rank among men it is best to hold, and, as a corollary of this, to understand that competitive rankings of superiority, power and riches bring only illusory gains and false rewards:

> He is a man; he is interested in his brothers; he is equitable; he judges his peers. Surely, if he judges them well, he will not want to be in the place of any of them; for since the goal of all the torments they give themselves is founded on prejudices he does not have, it appears to him to be pie in the sky . . . He pities these miserable

kings, slaves of all that obey them. He pities these false wise men,
chained to their vain reputations. He pities these rich fools, martyrs
to their display.

(E IV: 244, OC IV: 536)

Émile will be happy to have health, moderation, few needs, the
means to satisfy them, to be in the common order of men; he will
know and feel that this is a sufficient and complete life and that the
determination to ascend and outdo yields only delusive rewards
and causes pervasive ills.

What follows from this? It is that the central demand of *amour-propre*, to receive our due recognition and respect from other people,
is capable of being met providing we are clear about what is our due
from others – not servility and fawning adulation but a position
among men of common regard and common respect, recognising
our equality as humans. This has a key further implication, which is
that the demands of any one individual's *amour-propre* can be met
consistently with those of each and every other person; it is not
necessary that my sense of self-worth should be be derived from
the domination of others and their immiseration as inferiors (see
E IV: 251, OC IV: 545), the nature and consequences of which idea
we have looked at carefully earlier, in Chapter 3. What ensues is
people relating to one another on a footing of equality and mutual
respect, this being a full acknowledgement of what is due when the
delusions of self-aggrandisment linked to the destitution and
ignominy of others are set aside. Kant, in his own idiom, makes a
closely related point very concisely, clearly drawing on Rousseau:

The predisposition to humanity can be brought under the general
title of a self-love which is physical and yet *compares* . . . that is to
say, we judge ourselves happy or unhappy only by making
comparisons with others. Out of this self-love springs the
inclination *to acquire worth in the opinion of others*. This is originally
a desire merely for *equality*, to allow no one superiority above
oneself, bound up with a constant care lest others strive to attain

such superiority; but from this arises gradually the unjustifiable craving to win it for oneself over others.

(Kant, *Religion* Book I, Section I, 22)

Where there are differences in the honour and favour paid to people – which Rousseau does not at all rule out completely – his insistence is that these should be proportionate to the services such persons have paid to the common good and the community, and in no way be dependent on depriving anyone of the basic respect which is everyone's absolute due.

So what emerges from these key pages in Rousseau's text is an account of the way in which we can enter society and have a position among other human beings, as they too have a position in our life, which does not automatically involve competition for dominance with the consequences for self-estrangement and unhappiness that brings in its train. It follows that Rousseau can, without self-contradiction or desertion of his primary principles, go on to reason about the best forms for human community to take without this necessarily involving a desertion of nature and man's corruption. It also follows, more scholastically, that it is a mistake to represent *amour de soi* and *amour-propre* as exclusive and opposed; the latter, so long as it is grounded in a just estimate of one's due, is a necessary and good element in one's well-being, completion as an individual and a full participant in society, benefits one seeks for oneself out of *amour de soi*.

This, I believe, is the climax of Rousseau's central argument of *Émile*; the individual is not necessarily corrupted by society, but a society in keeping with man's nature and promising happiness and wholeness of life would look very different indeed from those we are familiar with. We shall look closely at Rousseau's blueprint for this new kind of human community in the next chapter. But before moving to that, there are other aspects of Émile's education and development that Rousseau considers, and these merit attention. They are Émile's religious education; his love for a woman; and the beginnings of his political education. I shall say something about each of these in turn.

THE PROFESSION OF FAITH (CREED) OF THE SAVOYARD VICAR

In Book IV of E Rousseau incorporates a long more or less self-contained passage he calls 'The Profession of Faith (Creed) of the Savoyard Vicar' (E IV: 266–313, OC IV: 565–635). In this, he gives his most substantial account of the nature and basis of religious belief and sentiment treating of the nature of God, of God's relations with His creatures, and also considering the connections between religious belief and morality. Rousseau is very critical of the significance often ascribed to miracles and to revelation in religion, and of the intolerance between different religious denominations. This is the most important discussion for understanding Rousseau's religious ideas as they relate to the faith and conduct of an individual; his treatment of the role of religion in civil society will be considered later on; see below Chapter 6. Plainly these two matters are closely connected, but the considerations Rousseau brings to bear on each are substantially different and they merit separate discussion.

His pretext for including the *Creed* at this point in the text of E is the need to introduce Émile to ideas of religion and to give an account of the kind of personal belief and allegiance that would be proper to his education in accordance with the requirements for the cultivation and preservation of his intact nature. It was this section of *Émile* that was above all responsible for the book's being condemned and for the misfortunes that befell its author as a result, as considered earlier on (see Chapter 2). Great offence was taken to his criticism of the authority afforded to miracles, and to his denunciation of the cruelty of various churches, quite especially the Catholic Church.

The ideas presented in the *Creed* are put forward through the figure of an imagined priest from Savoy who is engaged in earnest conversation with the young Rousseau who makes his appearance in the book at this point. It is said that the figure of the priest, and some of the thoughts he expresses, are based in part on two people Rousseau encountered earlier in his life, the Abbé Gaime, whom he met in Turin, and the Abbé Gâtier, with whom he studied briefly on his return to Annecy in 1729–30 (see The Confessions III: 117–9, OC I: 118–120). It is to this last that Rousseau attributes the sexual indiscretion that he has his imagined priest commit such that he lost his office and was provoked into the intense meditations set down in the Creed. Because Rousseau does not present these reflections straightforwardly in his own voice, the question has been raised whether the views expressed are truly his own. However, it seems pretty apparent from what he says elsewhere about the Creed that it does contain his own considered ideas by which he was prepared to stand (see for instance, RSW III: 55, OC I: 1018; compare O'Hagan: 238). I turn now to giving a brief account of the vicar's ideas.

Thrown into a state of indecision and distress as a result of his disgrace, the vicar turned first to the ideas of philosophers for aid in recovering his faith and a cogent form of religious belief. However, in terms that clearly echo DSA (see, for instance, DSA: 16–17, OC III: 18–9) he finds them 'to be good only at destructive criticism' (E IV: 268–9, OC IV: 568–9). But from this the vicar takes an importance cue, that the scope of human understanding of such matters is limited and that we should confine ourselves only to what we need to know for our essential interests, testing all ideas against our most basic feelings, eschewing speculations and grand theory: 'I am resolved to accept as evident all knowledge to which in the sincerity of my heart I cannot refuse my consent; to accept as true all that which appears to me to have a necessary connection with this first knowledge; and to leave the rest in uncertainty' (E IV: 269–70, OC IV: 570). Working on this basis, we learn first that human beings are not just sensitive and passive but also active and intelligent. Going beyond human beings, it appears that material objects are only passive, not being capable of spontaneous motion. It follows then that because there is motion in the material world that must be the result of spontaneous movement originating elsewhere which is the outcome of an exercise of will. This provides the basis for the vicar's first dogma or article of faith: 'I believe therefore that a will moves the universe and animates nature' (E IV: 273, OC IV: 576). Moreover, the motion that matter has is not random, but lawful. From this, the second article is derived: 'If moved matter shows me a will, matter moved according to certain laws shows me an intelligence. This is my second article of faith. To act, to compare, and to choose are operations of an active and thinking being. Therefore this being exists' (E IV: 275, OC IV: 578). Developing this thought, the vicar (Rousseau) concludes:

I believe therefore that the world is governed by a powerful and wise will. I see it or, rather, I sense it . . . This Being which wills and is powerful, this Being active in itself, this Being, whatever it may be, which moves the universe and orders all things, I call *God*. I join to this name the ideas of intelligence, power and will which I have brought together, and that of goodness which is their necessary consequence. But I do not as a result know better the Being to which I have given them; it is hidden equally from my senses and from my understanding.

(E IV: 276–7, OC IV: 580–1)

Before coming to the third and last dogma, the vicar reflects further on the nature of man and man's place in God's ordered universe. The human species is, he says, 'incontestably in the first rank' in the order of things that is divinely governed (E IV: 277, OC IV: 582), because of the range of powers and of understanding that we have in comparison with other species. This, he argues, should be sufficient for us to be moved by gratitude towards and to bless the beneficent deity; but when we look at actual human societies we do not find common rejoicing in the divine harmony but chaos, conflict and confusion. How has this come about?

To address this issue, the vicar/Rousseau at this point gives an account of the composition of human nature that is surprisingly at odds with a great deal of his other argumentation elsewhere. I shall consider the contrasts later on. Here he says there are 'two distinct principles' in man: 'one ... raised him to the study of eternal truths, to the love of justice and moral beauty, and to the regions of the intellectual world whose contemplation is the wise man's delight; while the other took him basely into himself, subjected him to the empire of the senses and to the passions which are their ministers' (E IV: 278, OC IV: 583). But it lies in our own hands which of these 'principles' governs our actions, dominates our life; as intelligent, willing beings we determine our own choices and deeds. This is the vicar's third article of faith: 'Man is therefore free in his actions and as such is animated by an immaterial substance' (E IV: 281, OC IV: 586–7). The disorder and distress of human life need not, therefore, be attributed to failures in God's providence:

> Providence does not will the evil a man does in abusing the freedom
> it gives him; but it does not prevent him from doing it, whether
> because this evil, coming from a being so weak, is nothing in its
> eyes, or because it could not prevent it without hindering his
> freedom and doing a greater evil by degrading his nature.
>
> (E IV: 281, OC IV: 587)

It is our abuse of our faculties that causes unhappiness and wickedness. Rousseau concedes that in this world the wicked often prosper, but the immateriality of the soul permits us at least to consider that after death the balance will be restored. Or, rather, the case is better put the other way about:

> If I had no proof of the immateriality of the soul other than the
> triumph of the wicked and the oppression of the just in this world,
> that alone would prevent me from doubting it. So shocking a
> dissonance in the universal harmony would make me seek to

resolve it . . . When the union of body and soul is broken, I conceive
that the former can be dissolved while the latter can be preserved.

(E IV: 283, OC IV: 589–90)

The vicar then considers what rules of conduct should emerge from
acceptance of these articles of faith. He presents an account of the
nature and role of conscience as the capacity to sense whether something is or is not suitable to our nature, a nature we know to be good
and healthy because of God's provident work in ordering things in
fit harmony which only our abuse of our freedom disrupts:

> Conscience is the voice of the soul; the passions are the voice of the
> body. Is it surprising that these two languages often are
> contradictory? And then which should be listened to? . . .
> conscience never deceives . . . he who follows conscience obeys
> nature and does not fear being led astray
>
> (E IV: 286–7, OC IV: 594–5)

The vicar/Rousseau's depiction of conscience rises to exalted
heights; he refers to it as a 'divine instinct, immortal and celestial
voice, certain guide of a being that is ignorant and limited but
intelligent and free' (E IV: 290, OC IV: 600–1); he uses the same
terms when concluding the Fifth of the *Lettres Morales* he wrote for
Sophie d'Houdetot in the winter of 1757–8 (see OC IV: 1111). In a
striking passage, the vicar summarises the differences between
good and evil men:

> The difference is that the good man orders himself in relation to the
> whole, and the wicked orders the whole in relation to himself. The
> latter makes himself the centre of all things; the former measures
> his radius and keeps to the circumference. Then he is ordered in
> relation to the common centre, which is God, and in relation to all
> the concentric circles, which are the creatures. If the divinity does
> not exist, it is only the wicked man who reasons, and the good man
> is nothing but a fool.
>
> (E IV: 292, OC IV: 602)

Acknowledging that he may still be in error despite his sincerity, the vicar's exposition of his positive views concludes at this point. The young Rousseau says that what he has heard seems to amount to 'pretty nearly the theism or the natural religion that the Christians pretend to confound with atheism or irreligiousness' (E IV: 294, OC IV: 606). The vicar willingly agrees to this, but goes on to contend that nothing more is needed and that where we do find further dogmas insisted on these make 'man proud, intolerant and cruel' (E IV: 295, OC IV: 607). This is where he begins the criticism of miracles, revelation and separate religious orders that I referred to at the start. The vicar insists that the true worship of God comes from the heart, and that particular ceremonies or practices are not required as a condition of salvation. To affirm that they are would require finding extraordinary proofs that one only among the many forms that worship takes is meritorious, and that those who do not practice this are damned. But all such alleged proofs lack credibility; all we find in them on examination is a claimed authority, but deceptions and sophistry are everywhere used in an attempt to bolster those claims:

> See, then, what your alleged supernatural proofs, your miracles and prophecies come down to: a belief in all this on the faith of others, and a subjection of the authority of God, speaking to my reason, to the authority of men. If the eternal truths which my mind conceives could be impaired, there would no longer be any kind of certainty for me, and far from being sure that you speak to me on behalf of God, I would not even be sure he exists.
>
> (E IV: 301, OC IV: 617)

In any event, the vicar stresses, how could a loving or good God destine 'the great majority of His creatures to eternal torment' (E IV: 299–30, OC IV: 614)? It is not on human testimony or in man's books but in the book of nature, which is accessible to all alike, that we 'learn to serve and to worship its divine Author' (E IV: 306–7, OC IV: 625). There is one written book that is however exempt from these strictures, the Bible – or the four Gospels in particular – which depict a morality of love, compassion, mutual care and trust. This is the essential teaching of the love of God and it requires no special revelation or sectarian allegiance to recognise and respond to this:

> the true duties of religion are independent of the institutions of men; . . . a just heart is the true temple of the divinity; . . . in every country and in every sect the sum of the law is to love God above everything and one's neighbour as oneself; . . . no religion is exempt from the duties of morality; . . . nothing is truly essential other than these duties; . . . inner worship is the first of these duties; . . . without faith no true virtue exists.
>
> (E IV: 311–12, OC IV: 632)

It is easy enough to understand why these views were condemned by the Catholic authorities even though there is no great originality in much of what Rousseau brings forward, and his versions of the arguments from first causes, and from design, show little sophistication and have had even less impact. From the material presented, I want just to pick up three points. The first concerns what I referred to earlier as Rousseau's view of the composition of human nature here which I said was surprisingly at odds with much of his other thinking about this. Second, I want to say a bit more about Rousseau's account of conscience; and, third, to look at what he says about atheism.

To begin with the first point. As far as I am aware, we scarcely find elsewhere in Rousseau's writings any hint of the dualistic account of human nature that is presented in the Creed, allocating intellect and freedom to one 'principle' and the passions and subjection to another, opposed one. But not merely this, his attributing evil to our abuse of our freedom in allowing ourselves to be guided by the inclinations and desires of our body sits very ill with his painstaking and detailed accounts of the origins of vice in terms of the effect of alien causes on our dispositions that we considered closely earlier. O'Hagan, in a powerful account, finds in this another instance of what he sees as a tension pervading most of Rousseau's thinking:

Rousseau is driven by two opposing visions of what it is to lead a perfect life.

The first is a *naturalist* vision of the world. In terms of this vision, human beings are unique, endowed with properties which are not reducible to the properties of their material bodies, but at the same time . . . they should strive to realise an ideal of integrity, which can be attained only when an equilibrium is established (or re-established) between the individual and its environment.

The second is a *deontological* vision of duty and virtue, according to which the human being is an essentially divided creature, and the division within human nature is something to be mastered rather than transcended.

(O'Hagan: 271)

In the rest of my own account, I have presented what O'Hagan refers to as the naturalist vision, and I continue to believe that lies really at the centre of Rousseau's thinking as one of his strongest conceptions. But the disparity with this of the doctrines of the Creed cannot be denied, and it is far from plain that the two can comfortably co-exist.

Second, a few further comments on Rousseau's conception of conscience. Here, too, the consistency of the view of man's moral capacities presented in the Creed with the rest of Rousseau's thinking is not obvious. For he does not at all see conscience as the exclusive source of moral understanding and moral motivation in human beings; compassion, for instance, can direct us towards generosity, clemency and justice without need of recourse to conscience. However, at a deeper level, a degree of unity in his thinking about these matters is discernible. If an individual, guided by their conscience, uses their freedom to choose good, they can be assured that the good they choose will be in accord with the good order that God has created in them and in their relations with their world. The 'voice' of conscience is an expression of the demands of this proper inner order of man, preserving which constitutes the individual's true need and good and which directs them to act well in accordance with God's overall providential design for all human beings. The voice of conscience is not a direct, personal revelation of the will of God to any one individual; it is, rather, the echo in everyone's soul of harmony that exists in the depths of the human personality and that if listened to will inspire the individual to proceed with God's loving work by their own actions. It is thus possible to see how it comes about that the sentiments engendered by compassion and the promptings of conscience have in the end a common root for Rousseau. In both cases, it is our own constitution directing us to follow our nature and good that is being expressed. In the case of conscience, it is the requirements of our whole nature as an element of God's overall design that is becoming manifest, whereas in the case of compassion it is only one part of the whole. But both derive from the good order which makes for harmony between the good proper to each individual, each individual's good acts, and promoting the good of others − or so Rousseau believes. He expresses his own confidence in this thus: 'I have only to consult myself about what I want to do. Everything I sense to be good is good; everything I sense to be bad is bad' (E IV: 286, OC IV: 594). This may be a rash thing to say, but it takes a peculiar perversity to read this − as has been done − as if Rousseau were claiming to be the creator and arbiter of good and evil and thus above obedience to any moral rules. What he is in fact acknowledging is that, at a fundamental level, he does not belong to himself; the character of his proper destiny and duty is imprinted on his given constitution, and what there remains for him to do is to recognise ('sense') this destiny and duly and freely to elect to follow its directions.

Third and finally, I want briefly to note what Rousseau says in the *Creed* about atheism. In a long note right at the end of that (E IV: 312−4, OC IV: 632−5) Rousseau is very emphatic that atheism is more deadly in its consequences than fanaticism since, in his view, it 'causes attachment to life, make souls effeminate and degraded, concentrates all the passions in the baseness of private interest, in the abjectness of the human I, and thus quietly saps the true foundations of every society' (ibid.). Whereas 'fanaticism . . . is nevertheless a grand and strong passion which elevates the heart of man . . . and gives him a prodigious energy that need only be better directed to produce the most sublime virtues'. These are strong statements and, to my mind, underestimate how difficult, to the point of impossibility, it is to 'better direct' a fanatic's grand and strong passion. However, what they do bear out is that whilst Rousseau sought a more tolerant religion in which forgiveness and love were paramount, he was never of the view that men and societies could survive and prosper without religious conviction and religiously inspired action having a central place. For him, the key issue is how to harness this to strengthening and preserving the social bond and men's commitment to justice and equality; we shall see how he tackles this in his discussion of civil religion (see below, Chapter 6).

Overall, as have indicated, I think there is much in the Creed that sits ill with Rousseau's other writings; and his own account of the grounds of religious conviction is far from compelling. On the other hand, he held a genuine and deep faith and was, I think, genuinely inspired by the message he took from the Gospels, 'to love God above everything and one's neighbour as oneself', as cited above.

ÉMILE: BOOK V – SOPHIE, OR THE WOMAN

The last book of E (Book V) concerns Émile's last years under the direction of his tutor as he comes to full maturity, though even at the last, Émile asks Jean-Jacques never to cease to advise and govern him (see E V: 480, OC IV: 868, and compare E IV: 316, 325, OC IV: 639, 651 on the changing terms of the relationship between master and pupil). The book treats of travel and of the basics of political understanding, but above all considers Émile's falling in love, preparation for marriage and establishing a family. Already in Book IV, Rousseau spoke of Émile's need for a companion, to whom he gives the name Sophie (E IV: 328–9, OC IV: 657) and a great part of Book V is given over to a description of Sophie's character and accomplishments and to her courtship by Émile. However, this is prefaced by a substantial account of the nature, education and role of women generally, and I shall begin by considering that.

Rousseau's ideas about women have attracted extensive criticism, and it is hard to deny they deserve this. He believes wholeheartedly in the patriarchal family, in men being active and strong, women being passive and weak; in women depending on men for their social position and honour; in women being necessarily preoccupied with appearances and people's judgement of them; in their being unsuited to abstract studies but fitted for practical and domestic occupations – and so on. The arguments he adduces for these views, such as they are, are weak and often sit uneasily with arguments he propounds elsewhere in his work. And such ideas as he puts forward that ameliorate this unfortunate account – of which there are a few – are not really sufficient to allay the unconvincing character of his predominant views. It could perhaps be argued that Rousseau was a creature of his time, and that to expect him to propose ideas more congenial to current thinking would be unrealistic. But this defence is not very powerful. First, Rousseau clearly thinks that in developing his ideas about women he is swimming against the tide of the current opinion of his time, so he is not in his own estimate just a creature of his day. And second, in most of the rest of his work he had little trouble in arguing against contemporary ideas, so his failure to think more radically about women cannot be attributed, without further explanation, to his somehow in this case being unable to rise above the customs and expectations of his age. I shall give a brief overview of his general ideas about this subject and of what I have called his ameliorative ideas concerning the relations of men and women in marriage, concluding with a glance at Émile and Sophie's courtship and marriage and its aftermath.

Rousseau begins by saying of men and women: 'In what they have in common, they are equal. Where they differ, they are not comparable' (E V: 358, OC IV: 693). But, it soon transpires, the differences appear to matter a great deal more than the similarities, and despite Rousseau's own comments the moral consequences of those differences are much to women's detriment. Rousseau attaches huge importance to what he believes to be unalterable differences between the roles of men and women in sexual union, and in the consequences of that. As noted already, men 'ought to be active and strong', women 'passive and weak' (E V: 358, OC IV: 693). From this we learn that 'a woman is made specially to please man . . . and to be subjugated' (ibid.). However, Rousseau infers from this that in the contest between the sexes, women are just as well able to control men as men women: 'an invariable law of nature . . . gives woman more facility to excite the desires than man to satisfy them. This causes the latter, whether he likes it or not, to depend on the former's wish and constrains him to seek to please her in turn, so she will consent to let him be the stronger' (E V: 360, OC IV: 695–6). 'Women', he goes on, 'possess their empire not because men wanted it that way, but because nature wants it that way' (ibid.). Finally: 'Woman is worth more as woman and less as man. Wherever she makes use of her rights, she has the advantage. Wherever she wants to usurp ours, she remains beneath us' (E V: 364, OC IV: 701).

It is hard to know what to make of this representation of a pattern of conduct between men and women supposedly the inevitable correlate of natural differences in forms of sexual arousal and satisfaction. Rousseau himself knows very well that many do not live like this. He routinely denounces the 'lascivious' habits of courtesans and libertines as being departures from this natural order, rather than accepting that no such order is readily discernible in this area. None of his ideas about what is 'natural', discussed earlier, have any real bite in this case.

With regard to the consequences of intercourse, Rousseau's account is no more convincing:

> The strictness of the relative duties of the two sexes is not and cannot be the same. When woman complains on this score about unjust man-made inequality, she is wrong. This inequality is not a human institution – or, at least, it is the work not of prejudice but of reason. It is up to the sex that nature has charged with the bearing of children to be responsible for them to the other sex. Doubtless it is not permitted to anyone to violate his faith, and every unfaithful husband who deprives his wife of the only reward of the austere duties of her sex is an unjust and barbarous man. But the unfaithful woman does more; she dissolves the family and breaks all the bonds of nature. In giving the man children which are not his, she betrays both. She joins perfidy to infidelity. I have difficulty seeing what disorders and what crimes do not flow from this one.
>
> (E V: 361, OC IV: 697)

The asymmetry Rousseau sees here seems to me to have no defensible foundation, and his attachment to this particular model of a patriarchal family does not appear to have justification, at least not on the grounds given.

So strongly does Rousseau take the view that 'appearances [are] among the duties of women' (ibid.) that he dilates on the theme thus:

> By the very law of nature women are at the mercy of men's judgments, as much for their own sake as for that of their children. It is not enough that they be estimable; they must be esteemed ... Their honour is not only in their conduct but in their reputation; and it is not possible that a woman who consents to be regarded as disreputable can ever be decent. When a man acts well, he depends only on himself and can brave public judgment; but when a woman acts well, she has accomplished only half of her task, and what is

thought of her is no less important to her than what she actually is
... Opinion is the grave of virtue among men and its throne among
women.

(E V: 364–5, OC IV: 702)

This distressing line of thought reaches its nadir in the following remarks:

Woman is made to yield to man and to endure even his injustice. You
will never reduce young boys to the same point. The inner sentiment
in them rises and revolts against injustice.

(E V: 396, OC IV: 750–1)

This is a sorry tale. There are, however, a few passages that hint at a more balanced account, and it is worth a moment to look at some of these. Not evidently in complete consistency with the above passages, Rousseau also says this:

To what will we reduce women if we give them as their law only
public prejudices? . . . A rule prior to opinion exists for the whole
human species. It is to the inflexible direction of this rule that all the
others ought to be related. This rule judges prejudice itself, and only
insofar as the esteem of men accords with it ought this esteem to be
authoritative for us.

(E V: 382, OC IV: 730)

However, even this position, which appears to provide women with a footing for independent judgment and separateness from men's opinion, is qualified by Rousseau who insists that the 'rule' directs obedience to a husband and to think otherwise is bad faith (ibid.). A few pages later Rousseau goes on to say that 'women are the natural judges of men's merit' (E V: 390, OC IV: 742), but again little is made of this and we do not see anything very substantial to correct the subordination that Rousseau designates as woman's proper place. I think it is apparent that Rousseau wasn't entirely comfortable with his overall position, but these hints at another way of thinking about the relations between the sexes and the rights of women are not given much development.

Fortunately, when we turn from the general to the particular we find in Émile's Sophie someone with a great deal more to her than we might have been led to expect. Although Rousseau repeats that the honour due to Sophie derives from her potential husband, and that she owes her rank and obedience to him, he equally stresses that Sophie is, as he puts it, interested in a man and not 'monkeys', that is, interested in those who possess virtue and integrity, not just those who will caper to attempt to delight her (E V: 404, OC IV: 761). Equally, despite the stress he has placed on a wife's acquiring her rank from her husband, he emphasises that the best unions are not those of people who 'suit each other only in a given condition', but those 'who will suit one another in whatever situation they find themselves, in whatever country they inhabit, in whatever rank they wind up' (E V: 406, OC IV: 764). There seems some hope, then, that despite the position prepared for Sophie by Rousseau's theories regarding women's place and role, she may still in fact be able to exhibit some independence and self-determination.

As noted in Chapter 2, Rousseau wrote a short sequel to Émile entitled *Émile and Sophie* or *The Solitaries*, not finished nor published in his lifetime. This takes the form of two letters addressed by Émile to his tutor, recounting the misfortunes that he and Sophie experienced. After the death of their daughter they move to Paris, but there Sophie is unfaithful and Émile leaves her and France. He is captured and enslaved by the ruler of Algeria, but shows so much ability that he rises to be a valued adviser. There is little of significance in these letters, except perhaps that they reveal that even in Rousseau's own estimation the chances of human happiness, of preserving oneself from the corruptions of city life, are very small indeed even when people have been brought up and guided with the utmost care. But it is hard to be sure what Rousseau's true intent in them was, and we do not need to share his own verdict (if that is what it is).

ÉMILE'S POLITICAL EDUCATION

In the closing pages of E, Émile sets out to travel, not least to test the solidarity of his love for Sophie and hers for him. But there is another, more significant, purpose also. In a helpful summary passage, Rousseau writes:

> Now that Émile has considered himself in his physical relations with other beings and in his moral relations with other men, it remains for him to consider himself in his civil relations with his fellow citizens. To do that, he must begin by studying the nature of government in general, the diverse forms of government, and finally the particular government under which he was born.
>
> (E V: 455, OC IV: 833)

and it is to learn about the diverse forms that government takes that travel is especially useful. However, setting aside the narrative incidentals, what we are offered in these pages is a succinct, but very helpful, summary of many of the principal ideas and arguments of The Social Contract, the text we shall be examining in the next chapter. I will not discuss this material here; its substance will be covered in the treatment given in SC. But it is useful to be aware of this presentation since it is in some respects clearer and more accessible than is the text of SC. What for now we should take away from this is a more general point, namely that it is clear that Rousseau sees no sharp discontinuity between Émile's prospects for a whole and happy life in regard to his 'physical relations' and in regard to his 'civil relations', though of course the issues and challenges pertinent to each will be different. This does, I think, clearly support the view I have put forward here overall that it was not Rousseau's view that every form of social or civil life was bound to be corrupting and immiserating; the question rather is one of the particular character or terms of that life, and his purpose is to identify the characteristics that will make it beneficial and enriching to people. We shall see what his ideas about this are in the next chapter.

FURTHER READING

Roger D. Masters, *The Political Philosophy of Rousseau*. Princeton: Princeton University Press, 1968, chapters I–II. Gives exceptional treatment of the argument of E.

N.J.H. Dent, *Rousseau*. Oxford: Basil Blackwell, 1988, chapter 4. Gives more detailed treatment of views expressed here.

Allan Bloom, 'Introduction' to *Émile* tr. Allan Bloom. New York: Basic Books, 1979; London: Penguin Books, 1991. An outstandingly interesting interpretative essay.

Joel Schwartz, *The Sexual Politics of Jean-Jacques Rousseau*. Chicago: Chicago University Press, 1984. A very full account of Rousseau's views on men, women and sex.

Laurence D. Cooper, *Rousseau, Nature, and the Problem of the Good Life*. University Park, PA: Pennsylvania State University Press, 1999. A very strong account of the role of conscience in Rousseau's thinking.

Ronald Grimsley, *Rousseau and the Religious Quest*. Oxford: Oxford University Press, 1968. A fine treatment of the Creed and other aspects of Rousseau's religious thinking.

K.F. Roche, *Rousseau – Stoic and Romantic*. London: Methuen, 1974. Good on Rousseau's conception of nature.

Five

The Social Contract

The remote origin of *The Social Contract* lies in a project Rousseau conceived while he was secretary to the French ambassador in Venice in 1743, to write a comprehensive work on political systems and processes to be called *Institutions Politiques*. He made little progress with this, however, but it is clear from the *Discourse on Political Economy* (of 1755/58), considered in Chapter 3, that several of the key ideas that are developed and utilised extensively in SC were, by that time, within Rousseau's grasp. He finally abandoned his grand scheme – as the foreword to SC indicates – in the mid to late 1750s and decided to 'extract from it whatever could be extracted and then to burn the rest' (C 10: 478, OC I: 516). Working up these 'extracts' into what became the text of SC proceeded alongside his work on E, and both books were published in 1762 within a month of each other, SC in April; E in May. *Émile*, as noted in Chapter 4, includes in Book V a highly compressed, but still helpful, summary of the central thinking of SC, ostensibly as part of Émile's political education in his maturity. Additionally, significant parts of earlier drafts of SC survive, including an important piece, originally intended for Book I of SC, usually referred to as 'The General Society of the Human Race' (in Cole *et al.*: 169 ff, OC III: 281 ff).

SC continues to be generally regarded as Rousseau's most important work and is certainly the most widely read. It holds its place as one of the classic works of political philosophy, alongside Plato's *Republic*, Hobbes' *Leviathan*, Hegel's *Philosophy of Right* and other permanently influential essays in this area. However, as we have seen earlier, Rousseau himself thought *Émile* his best achievement, and the contemporary reception of SC by no means matched the status now afforded to it. I do believe that we in fact gain a better understanding of SC if we bring an understanding of the core ideas of E to a reading of it, as well as drawing on Rousseau's critique of modern society most amply expressed in DI. Also, I think there are some respects in which the structure and organisation of SC are not absolutely clear, perhaps betraying something of its complex origin. There are, for instance, lengthy discussions in Book IV of the Roman republic, whose significance for the work's primary themes is far from clear; and the treatment given to perhaps the most important notion of the whole essay, the general will, is scattered throughout the work to the detriment of clarity and ready understanding.

In this chapter, I shall concentrate above all on Rousseau's account of the basis for a just and legitimate civil order and of what is connected with that. Rousseau also says a good deal about the social and cultural preconditions for establishing and maintaining such an order, a theme broached in DPE too as discussed in Chapter 3, and about the role of religion in the state. But I shall reserve fuller treatment of these aspects of the argument for Chapter 6. The work as we have it falls into four books. Broadly speaking, Book I considers the basic foundations of a legitimate civil body; Book II treats of law; Book III of the nature and role of government; and Book IV treats further of legislation, but also of the Roman republic and civil religion. I shall consider these books more or less in order although, as noted, Rousseau's discussion of the general will is spread throughout the work and requires pulling together; and as also noted I shall defer discussion of certain aspects of the argument, e.g. concerning civil religion, until the next chapter. My purpose will be to see if Rousseau succeeds in depicting a political community from which can be eliminated the deformations and miseries individuals suffer in most ordinary societies, as he believes, and in which instead people can live in union with one another on a footing which provides for the respect, integrity and happiness of each and all.

THE SOCIAL CONTRACT – BOOK I

Book I opens with Rousseau saying that his inquiry is 'if, in the civil order, there can be any sure and legitimate rule of administration, men being taken as they are and laws as they might be' (SC I: 181, OC III: 351). A few lines lower down, he makes one of his most famous statements: 'Man is born free; and everywhere he is in chains . . . How did this change come about? I do not know. What can make it legitimate? That question I think I can answer' (ibid.) Actually, of course, Rousseau thinks he does know how this change came about; both DI and E consider it at length. And note, too, the echo here of what Rousseau said almost at the start of DSA, written over a decade earlier: 'So long as government and law provide for the security and well-being of men in their common life, the arts, literature, and the sciences, less despotic though perhaps more powerful, fling garlands of flowers over the chains which weigh them down' (DSA: 4–5, OC III: 7). These two opening remarks highlight Rousseau's concern with legitimacy. He is not interested simply in how regulation and order is actually at work in society, but with finding a morally and rationally justified basis for rule and organisation. And, second, we see at once Rousseau's preoccupation with freedom in society. His views on this are complex and many faceted, and will be given specific attention later.

Rousseau begins by criticising two ways of trying to explain the basis of rightful rule in society. The first likens a state to a family, with the ruler as the father and the people as the children under his authority. (Rousseau also considers this, at rather more length, in DPE: 128–130, OC III: 241–3.) He argues that this familial union exists only so long as children need their father for their preservation, and as soon as this need ceases 'the natural bond is dissolved' (SC I: 2, 182, OC III: 352), and if they remain united it is only voluntarily and by convention. I dare say that few, if any, serious thinkers suppose any more that political legitimacy could be understood after this fashion, but equally we should not forget how common it remains for politicians and political leaders to be referred to or to refer to themselves as 'The father of the people' so it is clear that this way of thinking about the nature and basis of political authority and union still carries some if only emotional force. Of course, more broadly, many will argue that ethnic or religious ties may be necessary to underpin stable states, consent alone being insufficient to secure this. We shall see Rousseau's own assessment of the significance of such bonds in Chapter 6 below.

Rousseau then considers, in Book I Chapter 3, whether dominant strength or force creates a right to rule and an obligation of obedience. Again he deals with this briskly: 'To yield to force is an act of necessity, not of will – at the most, an act of prudence. In what sense can it be a duty?' (SC I: 3, 184, OC III: 354) Here, too, his view is compelling.

Having cleared the decks thus, Rousseau turns to his constructive ideas. He is, as I have said, concerned with the genesis and basis of a legitimate civil order. We need to ask what gives rise to the necessity for humans to come together in a 'conventional' union, i.e. one not established by bonds of affection or the imposition of superior force. And to ask on what terms they should do so, so that the rules that regulate their behaviour and interrelationships in that union are legitimate and properly command their obedience. In response to the first question, Rousseau identifies shortage of resources and limitations in our capacity to utilise them effectively as the principal cause. In such circumstances our 'primitive condition can then subsist no longer; and the human race would perish unless it changed it manner of existence' (SC I: 6, 190, OC III: 360). Here, as elsewhere in the text of SC, Rousseau presents man's 'primitive condition' as very much a matter of each individual having an existence independent of others, fending as best we can for ourselves or, at most, living and providing for ourselves as independent

families. In so doing he echoes the account of natural man in the
state of nature described in the early parts of DI. However, in the
chapter omitted from the final version of SC, 'The General Society
of the Human Race' referred to above, he emphasises also man's
cupidity and the jealous, competitive passions, considered in the
later parts of DI, as sources of difficulties in the way of human
preservation that a properly constituted civil order must address
and repair. It is important to note these more complex patterns of
human relationship and dependency at work before the establish-
ment of a settled civil society, because rightly ordering these is just
as much the concern of a just and well-founded political association, in Rousseau's view, as is meeting the material needs of its
members. Certain elements Rousseau includes in his final account
only make sense on this basis, as I shall show.

A variety of factors, then, make it necessary for human beings to
work together. But how can any individual leave his 'primitive
condition' and contribute to the common task without exposing
himself to the risk of harm and neglecting himself? For what
assurance can they have that they will not be taken advantage of by
others in making their contribution, and end up worse off than
before? Rousseau presents the issue thus:

> 'The problem is to find a form of association which will defend and
> protect with the whole common force the person and goods of each
> associate, and in which each, while uniting himself with all, may still
> obey himself alone, and remain as free as before'. This is the
> fundamental problem of which the social contract provides the
> solution.
>
> (SC I: 6, 191, OC III: 360)

And what are the terms of that social contract (or compact)? They
are these:

> 'Each of us puts his person and all his power in common under the
> supreme direction of the general will, and, in our corporate

capacity, we receive each member as an indivisible part of
the whole.'

(SC I: 6, 192, OC III: 361)

How this, what Rousseau calls an 'act of association', provides the
solution to the problem as he posed it is very far from transparent.
Key to understanding this will be to grasp the nature of the general
will and what it directs, and as yet we have been given no clue as to
what that might be. Before engaging with this issue head-on, it is
helpful to look at further aspects of this association-creating
undertaking.

Rousseau says that the act of association involves 'the total alienation of each associate, together with all his rights, to the whole
community' (ibid.) This statement is apt to cause alarm; it seems
that the individual is required to yield themselves without recourse or
defence to the control of the community, but in doing so they
appear to be exposing themself to potentially the most dreadful
risks and deprivations. How is this to advance beyond the threat to
our well-being, our survival we faced at the start? On one point, at
least, Rousseau's position is very strong. He points out that if in
relation to the act of association some individuals retained certain
rights, there would need to be a 'common superior to decide
between them and the public' if there were any dispute about e.g.
the scope or infringement of such rights. No such superior existing, the individual would be judge in their own case, so the association would cease to be effective or would need to resort to force to
exact compliance. Still, Rousseau himself seems conscious that talk
of 'total alienation' may cause unease, because he stresses two key
aspects of it. First, everyone entering into the association is in the
same boat, so it is not as if there were other members of the
association still possessed of the rights and powers one has oneself
just resigned who could then exert mastery over you. Second,
whatever the terms of the association may turn out to be, which are
as yet unspecified, they will be the same for all members and hence

no one will have any incentive to make them burdensome nor will have the scope to make them more burdensome for some rather than others.

This act of association creates a 'public' or a 'people' out of an 'aggregation' of persons. Rousseau calls it 'a corporate and collective body, composed of as many members as the assembly contains voters', or 'formed wholly of the individuals who compose it', and he introduces some key terminology to treat of its characteristics and functions, as follows:

> This public person, so formed by the union of all other persons, formerly took the name of *city*, and now takes that of *Republic* or *body politic*; it is called by its members *State* when passive, *Sovereign*, when active, and *Power* when compared with others like itself. Those who are associated in it take collectively the name of *people*, and severally are called *citizens*, as sharing in the sovereign authority, and *subjects*, as being under the laws of the State.
>
> (SC I: 7, 192–3, OC III: 361–2)

The central notion here is that of the sovereign, or bearer of sovereign authority. This is the final authority on this earth beyond which there is no further appeal, the decisions and determinations of which are therefore decisive and ultimate. The issue of appeal to superlunary authority beyond the civil sovereign will be considered when I discuss Rousseau's treatment of the role of religion in society; see below Chapter 6. It is, therefore, of the utmost importance that the constitution and mode of functioning of the sovereign body be determined with great care since everything else walks in its shadow, so to say. Thus far we know that the sovereign body is composed of as many members as the assembly contains voters, and Rousseau goes on to say that the primary though not exclusive function of this body is to declare laws to and for the whole community; or, more precisely, to declare what he describes as political or fundamental laws (SC II: 12, OC III: 393–4) which are 'the conditions of civil association' (SC II: 6, 212, OC III: 380) and which concern the relation of the whole to the whole, or of the sovereign to the state using the terminology Rousseau has introduced.

Now, conventionally laws take the form 'Thou shalt . . .' or 'Thou shalt not . . .', and these directives are ordinarily understood as the declaration of a will or intent that something be done or foregone. It thus follows that the sovereign body in declaring law should be understood as having and disclosing a will; and the will of the sovereign body when it determines the fundamental laws is the general will. Or, to put it slightly more precisely, the sovereign body in making law may declare its will for many different reasons, on many different bases. Particular and sectional interests – of which more below – may dominate the assembly and may find expression in its declarations. But when this is so, these declarations comprise binding law only in name and establish no obligation of obedience. They are only law in nature, that is to say are legitimate and create an obligation, when a truly general will is expressed in them: 'the general will alone can direct the State according to the object for which it was instituted, i.e. the common good' (SC II: 1, 200, OC III: 368). This at least locates the formal position of the general will in the composition and functioning of Rousseau's state; we have yet, of course, to be told anything about how it is determined and functions materially and substantively.

I have stressed so far the importance of the sovereign body and its exercise of authority in the declarations of the general will. The related idea of a 'citizen' should also be noted; this term and its complement 'citoyenne' came to play a key role in the rhetoric of the French Revolution as an appellation signifying equal membership of and participation in acts of sovereign deliberation and determination, a status eagerly if deludedly claimed by many previously disenfranchised townspeople and peasants.

The sovereign body, as the repository of final authority, normally has to have at its disposal dominant force also. If this were not so, then individuals or subgroups could flout the requirements of the sovereign body, the laws, with impunity, and whilst it might remain true that authority still resided in the laws they would have become empty for most practical purposes. Rousseau recognises this point, saying:

> In order then that the social compact may not be an empty formula, it tacitly includes the undertaking, which alone can give force to the rest, that whoever refuses to obey the general will shall be compelled to do so by the whole body.
>
> (SC I: 7, 195, OC III: 364)

This passage continues in a very striking way, Rousseau making one of his most notorious comments:

> This means nothing less than that he will be forced to be free; for this is the condition which, by giving each citizen to his country, secures him against all personal dependence . . . this alone legitimises civil undertakings, which, without it, would be absurd, tyrannical and liable to the most frightful abuses.
>
> (Ibid.)

Not only is it troubling to read that being subject to compulsion can make one free, which seems simultaneously near to being a contradiction in terms and yet very sinister in its implications; but also the reason he cites in support of this claim, namely that we are by this secured from 'all personal dependence' seems in no clear way to do this. Even were it to do so, how giving oneself to one's country is the only real alternative, and the one which makes you free, is far from transparent. Rousseau's thinking on this is, in fact, recoverable, but requires attention to arguments not fully present in the text of SC alone. But I shall defer engagement with this until later in this chapter, where I look explicitly at Rousseau's various ideas of freedom. (See also SC IV: 2, 278, OC III: 440.)

That Rousseau has much additional work to do here is also apparent if we return to the closing words of his 'solution' to the problem the social contract has to answer. They were: 'in our corporate capacity, we receive each member as an indivisible part of the whole'. Rousseau's basic thought here – which reaffirms the ideas expressed in his forceful comments in DPE considered in Chapter 3 above -- is that if there is any member of the civil community who is not in the relevant way part of the sovereign body and a participant in the processes and acts of sovereignty, then they are not true citizens, but merely enslaved, coerced into compliance – they are not properly *members* of the community at all, but merely constrained by its laws. However, as we have just been seeing, he allows the possibility of compelling an individual to obey the general will, and it needs explaining how this is not just a matter of enslavement of that person but continues to treat them as an 'indivisible part of the whole'. Their dissent appears to imply that they are treated as separate from the whole but are then forced back into line, so to speak. Rousseau needs to show how such enforced compliance does not involve abuse of the individual who is being sacrificed for the good of the multitude, to use his own words from DPE. I hope to show that despite the fact that it is very reasonable to have these initial doubts, in the end Rousseau mounts a powerful case for his position.

He begins to make that case in Book I, Chapter 8, which follows the remarks about being forced to be free cited above. He writes there that 'the passage from the state of nature to the civil state produces a very remarkable change in man, by substituting justice for instinct in his conduct, and giving his actions the morality they had formerly lacked'. He goes on to say that although by leaving the state of nature we lose some advantages, the rewards are even greater; man's:

> faculties are so stimulated and developed, his ideas so extended, his feelings so ennobled, and his whole soul so uplifted, that, did not the abuses of this new condition often degrade him below that which he left, he would be bound to bless continually the happy moment which took him from it forever, and, instead of

a stupid and unimaginative animal, made him an intelligent being
and a man.

(Ibid.)

This rather rhapsodic passage goes on with Rousseau saying: 'We
might, over and above all this, add, to what man acquires in the
civil state, moral liberty' and, I suggest, this obscure notion of
'moral liberty' holds the key to solving the questions I have just
been raising. However, unhelpfully Rousseau himself now concludes by saying: 'But I have already said too much on this head,
and the philosophical meaning of the word liberty is not what
concerns us here'. Quite the opposite is true; he has not said
enough, and we shall need to inquire into that philosophical meaning in order to resolve these difficulties. This I shall be doing later
on, as I have said.

THE SOCIAL CONTRACT – BOOK II

I turn now to the activity of the sovereign body undertaking its
proper task, determining and declaring fundamental laws for the
whole association through the expression of its will, the general
will. 'The people', Rousseau writes, 'being subject to the laws,
ought to be their author: the conditions of the society ought to be
regulated solely by those who come together to form it' (SC II: 6,
212, OC III: 380). But by what process, on what footing, are the
people to authorise law and regulate their own society? How, that
is to say, is the general will to be determined out of the ideas,
desires, hopes and fears of the people who comprise the society or
association?

Before turning to address this crucial issue it is worth pausing for
a moment to reflect that whilst today the proposition Rousseau
enunciates, that those subject to laws should be their author, may
seem almost definitive of a just and legitimate civil order he was
making this claim in a context where it was possible for Louis XV to
say, in 1766, admittedly not to universal acclaim:

It is in my person alone that sovereign power resides . . . it is from
me alone that my [sic] courts hold their existence and their
authority . . . public order in its entirety emanates from me, and my
people forms one with me, and the rights and interests of the
nation, of which people are daring to make a body separate from the
monarch, are necessarily united with mine and repose only in my
hands.

(Jones: 263)

Furthermore, throughout the nineteenth century and much of the
twentieth in many parts of the world, it was widely argued that 'the
people', variously described as the mass, a mob or rabble, were
wholly unfit to have any role in sovereign determinations at all.
Indeed, it is a principle which, though it might be viewed by many
today as a yardstick for assessing the legitimacy of law, more often
reveals how little existing sovereign arrangements measure up and
the extent to which they fail to satisfy the necessary criteria.

The general will

We know already the structural place of the general will in
Rousseau's argument. The sovereign body, composed of as many
members as the assembly contains voters, declares the fundamental
laws of their society. When that declaration is the expression of the
will of the whole body of the people, of the general will, then those
laws are just and legitimate, laws in nature as well as in name. But
how does the whole body of the people discover and declare its
will? How, given that this body is composed of individuals with
undoubtedly different needs, wishes, let alone visions of the terms
on which they want to live with others, is one will to emerge that
has a properly binding force on all and establishes a common obligation of obedience? To address such questions as these is to
address the question of the nature, basis and functions of the general will; no issue in the interpretation of Rousseau's political thinking has attracted more comment, but without any wholly clear and

uncontroversial assessment having been arrived at. The account I now offer makes, I hope, fair sense of most of what Rousseau says, and meshes with the overall character and intent of his thinking. But I do not pretend it captures everything to do with this issue, and other accounts are certainly possible, and actual.

A good place to begin is with the following:

> the general will, to be really such, must be general in its object as well as its essence; . . . it must both come from all and apply to all
> (SC II: 4, 205, OC III: 373)

The French reads literally 'must come from all *in order to* apply to all', which is a better expression of Rousseau's thought. The issue of the general will being 'general in its object' is reasonably straightforward, and is elucidated by Rousseau himself a few pages later when considering laws, the declarations of the general will:

> When I say that the object of laws is always general, I mean that law considers subjects *en masse* and actions in the abstract, and never a particular person or action. Thus the law may indeed decree that there shall be privileges, but cannot confer them on anybody by name. It may set up several classes of citizens, and even lay down the qualifications for membership of these classes, but it cannot nominate such and such persons as belonging to them.
> (SC II: 6, 211, OC III: 379)

It is much more problematic to understand what it is for the will to 'come from all', to be general in 'its essence'. It is very natural to understand the idea of 'coming from all' in terms of a process by which the principles for an association of persons are evolved, proposed and ratified by each and every individual who is going to be a member of that association and a true subject of it, rather than being merely coerced into compliance with its laws. And indeed Rousseau says a good deal about voting procedures, particularly in Book II, Chapter 3 (but also in Book IV, Chapter 2). He insists each citizen should be 'furnished with adequate information', 'should express only his own opinion' and 'have no communication with one another' (SC II: 3, 203, OC: 371). His principal concern at this point is to prevent the formation of factions, of interest groups, that may usurp or displace the role of the will of the whole body, and these comments by themselves get us little distance. But they do suggest an important point – that the views and decisions that come from those who make up the association, who comprise the sovereign, are not to be taken 'raw', so to speak. They must, Rousseau is saying, be views and decisions taken on the basis of proper information in an independent minded way if they are to carry weight, properly contribute to the determination of the general will. This leads to a more general point. Individuals may be, in varying ways and degrees, irrational, distracted, muddled, subject to temptation, short-sighted and – to take up a point Rousseau has argued for so intensively in his other works – they may see their own interests in terms of subjecting others. If we seek assent to a common rule for all that will 'come from all' in the sense that individuals so diverse, with such conflicting attitudes, could all actually give their agreement to it, then the prospects for finding one at all are very small indeed, let alone for finding one that will be conducive to the common good and basic equality for all. Rousseau is, in fact, quite explicit that the general will is 'fallible':

> How can a blind multitude, which often does not know what it wills, because it rarely knows what is good for it, carry out for itself so great and difficult an enterprise as a system of legislation? Of itself the people wills always the good, but of itself it by no means always sees it. The general will is always upright, but the judgment which guides it is not always enlightened.
>
> (SC II: 6, 212, OC III: 380)

From this, it really does seem to follow that whatever Rousseau has in mind when he speaks of the general will coming from all he does not have in mind an actual process where actual individuals give voice to their views; the scope for muddle and ignorance is too great.

What could stand in place of such a process? If we return to Rousseau's original statement of the problem the social contract is intended to solve we can get a good guide. That 'problem' involved, it will be recalled, defending and protecting 'with the whole common force the person and goods of each associate'. It was to secure at least these benefits that individuals seek to associate with one another. With this in mind, we can say that some sovereign declaration can be taken to come from all only if each and every associate has good reason to assent to it on the basis that its implementation better secures their person and goods. And they may have that good reason even if, through confusion, muddle or whatever they do not realise this and may (if asked) withhold their assent.

Clearly, this way of putting it carried the implication that some person or body of persons can identify whether or not individuals have good reason to assent to some declaration even should they believe they do not. And this is by no means a straightforward matter, in many cases. On the other hand, every community does and must have some normative standard of practical reasonableness by which to judge, and sometimes find against, the reasonableness some individual may claim for his views and actions. Someone who, for instance, believes they are the incarnation of Attila the Hun, possessed of immortality and able to communicate their thoughts solely by thinking them, will not – and should not – have any declaration taken into account however strenuously they might insist it should be. In most cases, in any event, it is not all that hard to identify with a good degree of certainty what would benefit people materially and in the security of their person in basic regards.

In sum, we can say that some rule or law is the authentic expression of the general will if and only if each and every associate has like good reasons to assent to that rule or law. The rule or law comes from all since all have good grounds for endorsing it, subscribing to it; its rationale is grounded in needs which all alike have. However, it is one thing to establish that this is what it is for a law to be the expression of the general will, and quite another to explain why laws having this character create an obligation of obedience on everyone. For an individual may reason thus: 'I understand that this rule for our association is such that every associate has like good reason to subscribe to it. But why should I comply with a rule of this kind? I should prefer a rule that gives me advantages, not one that places me on a par with others. I realise that if such a rule is enforced, some other people will be worse off. But what is that to me? Why should I be concerned with their predicament when I myself will be better placed than if I had to give their needs and interests equal weight along with my own?' Compare the words Rousseau puts into the mouth of the 'independent man' in 'The General Society of the Human Race', and the whole of this omitted chapter (see Cole *et al.*: 172–4, OC III: 284–6). These are wholly reasonable questions, and working out Rousseau's answers to them will helpfully uncover other important aspects of the nature and role of the general will.

First of all, Rousseau frequently says that it is only in a community where there is a strong sense of mutual interest, where each individual cares for and identifies with the lot of those around them, that we can expect rules which acknowledge the needs and good of all alike to be adhered to, to be welcomed indeed as rules that give concrete expression to the care of each for each. In many different places he speaks of the importance of the social spirit, the bond of union, of patriotism and love of one's country and compatriots; recall the discussion of this in DPE, considered earlier in Chapter 3. I shall explore these points more fully later in Chapter 6, but we should note that as a response to the questions raised this is rather platitudinous, saying little more than that if you do care for others then you will be happy to comply with rules that look after their interests as much as your own. It does nothing to establish that such rules have authority, have a claim to the obedience of someone in whom the social spirit is weak or absent. Why do rules that acknowledge the interests of others as being on a par with my own have authority over me? I shall suggest that this can be answered in terms of each of us securing 'moral liberty' only on this basis. But I shall present that argument only after having picked up on two other aspects of the nature and role of the general will.

Above, I cited Rousseau posing the question: 'How can a blind multitude, which often does not know what it wills, because it rarely knows what is good for it, carry out for itself so great and difficult an enterprise as a system of legislation?' (SC II, 6: 212, OC III: 380). But I did not give his own answer to this question. He responds to it by invoking the figure of 'a legislator', a strategy which raises more questions than it answers. Rousseau writes:

> In order to discover the rules of society best suited to nations, a superior intelligence beholding all the passions of men without experiencing any of them would be needed. This intelligence would have to be wholly unrelated to our nature, while knowing it through and through; its happiness would have to be independent of us, and yet ready to occupy itself with ours . . . It would take gods to give men laws.
>
> (SC II: 7, 213, OC III: 381)

Rousseau's having recourse to such a figure is one of the most perplexing points in his whole enterprise. Indeed, it is hard to be quite sure how seriously he took this concept himself; outside this one chapter, the legislator is nowhere else referred to or relied on. What, at root, is the problem this quasi-divine person is supposed to resolve? It is the question of identifying what is for the common good, what is in the interests of each and all alike, what, as I put it, each individual associate has good reason to assent to as a provision of law. Rousseau puts it thus:

> Each individual, having no taste for any other plan of government than that which suits his particular interest, finds it difficult to

realise the advantages he might hope to draw from the continual privations good laws impose. For a young people to be able to relish sound principles of political theory and follow the fundamental rules of statecraft, the effect would have to become the cause; the social spirit which should be created by these institutions, would have to preside over their very foundation.

(SC II: 7, 216, OC III: 383)

This is, of course, a real problem. If we are thinking back to the very fundamentals of political society, we cannot assume attributes and dispositions among the original associates the existence of which are dependent on the very institutions they are supposed to find the foundations far. And whilst it may possibly be true that some supra-human intelligence invoking quasi-divine authority might be able to make the plan and lead the way, it is surely more realistic to infer that a just and enduring civil association cannot be founded simply from scratch, taking an as it were completely random group of individuals with no prior sense of common life or commonality of feeling at all. And, I suggest, this is – apart from this one chapter – Rousseau's own view of the case. For, with no reference to the legislator, Rousseau writes in Chapter 10 of Book II as follows:

What people, then, is a fit subject for legislation? One which, already bound by some unity of origin, interest, or convention, has never yet felt the real yoke of law; one that has neither customs nor superstitions deeply ingrained, one which stands in no fear of being overwhelmed by sudden invasion . . . one in which every member may be known by every other, and there is no need to lay on any man burdens too heavy for a man to bear; one which can do without other peoples, and without which all others can do; one which is neither rich nor poor, but self-sufficient; and, lastly, one which unites the consistency of an ancient people with the docility of a new one.

(SC II, 10: 224, OC III: 390)

Rousseau follows this passage with his famous remark: 'There is still in Europe one country capable of being given laws – Corsica'. I shall return to the issue of Corsica in the next chapter.

This is a far cry from his earlier talk of the legislator's need to 'feel himself capable, so to speak, of changing human nature, of transforming each individual, who is by himself a complete and solitary whole, into part of a greater whole from which he in a manner receives his life and being; of altering man's constitution' etc. (SC II: 7, 214, OC III: 381). So whilst it may be right to greet this prospect with some scepticism, it may equally be right to believe that nothing quite so extraordinary is after all required. If the people have already some unity of interest, are known to one another, have a consistency dating from ancient times, then the task of devising an appropriate system of legislation for themselves may not be quite so far beyond their reach. In any event, this is how more or less blunderingly we do try to do it, and I do not think that Rousseau's case is really advanced by his recourse to the supposition that we might receive some supra-human guidance.

The second matter I want to look at briefly before picking up the major outstanding issue is the question of the relation between the general will and the 'will of all'. In a well-known passage Rousseau writes:

> There is often a great deal of difference between the will of all and the general will; the latter considers only the common interest, while the former take private interest into account, and is no more than a sum of particular wills: but take away from these same wills the pluses and minuses that cancel one another, and the general will remains as the sum of the differences.
>
> (SC II: 3, 203, OC III: 371)

This is a pretty inscrutable statement, and I am by no means certain I have caught Rousseau's meaning in it. A person's 'particular will' comprises what they want for themself alone, and from others in their relations and dealings with them, which directs their activities without any reference to whether their wishes could or would win the assent or compliance of anyone else.

What might we envisage as the objectives of someone's particular will, the content of his 'private interest'? Rousseau is surprisingly inexplicit about such things, but we might conjecture that as a wholly self-referential vision of a good life for myself I would want: ample material means procured with minimal effort on my part; the esteem and favour of all around me; long life and happiness all my days. And we could reasonably suppose that others want suchlike things for themselves also. Given a shortage of material goods, and the need to labour to procure these; and given that each person will seek esteem and will be reluctant to give it to others, it is clear that these visions cannot all be realised together. But, Rousseau says, if we take away 'the pluses and minuses that cancel one another' we will arrive at the general will 'as the sum of the differences'. What could this mean? Possibly this. My having ample material goods with minimal labour is a plus for me; but my prospect of having this is cancelled out by others' wanting the same for themselves on the supposition that material abundance is not a natural occurrence. My optimistic, extravagant wish is cancelled out, brought to nothing, by others' like wish, as theirs is also. Does anything remain? We each want material well-being; we each are prepared to invest some labour, and this is a realisable objective which we might all adopt once our respective extravagant projects are abandoned, And, furthermore, this upshot is an objective which more or less corresponds to what the general will, concerned with the common interest, would direct, though there remains an ambiguity over whether the objective is to be understood collectively or severally.

Kant, in his essay *Perpetual Peace*, is clearly considering this same matter when he write that a 'good organisation of the state' may be achieved if it is arranged so that men's 'self-seeking energies are opposed to one another, each thereby neutralising or eliminating the destructive effects of the rest. And as far as reason is concerned, the result is the same as if human beings' selfish tendencies were non-existent, so that the individual, even if not morally good in himself, is nevertheless compelled to be a good citizen' (*Perpetual Peace*: 112–3).

Even if an interpretation along these general lines is correct, I do not think anything of decisive importance for the understanding of Rousseau's argument overall, or for the general will, hangs on this passage. For even should it be somehow possible to determine the content of the common good along these lines, there is nothing in what Rousseau says here to explain why an individual should want to, or be under any obligation to, place pursuit of the common good above pursuit of their own private interest; that matter remains unaddressed by this. And it is striking perhaps that Rousseau makes no further reference to the 'will of all', suggesting that he himself placed little weight on this perplexing passage.

We are left, then, with one last major issue, regarding the individual's obligation of obedience to the requirements of the general will which demand that I should adhere to rules that give like weight alongside my own to the interests of others with whom I am in community. How do suchlike rules have a claim on me? Why should I not favour rules that privilege me, or me and my family or friends etc.? To answer this, I suggest we needed to look at Rousseau's notion of 'moral liberty' for all that he passes over it so quickly; and to understand that, we need to consider more generally his assessment of the various ideas of freedom.

Rousseau on freedom and liberty

Rousseau attaches enormous importance to human freedom, quite especially in the arguments of SC though also elsewhere. I have already cited his famous words about man being born free, but everywhere in chains; just a few pages later on, he writes:

> To renounce liberty is to renounce being a man, to surrender the rights of humanity and even its duties.
>
> (SC I: 4, 186, OC III: 356)

We have also noticed two other places where Rousseau gives free-dom a key significance. The problem to which the social compact is to provide the solution is to find a form of association in which, among other things, 'each, while uniting himself with all, may still obey himself alone, and remain as free as before' (SC I: 4, 191, OC III: 360). So securing that freedom is a key desideratum directing Rousseau's overall thinking about the proper character of a good society. Further, we noted his saying that the social compact 'tacitly includes the undertaking, which alone can give force to the rest, that whoever refuses to obey the general will shall be compelled to do so by the whole body. This means nothing less than that he will be forced to be free' (SC I: 7, 195, OC III: 364). Indeed, elucidating this last remark is one of the principal objectives of this section, although the previous one poses almost as many questions: how can a person in union with others still obey themself alone? The very idea seems self-contradictory; if someone obeys themself alone, then they are a 'lone operator' and not in union with anyone else. Finally, I have been suggesting that Rousseau's notion of 'moral liberty', which alone makes man 'truly master of himself . . . obedience to a law we prescribe to ourselves is liberty' (SC I: 8, 196, OC III: 365) holds the key to understanding why we have an obligation of obedience to the law, to the declarations of the gen-eral will. Clearly there is a great deal that needs thinking out here, and I shall try to offer a way through the maze.

I shall begin with Rousseau's notion of 'natural liberty'. There are two aspects to this. First and foremost, to enjoy natural liberty means not being subject to command, control or other direction by any other person or agency, but being the self-determining judge and director of what one is going to do and why (see, for instance, SC I: 2, 182; 8, 196, OC III: 352, 364–5). When enjoying natural liberty one is – to use a familiar phrase – one's own master. Of course, enjoying such liberty may not be an unalloyed advantage. Being the sole judge of what one shall do, when, why and how could well bring great harms down on one's head. But however that may be, the enjoyment of uninterfered-with non-accountable discretion is normally regarded as a great good, and certainly better than being subject to someone else's will, and the capability to be the self-deviser and director of one's purposes is often taken to be a defining mark of mature humanity, of an autonomous being.

In addition – and this is the second aspect of the case – one needs scope for the exercise of one's right and power of self-direction. This may be circumscribed by one's lack of skills, resources or opportunities so that one is able to make little productive use of the power of independent self-direction. Indeed, it is that very predicament that, as we saw, Rousseau identifies in SC as the principal spur for individuals to unite into an ordered and regulated society. One could say in this case either that one possessed natural liberty but could make very little use of it; or that, in lacking the opportunity etc. to exercise one's power of self-determination, one's natural liberty was reduced or absent. Rousseau's usage doesn't fall clearly either way; but nothing hangs on this. Lastly, one other limit on one's natural liberty may well be that this brings one into conflict with others similarly placed in seeking e.g. food or shelter, so the actual level of well-being people enjoy through the exercise of their natural liberty may be quite low.

Now, when each person joins together with others to form a civil society they renounce, according to Rousseau, the right to be sole judge of what they shall do; what they shall do is limited by the direction of the general will, that is by law. It does not follow that every action will be the subject of a legal directive; Rousseau writes: 'Each man alienates . . . by the social compact, only such part of his powers, goods and liberty as it is important for the community to control' (SC II: 4, 205, OC III: 373). But he goes on at once to say, quite correctly, 'but it must also be granted that the Sovereign is the sole judge of what is important' [for the community to control] (ibid.). If it were not the sovereign, then the individual would be retaining the right of final judgement to himself, and that would mean the dissolution of the association. Rousseau calls this scope for action circumscribed by the general will 'civil liberty', and one might try to argue that by enjoying civil liberty in society people are as free, all things considered, as they were before. This is because, before joining together in civil community, it was by no means true that they could actually do just what they wanted when and as they wanted because of weakness, lack of resources etc., as we have noted. So for their scope to be limited by law seems no exceptional burden, particularly if by submitting to law their person and goods are protected by the 'whole common force', for this will give them powers and resources they previously lacked and they may be able to do more of what they wanted to do overall. And Rousseau does highlight this from time to time (see, particularly, SC II: 4, 207–8, OC III: 375).

However, this would not appear to be a sufficient response. Each individual, in submitting to the general will, has given up the right of independent personal judgment, answerable to no one else – and isn't this the essence of natural liberty that has been yielded? A response to this challenge may seem to be possible if we remember how the sovereign body, which devises and enforces the law, is constituted and functions. The sovereign comes into being by a voluntary act of all associates, that is to say, by an exercise of their natural liberty electing to submit themselves to the deliberations and decisions of the sovereign body as it declares its will, the general will. So, at one remove so to speak, whilst individuals' choices and actions are circumscribed by the law it is a circumscription they have chosen for themselves and is therefore not a limitation of their liberty but an exercise of it. Perhaps by 'obedience to a law which we prescribe to ourselves' Rousseau means no more than this. But it is hard to find this response fully satisfactory. A person may voluntarily submit to brainwashing or confinement. Does it then follow that when brainwashed or confined they are free because this is a state they freely chose to be in? It is hard to agree that they are; and Rousseau's discussion of slavery in Book 1, Chapter 4 suggests he would agree, for this is the very place he speaks of renouncing liberty being to renounce being a man human being. Just because your present state is the upshot of an exercise of natural liberty, it does not follow that it is a state in which you continue to enjoy natural – or any other kind of – liberty.

However, this attends only to one aspect of the character of the sovereign body, the act of association by which it comes into being. If we recur to the point made earlier that a person will benefit from the protection of their person and goods, which is what the sovereign body directs as the principal purpose of the law, then surely we can say that these are precisely improvements in my circumstances I would seek through the exercise of my natural liberty, so I am doing, when I submit to law, just what I would want in the circumstances obtaining. This is not a case of my choosing to be in a condition which then dispossesses me of my natural liberty, but choosing to be in a condition which comprises the optimal exercise of that when we can no longer exist as separate and independent beings. Yet there are reasons to remain unhappy with this emollient proposal. It remains true that I have resigned my right of independent judgement, and that does seem a sharp diminution in my freedom even if the opportunities to make use of what remains to me are enhanced. But, also, it isn't at all obvious why enjoying my increased security and well-being alongside my fellow citizens doing so also does really comprise what I would want for myself through an exercise of my natural liberty. Would I not seek to promote my own greater good without any particular regard to how anyone else fared? Does not being forced by the requirements of law to attend to the situation of others and bring my own wishes into balance with theirs diminish my freedom? This is, of course, just the same issue we began with, of the source of the obligation of obedience to the requirements of the general will, viewed from another angle.

Struggle as we may, then, there seems to be no way in which we can make sense of how, being subject to the general will, we remain as free as we were before if we just deploy Rousseau's notions of natural liberty and of civil liberty. Richer notions are required here. They lie at hand, in fact, if we recall the arguments of Book 4 of *Émile* considered in the previous chapter. There I presented Rousseau's view that it is only through acknowledging other people as standing on level terms with oneself that one acquires the human recognition and respect for oneself that one seeks. So far from its being the case that the claims of others for regard and one's own claims being in inevitable conflict, Rousseau argues that the satisfaction of one requires the satisfaction of the other. The struggle for recognition is resolved through mutual acknowledgment and esteem. Living in accordance with the requirement of consideration for others is therefore living according to the principle of one's own being as a member of a community of persons. It is the mode of life proper to one's having that place and life, and giving regard to and receiving respect from others likewise positioned is to do just exactly what accords with one's need and character as such. It is, in short, to be free and act freely in one's character as a moral being, which is one's constitution in one's completed humanity. This, I suggest, is what Rousseau means by 'moral liberty', and it is after this fashion that compliance with the requirements of the general will makes one free.

It is worth unpacking this response a little more. Let us consider how things would stand if one did not join an association in which there was a fundamental equality of recognition and status offered to each and every member. In such a society, there would be a basic distinction or several distinctions between those who had wealth, power, status etc. and those who did not. The harm to the latter group is obvious. Not only would they suffer materially in all sorts of ways, they would also be marginalised, denied human recognition, be in no way treated as an 'indivisible part of the whole' but in fact be clearly divided from that. Their loss in terms of freedom too, understood in a wholly untendentious way, is also obvious; they would be subject, directly and indirectly, to the command and control of others with very little scope for the exercise of independent self-direction. The losses the dominant group of people suffer is less obvious. Indeed, it may seem plain that they are very well off, and the fact that they do not have to take into account all of those with whom they live, in some sense, in one society may seem only to be a bonus. However, if we find anything at all cogent in Rousseau's arguments put forward in DI and E, it can be said that, in more subtle ways, those in the dominant position are themselves still subject to control and direction by others. The meaning and value of the distinctions they seek and the privileges they covet depend on the public's esteem of those under whose judgement, therefore, the significance of their lives and achievements lies. In different ways, then, both those in a dominant and in a subordinate position are subject to 'personal dependence' (SC I: 7, 195, OC III: 364), and their scope for independent self-direction is circumscribed by this. This is why Rousseau cites being secured against personal dependence as a key point when he explains why being compelled to obey the general will forces people to be free. But is not simply relief from such dependence that makes obedience to the general will a condition of freedom, for conceivably such obedience might involve a yet greater if different servitude. It is also that obedience to the general will establishes a footing between people appropriate to the enactment of their full humanity in relation to one another, provides the terms for the free expression of that. Its requirements provide the form in which each can give and receive moral recognition from each, a recognition inherent to one's standing as a human person among human persons. Rousseau, at a number of places, tries to cast up the gains and losses we experience by joining together in civil society under the direction of the general will saying, at one point, 'Let us draw up the whole account in terms easily commensurable' (SC I: 8, 196, OC III: 364). But it is hard, in fact, to find such terms to compare natural with moral liberty, for the powers, capabilities and standing of the persons involved in each case is very different. One who enjoys natural liberty does so as an independent, self-directing being who encounters others only on terms of power and opportunity. The possessor of moral liberty encounters others as bearers of moral dignity deserving of respect and regard, and expects the same standing for himself with others. There is no straightforward answer to the question 'Who is the more free?' since the 'Who' in question is different in the two instances.

In attempting to give sense to Rousseau's idea of 'moral liberty', and to try to explain in relation to that how and why obedience to the general will forces one to be free in requiring one to do just what one would want to do as a moral being, I have drawn considerably on his other writings. I do not pretend that the line of argument I have mounted could be constructed from materials in SC alone; but neither, I believe, does SC provide alternative materials for any such argument. I have maintained all along that the text of SC requires supplementation from Rousseau's other works if it is to be well understood. I hope what I have brought forward here bears out this claim. On the other hand, it must be admitted that the notion of 'moral liberty' I have sketched out here does not enjoy wide acceptance. Virtually all contemporary discussions of freedom in society concentrate on some form of 'natural liberty', to use Rousseau's phrase, in the form of what is often called 'negative liberty'. Such liberty is called 'negative' since it emphasises the negation, removal, of as many constraints on the scope of action of the individual as possible as the key to maximising his liberty. In terms of such an idea, to be required by law to respect the life, goods, reputation etc. of another person can only be seen as being subject to a constraint, as having one's liberty diminished. However, so to view the kind of accommodation one makes with others when living together in society strongly implies that others are present in one's life as nothing more than a threat or burden that must be contained. It is hard to see that considering the matter so amounts to any real community or union of persons at all – certainly not the kind of community Rousseau sought. Indeed, that one is a member of one society with others if their very existence is viewed as a limit on one's freedom seems questionable; this is a mere aggregate, not an association (see SC I: 5, 190, OC III: 359). But it may be said that in many respects that is in fact all we have; our society displays high levels of alienation, a great want of mutual moral recognition, and we often subsist as atoms jostling and impeding one another in a ceaseless struggle for dominance. Things have not, I think, moved on much beyond the society Rousseau knew and to which he hoped to describe an alternative.

Summary

Rousseau's position concerning the character and role of the general will may, I am suggesting, be understood thus. The general will is expressed in political or fundamental laws that consider subjects en masse and actions in the abstract. The general will requires that each member of the association respects and protects the person and goods of each associate and that their own person and goods be likewise respected. In requiring this, the general will establishes a condition of basic equality between associates, and acknowledgment of that equality is a condition of the acceptance of the humanity, moral dignity, of each associate by each. That acknowledgment is also the condition for the freedom of each and every associate. First, it relieves them of personal dependence; second, it accords with the behaviour properly expressive of our full humanity in mutual union.

To understand and accept the terms of civil life that the general will prescribes does not come easily to people, as Rousseau fully acknowledges. He writes:

Each individual, as a man, may have a particular will contrary or dissimilar to the general will which he has as a citizen. His particular interest may speak to him quite differently from the common interest: his absolute and naturally independent existence may make him look upon what he owes to the common cause as a gratuitous contribution, the loss of which will do less harm to others than the payment of it is burdensome to himself.

(SC I: 7, 194, OC III, 363)

We have looked at some aspects of this tension or conflict between particular and general wills, particular and common interests, when considering Rousseau's notion of the legislator above. There he emphasises, as he does in DPE also, the importance of the development of the 'social spirit' in each individual to overcome these conflicts. I shall be examining this further in the coming chapter, but some of the key issues come to the fore in Rousseau's account of the nature and role of government, to which I now turn.

THE SOCIAL CONTRACT - BOOK III

Rousseau makes a sharp distinction between the business of legislation, which is the task of the sovereign through the determinations of the general will, and the activities of government or the executive power. His own words are these:

What then is government? An intermediate body set up between the subjects and the Sovereign, to secure their mutual correspondence, charged with the execution of the laws and maintenance of liberty, both civil and political.

The members of this body are called magistrates or *kings*, that is to say *governors*, and the whole body bears the name *prince*. Thus those who hold that the act, by which a people puts itself under a prince, is not a contract, are certainly right. It is simply and solely a commission, an employment, in which the rulers, mere officials of the Sovereign, exercise in their own name the power of which it makes them depositaries. This power it can limit, modify or recover at pleasure . . . I call the *government*, or supreme administration, the legitimate exercise of the executive power, and *prince* or *magistrate* the man or the body entrusted with that administration.

(SC III: 1, 230, OC III: 396)

Rousseau openly admits that legislative and governmental authority and power are not normally so clearly distinguished in language or in fact, and his own expression is sometimes a bit loose. But the distinction he is making here is important and useful.

Having made it, Rousseau then devotes considerable space to considering what is the best form for the prince or magistrate to take, for the person or body charged with the supreme administration to have. He argues that no one form is suitable alike for all states, the size of the state in particular being a crucial variable. However, in a fairly conventional fashion, he distinguishes three forms of governmental body insisting that each of these forms can allow for considerable variations:

> In the first place, the Sovereign may commit the charge of the government to the whole people or to the majority of the people, so that more citizens are magistrates than are mere private individuals. This form of government is called *democracy*.
>
> Or it may restrict the government to a small number, so that there are more private citizens than magistrates; and this is named *aristocracy*.
>
> Lastly, it may concentrate the whole government in the hands of a single magistrate from whom all others hold their power. This third form is the most usual, and is called *monarchy*, or royal government.
>
> (SC III: 3, 237–8, OC III: 403)

Rousseau must, of course, have been writing about monarchy with his tongue in his cheek; monarchs then, if not now, saw themselves as sovereign, not as holders of an employment revocable at pleasure by the sovereign people.

In the following chapters, Rousseau goes on to discuss the strengths and weakness of each of these forms, stressing as noted above that no one form is as it were a universal ideal but that different circumstances make different forms more or less apt (see especially Book III, Chapter 8). I shall not follow him in the details of these discussions – which are readily accessible – except to comment on his treatment of democracy. It might be anticipated that since for Rousseau sovereignty lies with the whole body of the people, then a form of government in which, if not quite all, at least a substantial number of citizens participated and took responsibility would draw his favour. For this would seem to embody the same principles of equality and commitment to the common good which are at the core of his political thinking. But this is not in fact his position. He argues (in SC III: 4) that for the body of the people to 'turn its attention away from a general standpoint and devote itself to particular objects' in executing the laws dangerously mixes private and general interests. Additionally, the people cannot remain continually assembled 'to devote their time to public affairs', and if they devolve responsibility to commissions then these gradually assume greater authority. Also, complex and thorny issues do not lend themselves to determination by large groups of people; they need to be considered carefully and in detail. He concludes: 'were there a people of gods, their government would be democratic. So perfect a government is not for men'. In so far as Rousseau does identify a best form for the governmental body to take, with the caveats noted borne in mind, it is elective aristocracy: 'In a word, it is the best and most natural arrangement that the wisest should govern the many, when it is assured that they will govern for its profit, not for their own' (SC III: 5, 242, OC III: 407).

Rousseau's adding this rider ('when it is assured. . .') takes me back to the point which led into this section, namely the nature of the possible conflicts between the particular will of an independent individual and the general will he has as a citizen. For a key issue for Rousseau in his discussion of forms of governmental body is how to check the tendency of the prince to usurp sovereign power, taking advantage of his authority in the state to assume authority *over* the state. Rousseau writes:

In the person of the magistrate we can distinguish three essentially different wills: first, the private will of the individual, tending only to his personal advantage; secondly, the common will of the magistrates, which is relative solely to the advantage of the prince, and may be called corporate will, being general in relation to the government, and particular in relation to the State, of which the government forms part; and, in the third place, the will of the people or the sovereign will, which is general both in relation to the State regarded as the whole, and to the government regards as part of the whole.

In a perfect act of legislation, the individual or particular will should be zero; the corporate will belonging to the government should occupy a very subordinate position; and, consequently, the general or sovereign will should always predominate and should be the sole guide of all the rest.

According to the natural order, on the other hand, these different wills become more active in proportion as they are concentrated. Thus, the general will is always the weakest, the corporate will second, and the individual will strongest of all: so that, in the government, each member is first of all himself, then a magistrate, and then a citizen – in an order exactly the reverse of what the social system requires.

(SC III: 2, 235, OC III: 400–1)

So what we have here is, in fact, not just two 'wills', the particular and general, but three – the corporate will someone has as a member of and identifying with an intermediate or partial body within the state with its own sectional interests (in this instance, the interests of the prince; see also SC II: 3, 203, OC III: 371). What Rousseau is speaking of is, of course, very familiar to us. Members of a society will have interests not just as private individuals but also as, for instance, farmers or commuters or gardeners, and people with these characteristics may act as a group to lobby government. And the government itself may – will – wish to retain power whether or not it is genuinely serving the interests of the people; and, lastly, we may have reason to believe that certain interest groups have, more or less indirectly, taken over the executive power itself bending it to serve these sectional concerns rather than its professed object, the common good. It must, then, be a major concern for Rousseau how to reverse the 'natural order' of activity of these three wills in each individual so that the general will should predominate, and this is where the role of the 'social spirit' is so important. This will be at the centre of the discussion of the next chapter, and we see now that this bears not only on the reconciliation of the particular and general will, but on locating the proper place for corporate, or sectional, interests within the state.

OVERVIEW AND CONCLUSION

Let us now take, in conclusion of this chapter, a brief overview of Rousseau's account of the character of a legitimate civil association as this has been so far considered. His assessment of existing states focussed above all on the massive and pervasive inequalities present in them, which – in earlier works – he traced to people's aggressive desire to gain ascendancy over each other, to the excesses of their *amour-propre*. These inequalities were not only harmful to those in inferior positions, deprived of money, status and power but also to those 'on the pinnacle of fortune and grandeur' (DI: 112, OC III: 189) who remain dependent on the esteem of others for their scope to think themselves better than others. Or so Rousseau argues. Any just and humane community must, therefore, address the issue of inequality above all, and this Rousseau tries to do by insisting that the sovereign body comprises all those who live in the community determining the laws of the community on a level footing:

I shall end this chapter and this book [Rousseau writes at the end of Book 1 of SC] by remarking on a fact on which the whole social system should rest: i.e. that, instead of destroying natural inequality, the fundamental compact substitutes, for such physical

> inequality as nature may have set up between men, an equality that
> is moral and legitimate, and that men, who may be unequal in
> strength or intelligence, become every one equal by convention and
> legal right.
>
> (SC I: 9, 199, OC III: 367)

Only in this way can the distress and destitution, self-estrangement and dependency on others that people ordinarily suffer in society be avoided and they retain their integrity and hopes of happiness in community with others.

Through the working of the general will, which has supreme authority in the state, the interests of each person alike are addressed and met; the laws do not operate to promote the benefit of just a few but the person and goods of each associate are protected and defended by the whole common force, to use Rousseau's own words. Neither is it a loss or burden for each person to be obliged to consider and respect others; only by doing so are the demands of *amour-propre* for honour and respect to be given to each by all capable of being properly and enduringly met. A union of equals, bearing one another in mutual regard, governing their own affairs according to laws directed to promoting the common good, is the vision of a good society that Rousseau tries to spell out.

That there are difficulties in much of what he says – and many problems and issues he doesn't fully engage with – cannot be denied. Neither can it be denied how far removed from this vision is the actuality of the social and political life we mostly know. But it remains a vision which is capable of stirring the moral sense and inspiring a wish for things to be different, and that testifies to its continuing force. I turn now to filling out some further aspects of it, especially concerning the development and role of the 'social spirit' in maintaining a just and equal society.

FURTHER READING

Christopher Bertram, *Rousseau and The Social Contract*. London: Routledge, 2004.
A very lucid, full and detailed treatment of the entire text.

Hilail Gildin, *Rousseau's Social Contract*. Chicago: Chicago University Press, 1983. Another full-length treatment of the argument.

Andrew Levine, *The Politics of Autonomy: A Kantian Reading of Rousseau's Social Contract*. Amhurst, MA: University of Massachusetts Press, 1976. As the title states, a reading influenced by Kant's themes.

J.B. Noone, *Rousseau's Social Contract*. London: Prior, 1980. Another reading of the work as a whole.

Timothy O'Hagan, *Rousseau*. London: Routledge, 1999. Chapters IV–VI. Careful treatment as part of an overall account.

Roger D. Masters, *The Political Philosophy of Rousseau*. Princeton: Princeton University Press, 1968, Chapters VI–VIII. An important account as part of a general interpretation.

Maurizio Viroli, *Jean-Jacques Rousseau and the 'Well-Ordered Society'*. Cambridge: Cambridge University Press, 1988. An admirable account of Rousseau's political thinking, laying special emphasis on the notions of order and disorder.

Judith N. Shklar, *Men and Citizens*. Cambridge: Cambridge University Press, 1985. A influential and substantial study of Rousseau's social theory overall.

Alfred Cobban, *Rousseau and the Modern State*. London: George Allen & Unwin, 1964. A classic study still of great interest.

Six

Culture, Religion and Politics

THE PURPOSE OF THIS CHAPTER

The purpose of this chapter is, in the first instance, to consider further the issue of the development and consolidation of 'the social spirit' (SC IV: 8, 305, OC III: 465) to which Rousseau attaches so much importance as a condition for the emergence and maintenance of a just and humane civil community. As will be seen below, his discussion of 'civil religion', in the last chapter of SC from which the reference to 'the social spirit' is taken, which I have not so far discussed, is also centrally concerned with this issue and thus is treated here too. Finally, I shall look at Rousseau's excursions into 'applied politics' as contained in his essays on Poland and Corsica to see how these works may deepen our understanding not only of the significance Rousseau attaches to the cultivation of the social spirit but also of how the general principles of legitimacy and justice argued for in SC may need to be qualified or compromised in the face of the recalcitrant facts of an actual social and political situation. By doing this we may hope to round out a sense of the scope and limits of Rousseau's political thinking overall.

CUSTOM AND CULTURE

In the last chapter, we saw that obedience to the general will required each member of the community to attach weight to the person and goods of every other member of that community. And, despite the fact that doing so is, in Rousseau's estimation, the key to living in and enjoying the benefits of a stable, just, egalitarian and prosperous community, and one that meets each person's need for recognition and respect compatibly with everyone else's, he plainly and surely rightly believes that such obedience does not come readily. Certain conditions need to obtain if such obedience is not to be merely coerced, or mechanical, but the gladly embraced spring of each citizen's conduct. A key passage, cited before, highlights some of the issues here:

> Each individual, as a man, may have a particular will contrary or dissimilar to the general will he has as a citizen. His particular interest may speak to him quite differently from the common interest: his absolute and naturally independent existence may make him look upon what he owes to the common cause as a gratuitous contribution, the loss of which will do less harm to others than the payment of it is burdensome to himself . . . he may wish to enjoy the rights of citizenship without being ready to fulfil the duties of a subject.
>
> (SC I: 7, 194–5, OC III: 363)

How can the sense that the contribution one makes to the common cause is 'gratuitous' be overcome, and a greater congruence or compatibility between the individual's particular will as an independent being and the general will they have as a citizen be secured?

Rousseau considers this issue at some length in DPE, as we saw earlier (Chapter 3; see DPE: 140–50, OC III: 252–62), saying: 'If you would have the general will accomplished, bring all the particular wills into conformity with it; in other words, as virtue is nothing more than this conformity of the particular wills with the general will, establish the reign of virtue' (DPE: 140, OC III: 252). And he goes on:

> It is not enough to say to the citizens, *be good*; they must be taught to be so; and even example, which is in this respect the first lesson, is

not the sole means to be employed; patriotism is the most
efficacious: for, as I have said already, every man is virtuous when
his particular will is in all things conformable to the general will,
and we voluntarily will what is willed by those whom we love . . . Do
we wish men to be virtuous? Then let us begin by making them love
their country.

(DPE: 142, OC III: 254)

As we shall soon see, such views are strongly present in Rousseau's essays on Poland and Corsica, and although and perhaps surprisingly there is no discussion of patriotism in *The Social Contract*, similar considerations but in a different form are clearly present in the argument of that.

Before taking this further, it will be useful to make some distinctions. Broadly and roughly, we can distinguish four attitudes an individual (as an independent being) could take towards complying with the requirements of the general will, of the law, as follows. First, their compliance could be merely coerced, undertaken simply because of the threat of punishment. In this instance, were they to see the opportunity, it is reasonable to suppose that they would try to evade these requirements, and the likelihood of any stable and enduring community existing where this is the attitude of many members is very small or non-existent. Second, compliance could be viewed as a trade-off; this is roughly the attitude expressed in the quotation from SC Book 1, Chapter 7 cited above. But here too, should it appear that the benefits can be secured without the cost being paid then continued compliance is not to be expected, with similar consequences for the maintenance of a stable and just society as indicated in the first case. Third, compliance may have become largely mechanical, a not-thought-about way of behaving. This at first sight appears to indicate perfect conformity (and Rousseau does often enough speak of the importance of force of habit). But there are two reasons for thinking that this still comprises an unsatisfactory relationship between the individuals' will and the general will. First, unreflective habits are apt to be disrupted or lost if circumstances change much or other interests enter the picture. They lack vitality and adaptability, making them appropriate only to very fixed conditions. But also, second, this way of looking at the matter suggests that, somehow, the requirements of the general will are there and in place for citizens to become habituated to. But, as we know, such requirements are supposed in complex ways to emerge from and relate to the concerns and commitments of all the members of the community, and unless there were some more active form of engagement with the common good sufficient to enable the requirements of the general will to be established in the first place there could be nothing to become habituated to.

This, then, brings us to the fourth possibility: that compliance could emerge from an understanding and active embrace of the ends that the law fosters, that is, the equal basic well-being and respect of all members of the community alike. Recall Rousseau's words: 'We voluntarily will what is willed by those whom we love'. This is plainly the kind of attitude that he thinks is most important to enable and sustain a just society, involving some identification by the individual members of their own good with the good of those others who comprise their community.

But how deep and pervasive should such 'identification' be? When Rousseau speaks of the 'conformity' of particular wills and the general will, what character should that take? A further distinction here is useful. On the one hand, what could be intended could be the reduction of private, individual goals and enjoyments to the minimal with each person giving themself over to communal pursuits and activities concentrating their efforts, their ideas of what is worthwhile, on the promotion of the common good of the whole society, maximally identifying themselves with that. On the other hand, all that may be in view is that where there is conflict between an individual's pursuit of their particular interest and the pursuit of the common good through obedience to law, the latter is gladly afforded priority but without there being any question overall of the erasure of private concerns.

There are passages where Rousseau seems strongly to favour 'maximal identification' as I have roughly outlined the character of that. Thus, when discussing the task of the legislator he writes:

> He who dares to undertake the making of a people's institutions ought to feel himself capable, so to speak, of changing human nature, of transforming each individual, who is by himself a complete and solitary whole, into part of a greater whole from which he in a manner receives his life and being . . . of substituting a partial and moral existence for the physical and independent existence nature has conferred on us all . . . if each citizen is nothing and can do nothing without the rest . . . it may be said that legislation is at the highest possible point of perfection.
>
> (SC II: 7, 214, OC III: 381–2)

And in the opening pages of *Émile* he writes:

> Good social institutions are those that best know how to denature man, to take his absolute existence from him in order to give him a relative one and transport the / into the common unity, with the result that each individual believes himself no longer one but a part of the unity and no longer feels except within the whole.
>
> (E I: 40, OC I: 249)

However, there are other passages that suggest only that priority need be given to the demands of the common good though, of course, the willingness to grant that will have its preconditions in terms of some sense of unity with others. Thus in Book II, Chapter 4 of SC, Rousseau writes:

> Each man alienates . . . by the social compact, only such part of his powers, goods and liberty as it is important for the community to control . . . the Sovereign . . . cannot impose upon its subjects any fetters that are useless to the community.
>
> (SC II: 4, 204, OC III: 373)

This would make no sense unless it was accepted that it was fit and proper for human beings to retain scope for the use and enjoyment of their powers, goods and liberty without reference to the community at least in some instances. Even in his most intensive writing about patriotism, referred to already, Rousseau says only that 'a carefully and well intentioned government' should keep 'within narrow bounds that personal interest that so isolates the individual' (DPE: 150, OC III: 262). And, late in Émile, Rousseau makes a powerful point, that love of country and community requires a 'natural base' and could not exist without it. In criticising Plato's removal of private families from his ideal republic, Rousseau says:

> I speak of that subversion of the sweetest sentiments of nature, sacrificed to an artificial sentiment which can only be maintained by them – as though there were no need for a natural base on which to form conventional ties; as though the love of one's nearest were not the principle of the love one owes the state; as though it were not by means of the small fatherland which is the family that the heart attaches itself to the larger one.
>
> (E V: 363, OC I: 700)

This being so, at least as Rousseau sees it, there cannot be any question of private ties and affections being wholly or even very substantially displaced and suppressed in the name of maximal identification with the interests of the state as a whole.

What, then, is Rousseau's considered view of this? It is, I think, that the cultivation and maintenance of a significant measure of engaged concern with the well-being of one's fellow citizens is certainly essential to sustaining a just and humane community, and achieving this requires a great deal of attention and detailed provision because the tendency for private or sectional interests to dominate goes deep. But he did not think that this concern for, love of, one's fellows should displace almost all other concerns becoming a nearly exclusive interest. What has to be secured is that it has priority where there is conflict, not that it becomes all-encompassing.

What affording it such priority will concretely require will plainly depend on the range and character of the requirements that concern for one's fellows under the direction of the general will involves. Even should these be fairly limited – and Rousseau is nowhere very explicit about this – if they are to engage one's full-hearted commitment one's fellow citizens must be more to one than simply people it happens that one is thrown together with. They will be, rather, people with whom one has some sense of shared life, pleasures, attitudes and values, to put it no more exactly than this.

We find Rousseau exploring these issues at some length in his *Letter to d'Alembert on the Theatre*. This substantial essay, which Bloom has called 'like a morality play, entitled "the Spirit of Enlightenment against the Spirit of Republican Virtue" ' (Bloom: PA xv) was prompted by the publication in 1757 of an article on Geneva by d'Alembert in his and Diderot's *Encyclopedia*. In this, he had argued that the life of the city of Geneva would be improved by allowing theatrical performances, which were not at that time permitted. d'Alembert writes that providing the conduct of the actors themselves was duly regulated by law:

> Geneva would have theatre and morals [manners], and would enjoy the advantages of both; the theatrical performances would form the taste of the citizens and would give them a fineness of tact, a delicacy of sentiment, which is very difficult to acquire without the help of theatrical performances . . . Geneva would join to the prudence of Lacedaemon the urbanity of Athens.
>
> (Bloom: PA 4)

As noted earlier in Chapter 2, Rousseau saw – and probably rightly – the hand of Voltaire in these comments. Voltaire had settled just outside Geneva in 1755, and it is likely that he was seeking a larger stage for the performance of his plays than his own home allowed for.

Rousseau argued strenuously against d'Alembert's proposal. He insisted that a theatre could only flourish if it provided amusement for the audience. Yet in amusing them, he asserted, it diverted them from finding their pleasure in performing their civic duties and thus weakened the customs and sentiments that made them the good people they really were. The theatre, Rousseau argues, is decidedly not an agent of moral improvement; it panders to and consolidates existing tastes and engenders no real passions but only ersatz feelings that take the place of real, engaged involvement with important concerns. In an extended critical treatment of Molière's *Le Misanthrope*, Rousseau objects to the fact that Alceste, a good, honest lover of his fellow men, is made to look ridiculous and contemptible whereas Philinte, the smooth man of the world, is shown as superior and as getting the better of him. Rousseau stresses that this play is a work of genius demonstrating the power of the theatre at its strongest; yet because it shows human goodness and virtue being mocked it can scarcely be said to show the role of the theatre as a force for good.

Rousseau also holds that undue prominence is given in plays to the 'love interest', and that this encourages the preoccupations of women in unacceptable ways. What will happen with regard to the wishes and enjoyments of women if a theatre is established? In one of his least edifying passages of argument, Rousseau says that theatregoers will all demand finery and want to go out to see and be seen in their outfits. As before, all pleasure will be taken away from the necessary and beneficial tasks of the family and community; expense and idleness will take their place. Nor can legislation work effectively to curb these ill effects. Even supposing that the effects were, after moral decay had begun to set in, still seen as ill and hence as needing legislative control, such legislation would only be successful if most people shared the concerns that it intended to foster. But, as the whole bent of his argument has shown, the establishing of a theatre, attendance at performances and the content of the plays themselves all work against a sense of common life and loyalty which the law needs to draw on in order to secure obedience. Sitting shut up in the dark as isolated individuals counteracts the need for people to live and work together to sustain a just and prosperous community. Yet it does not follow that in a republic there should be no entertainment:

> On the contrary, there ought to be many. It is in republics that they were born, it is in their bosom that they are seen to flourish with a truly festive air. To what peoples is it more fitting to assemble often and form among themselves sweet bonds of pleasure and joy than to those who have so many reasons to like one another and remain forever united? . . . It is in the open air, under the sky, that you ought to gather and give yourselves to the sweet sentiment of your happiness . . . Plant a stake crowned with flowers in the middle of a square; gather the people together there, and you will have a festival. Do better yet; let the spectators become an entertainment to themselves; make them actors themselves; do it so that each sees and loves himself in the others so that all will be better united.
>
> (Bloom, PA: 125–6, OC V: 114–5)

However strained Rousseau's arguments may appear to be (and be) at points, and however little his republican festivals may attract, the depth of his concerns here is undeniable. Indeed, they have an echo in many current concerns with the displacement of local cultural customs and festivals by forms of global entertainment, and in concerns that entertainment has become very much a matter of passive consumption rather than active participation.

The absolutely key issue here for Rousseau is ensuring that the customs, opinions and sentiments which are common and accepted among all the citizens are those that make accepting and adhering to laws requiring respect and equality a welcome expression of what each wants their fellow citizens to enjoy. Returning to the text of SC, Rousseau encapsulates his ideas when discussing what he calls a fourth kind of law, after fundamental laws, civil laws and criminal laws:

Along with these three kinds of law goes a fourth, most important of
all, which is not graven on tablets of marble or brass, but on the
hearts of the citizens. This forms the real constitution of the State,
takes on every day new powers, when other laws decay or die out,
restores them or takes their place, keeps a people in the ways in
which it was meant to go, and insensibly replaces authority by the
force of habit. I am speaking of morality, of custom, above all of
public opinion; a power unknown to political thinkers, on which
none the less success in everything else depends.

(SC II: 12, 228, OC III: 394)

Yet religion has a very central place in this as well, and it is to this
matter that I now turn.

CIVIL RELIGION

Rousseau's views on 'civil religion' – 'a purely civil profession of
faith of which the Sovereign should fix the articles, not exactly as
religious dogmas, but as social sentiments without which a man
cannot be a good citizen or a faithful subject' (SC IV: 8, 307, OC III:
468) – are presented in the penultimate chapter of *The Social Contract*.
I considered his treatment of individual religious conviction in the
discussion of 'The Profession of Faith of a Savoyard Vicar' in Chapter 4 and will not refer further to that, except with regard to one
point concerning atheism in a while.

It is appropriate to take up this matter at this point, since, as will
soon be seen, it is the role of religion in reinforcing, or undermining, the social bond between citizens and in sustaining or dis-
couraging commitment to obedience to the law that is at the heart
of Rousseau's concerns when discussing these issues. Many critics
have read his arguments in favour of the need for a civil profession
of faith as displaying what may be interpreted as totalitarian elements in his thinking. He writes, for instance, that the sovereign can
'banish from the State whoever does not believe' the articles of
that profession; and he goes on: 'If any one, after publicly recognising these dogmas, behaves as if he does not believe them, let him

be punished by death' (SC IV: 8, 307, OC III: 468; all subsequent quotations will be taken from Book IV, Chapter 8 of The Social Contract). These remarks seem plainly to say that religious observance will be enforced by the threat of very severe sanctions in a way that involves extreme intrusion by the state. On the other hand, Rousseau says that the civil religion will contain one 'negative dogma', the rejection of intolerance. So either he is all but contradicting himself, or there is more here that needs working out. I shall proceed on the latter supposition.

I said a moment ago that Rousseau's dominant concern in this chapter is with the need to consolidate the bonds of union between the members of a civil community, so that they will treat the good of all as having priority over their own exclusive, individual good and gladly treat their fellows with equal respect and care. Now, he holds that religious allegiance is one of the great sources shaping an individual's values and ends, and it is therefore necessary to determine how such allegiance comports with the central values incorporated in civil association as he has identified those and the commitment of citizens to them. If we follow the pattern of his argument, we will see that it is this concern that guides his assessment of the actual and possible relations between obedience to civil authority and the requirements of religious commitment.

In Rousseau's view, there are four possible types of relations here. First, religious allegiance and what it dictates could remain wholly unregulated by civil authority, by the Sovereign. Second, such allegiance could, as far as possible, be marginalised, treated as a purely personal matter of no import for the well-being and order of the civil community. Third, it may be regulated by the civil power; and lastly, religious allegiance could, in some key respects, be linked to sustaining the requirements of the civil order. Rousseau favours this last possibility, both because of what he believes are the great benefits for a just and prosperous community that would result but also because of serious problems with the other possibilities indicated. The primary benefits, in his estimation, are these. If religious sentiments become attached to the requirements of mutual respect and care that are fundamental to the character of civil society as he has characterised it, then acceptance of these requirements will be felt to carry with it divine favour and blessing, and rejection of them or failure to abide by them divine displeasure in addition to any civil rewards or punishments. Such sentiments invest civil obedience with a deeper significance so that it becomes more complete and fully embraced. But this is not to give to the laws an authority which otherwise they would be devoid of, by conjuring up fears of divine retribution to enforce compliance with some otherwise groundless requirement. Rather, it is a question of an 'addition' to 'the force [the laws] have in themselves'; and since this is the purpose it determines also the limits to the place for religious prescription in connection with civil requirements. Thus Rousseau writes:

> The right which the social compact gives the Sovereign over the subjects does not . . . exceed the limits of public expediency. The subjects then owe the Sovereign an account of their opinions only to such an extent as they matter to the community. Now, it matters very much to the community that each citizen should have a religion. That will make him love his duty; but the dogmas of that religion concern the State and its members only so far as they have reference to morality and to the duties which he who professes them is bound to do to others. Each man may have, over and above, what opinions he pleases, without its being the Sovereign's business to take cognisance of them.

If, in the light of this, we return to the apparently alarming remarks about banishment and death for those who do not accept the articles of the civil profession of faith, cited above, they can perhaps be seen to wear a somewhat less disturbing meaning. For one who rejects the dogmas of the civil religion is not banished as impious, but as 'an anti-social being, incapable of truly loving the laws and justice'. We may, of course, still find this very objectionable, not least because we are entirely used to the idea of people's capacity to love the laws and justice without the involvement of religious sentiments, though there are, of course, many millions of people for whom there remains a very close connection indeed. But if this is so then the root of the objection is to Rousseau's being excessively concerned with shaping all the resources that make for good citizenship rather than to the enforcement of religious conformity. If the dogmas of a civil religion did attach to the observance of the basic requirements of law, than a rejection of those dogmas would be apt to signal a person's intent to flout the law. And no civil authority can remain indifferent to that.

What, then, of Rousseau's objections to the three other possible types of relationship between civil authority and obedience to law and religious allegiance? Rousseau emphasises that if religious allegiance is unregulated by, or not connected with the maintenance of, the civil authority it will comprise a commitment that will be socially disruptive or subversive of loyalty and commitment to the community. It may be contended, for instance, that religious requirements preclude, or exempt one from, obedience to some or other laws of the state. Even if conflict of this kind is avoided, Rousseau argues that the divisions of loyalty will result in a weakened commitment to the preservation of the civil body. In addition, religious zeal is apt to divide the peoples of the world into the saved and the damned, and to spur the former to doing whatever they deem fit to 'redeem' the latter and rid the world of the pestilence they represent. Such persecutions cannot but threaten the stability and prosperity of a society. Rousseau's criticisms of religious intolerance considered in the *Creed* are clearly echoed here.

Rousseau thus distinguishes three 'kinds of religion'. The first is 'confined to the purely internal cult of the supreme God and the eternal obligations of morality'; the second is 'codified in a single

country, [and] gives it its gods, its own tutelary patrons'. The third
Rousseau calls 'the religion of the priest', in which there is a 'theo-
logical system' separate from the political system. In this instance,
the clergy of a religious denomination comprise a corporate body
with a corporate will distinct from the sovereign general will but
claiming an authority at least equal to that. Rousseau objects to this
last that it subjects men to contradictory duties so that they cannot
be 'faithful both to religion and to citizenship'. To the second, he
says that whereas it provides a support to the community in that it
'teaches . . . that service done to the State is service done to its
tutelary god' it also deceives men and becomes tyrannical. It makes
'a people bloodthirsty and intolerant . . . and regards as a sacred act
the killing of every one who does not believe in its gods'.

The first kind of religion, with its emphasis on the obligations of
morality, might seem to be more congenial to Rousseau's thinking.
But he argues that it leads to indifference to the earthly prosperity
and safety of the citizens and leaves the state open to usurpation of
public authority since 'in this vale of sorrows, what does it matter
whether we are free men or serfs?' Finally, it also leaves the state
easy prey in time of war for 'What does it matter whether they win
or lose? Does not providence know better what is meet for them?'
What Rousseau has in view in connection with these comments is,
of course, particularly Christianity, and he writes:

> But this religion [Christianity], having no particular relation to the
> body politic, leaves the laws in possession of the force they have in
> themselves without making any addition to it; and thus one of the
> great bonds that unite society considered in severalty fails to
> operate. Nay, more, so far from binding the hearts of citizens to the
> State, it has the effect of taking them away from all earthly things.
> I know of nothing more contrary to the social spirit.

It was from this passage that I drew the reference to 'the social
spirit' with which this chapter began. We amply see now how
central is Rousseau's concern with fostering and strengthening this.

In concluding this section, I want to return, as I indicated, to one relevant point in the *Creed* concerning atheism. In the long footnote almost at the end of the text of that we considered earlier in Chapter 4, Rousseau, whilst agreeing that religious fanaticism is more 'pernicious' than atheism, went on to say that it is a 'grand and strong passion which elevates the heart of man' whereas atheism, 'makes souls effeminate and degraded, concentrates all the passions in the baseness of private interests, in the abjectness of the human I, and thus quietly saps the true foundations of every society' (E IV: 312 note, OC IV: 632–3). O'Hagan, in a fine discussion of this material, comments:

> This apocalyptic passage targets atheists for being necessarily selfish, unwilling to strive for their fellow human beings, or even to reproduce them. In contrast to this image of moral decay, the image of the healthy, if barbarous, fanatic is relatively attractive . . . There he stands, more as a brutal contrast to the degeneracy of modern society than as a model of the citizen to come.
>
> (O'Hagan: 234)

The closing words are surely right. As we have seen, whilst Rousseau thinks that each citizen should have a religion it should throughout be constrained by the 'negative dogma' of the prohibition of intolerance.

POLAND AND CORSICA

Finally in this chapter I want to take a selective look at Rousseau's two essays in what I called 'applied politics', the *Considerations on the Government of Poland* and the *Constitutional Project for Corsica*, from the same general perspective – Rousseau's concern with the maintenance of the bonds of union among citizens – that I have deployed in my consideration of elements in the *Discourse on Political Economy*, the *Letter to d'Alembert* and the treatment of civil religion. Neither of these works was published in Rousseau's lifetime (the essay on Corsica is, in fact, an unfinished fragment). GP was completed in 1772, written in response to an approach from Count Wielhorski, a representative of the Confederation of Bar, a body dedicated to the preservation of Polish identity against Russian imperialism. PCC was begun in 1764 after Rousseau had been contacted on behalf of the leader of the Corsican rebels, Pasquale Paoli, to propose a new constitution for what they hoped would soon be an independent Corsica. Rousseau had written, as cited earlier, in striking terms of Corsica in Book II Chapter 10 of SC:

> There is still in Europe one country capable of being given laws – Corsica. The valour and persistency with which that brave people has regained and defended its liberty well deserve that some wise man should teach it how to preserve what it has won.
>
> (OC III: 391)

If Rousseau was pleased to be seen as that 'wise man' his endeavours, such as they were, came to nothing. In 1768 the rebellion was suppressed by the French, who had bought the island from the Genoese.

Although there are naturally enough marked differences of content between these works, there are strong thematic similarities and I shall try to bring these out. Rousseau stresses, right at the start of GP, that an institution needs to 'conform . . . to the people for whom it is intended' (G P: 177, OC III: 953). A few pages later on, he writes:

> It is national institutions which form the genius, the character, the tastes, and the morals of a people, which make it be itself and not another, which inspire in it that ardent love of fatherland founded on habits impossible to uproot, which cause it to die of boredom among other peoples in the midst of delights of which it is deprived in its own.
>
> (G P: 183, OC III: 960)

He follows this with scorn of the cosmopolitan spirit which echoes remarks made at the start of Émile (see E I: 40, OC IV: 249–50):

> There are no more Frenchmen, Germans, Spaniards, even
> Englishmen, nowadays, regardless of what people may say; there
> are only Europeans. All have the same tastes, the same passions,
> the same morals, because none has been given a national form by
> a distinctive institution. All will do the same things under the same
> circumstances; all will declare themselves disinterested and be
> cheats; all will speak of the public good and think only of
> themselves; all will praise moderation and wish to be Croesuses;
> they have no other ambition than for luxury, no other passion than
> for gold.
>
> (G P: 184, OC III: 960)

Rousseau's thought here is that when and where bonds of attachment and common life are attenuated we do not find in fact a widening of the sense of belonging but rather a reversion to an atomised, egoistic individualism. So, Rousseau continues, 'begin by giving the Poles a great opinion of themselves and their fatherland' (G P: 184, OC III: 961). In a similar vein he writes, in PCC:

> The first rule to be followed is the principle of national character; for
> each people has, or ought to have, a national character; if it did not,
> we should have to start by giving it one.
>
> (PCC: 293, OC III: 913)

What is the key to the formation of national character? Rousseau gives paramount emphasis to education:

> It is education that must give souls the national form, and so direct
> their tastes and opinions that they will be patriotic by inclination,
> passion, necessity . . . Every true republican drank love of
> fatherland, that is to say love of the laws and of freedom, with his
> mother's milk. This love makes up his whole existence; he sees only
> his fatherland, he lives only for it; when he is alone, he is nothing:
> when he no longer has a fatherland, he no longer is, and if he is not
> dead, he is worse than dead.
>
> (G P: 189, OC III: 966)

Recalling points made earlier in this chapter, Rousseau's language in this passage is very much in terms of 'maximal identification' by the individual of their good with the good of the whole. And the overriding purpose of this is to 'attach citizens to the fatherland and to one another' so that the requirements of law are not a burden or constraint, but the direction of each person's wish for themself and others.

Rousseau fully recognises that with neither Poland nor Corsica is one beginning with a 'blank sheet' but with long-established customs, and particularly orders of precedence and hierarchies among the subjects. Interestingly enough, despite the very great stress on equality among citizens in the arguments of SC, he advises caution in the process of freeing the peasants of Poland:

> To emancipate the peoples of Poland is a grand and fine undertaking but bold, dangerous, and not to be attempted thoughtlessly. Among the precautions to be taken, there is one that is indispensable and that requires time. It is, before everything else, to make the serfs who are to be emancipated worthy of freedom and capable of tolerating it . . . It would be rash of me to guarantee . . . success . . . But regardless . . . recognise that your serfs are men like yourselves, that they have in them the stuff to become all that you are.
>
> (G P: 197, OC III: 974)

For myself, I do not see in this any real compromise of Rousseau's theoretical principles, but rather a recognition that their realisation requires preparation and an appropriate context. His conviction seems to me unchanged, and his message will have been a challenging one for Count Wielhorski and his confederates. Throughout, in fact, Rousseau advocates working with existing ideas of honour and prestige and causing these to be turned gradually to new objects, new achievements. If the desire for distinction is ineradicable from the spirit of a people, then it is on the basis of accomplishments of service to all that these distinctions of persons will best be made since in that way all may benefit.

With the same intent of ensuring that destructive and invidious inequalities do not persist, Rousseau devotes a considerable amount of time to the corrupting influence of money, arguing that it is devious and secret in its workings concealed from public view and accountability. He urges as far as possible payment in kind for public services and the reintroduction of the corvée not, of course, on feudal principles, always with a view to preventing the corruption of competitive private interests. One of his most spectacular suggestions comes from the same root. In Chapter IX of GP, Rousseau considers the right of veto of proposed legislation that was, at that time, possessed by individual members of the legislative body in Poland. Whilst agreeing that it has an important role to play, Rousseau contends that it has been exploited for petty, personal reasons and has made legislative and indeed administrative action almost impossible. In the light of this, Rousseau suggests the following:

> If, then in the event of an almost unanimous resolution, a single opponent retained the right to annul it, I would wish him to be answerable for his opposition with his head, not only to his constituents in the post-session Dietine, but also subsequently to the entire nation whose misfortune he brought on. I should like it to be required by law that six months after his opposition he be solemnly tried by an extraordinary tribunal established solely to this end, made up of all the nation's wisest, most illustrious and most respected persons, which could not simply acquit him, but would either have to condemn him to death without possible pardon, or to bestow upon him a reward and public honours for life, without ever being able to adopt a middle course between these two alternatives.
>
> (GP: 219, OC III: 997)

This amazing idea would certainly have the effect of ensuring that anyone who intended to exercise their veto was doing so for reasons which, at the very least, a panel of their peers would find compelling. And, in that way, we might expect generality of interest to be finding voice in the veto, not just some private caprice. Rousseau is at least honest enough to accept that 'Institutions of this kind . . . are too remote from the modern spirit to allow the hope that they might be adopted or appreciated' (ibid.), but it is pleasant to speculate what, for example, the conduct of the members of the Security Council of the United Nations would be like if something of this kind could be made to apply to the exercise of national vetoes in that.

In this brief review of these works, we have seen a recurrence of Rousseau's central concern: a concern with the development and direction of a national or civic culture which makes each citizen's duty to acknowledge the rights and needs of others not a burdensome requirement but more nearly what they would design and wish for as their own way of realising their union with and care for their fellows. It is to be doubted that many view their obedience to law in these terms nowadays. But Rousseau is surely right in his conviction that if the sense of union, the social spirit, becomes very attenuated then a society is near to dissolution, or at best inequality and injustice will be widespread with many merely coerced by law and not true subjects. Perhaps it was ever so, but – as remarked at the end of the preceding chapter – Rousseau here offers a vision which remains capable of stirring the moral sense and inspiring a wish for things to be different. It is possible that his own strong personal sense of social exclusion made him particularly concerned with the conditions for and character of belonging, but his general thought that without a fairly widespread sense of belonging shared by many citizens we have a fragile society little concerned for the benefit of all is a powerful one. How that sense is sustained and consolidated must, therefore, be an urgent concern for anyone interested in a just society.

FURTHER READING

Zev M. Trachtenberg, *Making Citizens: Rousseau's Political Theory of Culture*. London: Routledge, 1993. Lays special emphasis on significance of culture.

Anne M. Cohler, *Rousseau and Nationalism*. New York: Basic Books, 1970. A good account of Rousseau's views on patriotism and the nation.

Timothy O'Hagan, *Rousseau*. London: Routledge, 1999, Chapters X–XII. A good account of civil religion, and of Rousseau's religious thinking generally.

F.M. Barnard, *Self-Direction and Political Legitimacy: Rousseau and Herder*. Oxford: Clarendon Press, 1988. Gives a particular place to national culture.

Seven

Autobiography

The great upsurge of creativity that began in 1749 with Rousseau's 'illumination' on his way to visit Diderot and which, during the next twelve years, had resulted in the writing of the *Discourse on Inequality*, *Émile*, *La Nouvelle Héloïse*, *The Social Contract* and a host of other works, ebbed somewhat after he fled Paris in 1762 to escape the threatened persecution that followed the publication of *Émile*. Not that Rousseau ceased to write – far from it. But his major essays in social and political philosophy were done and, with some exceptions such as for example the completion of his *Dictionary of Music*, and the preparation of his essay *Considerations on the Government of Poland* looked at in the preceding chapter, his output over the following years was predominantly devoted to self-explanation and self-justification in a variety of different modes. The year 1763 saw the publication of his *Letter to Christophe de Beaumont*, and 1764 his *Letters Written from the Mountain*. Both of these were written to defend himself against specific accusations laid against him as a result of ideas expressed in E and SC. And although there is material of enduring interest in these works, their scope and purpose is largely governed by the controversial circumstances of the moment and we do not find in them major new ideas nor important changes in the character and direction of Rousseau's work. The real new departure in the progress of his creative life came with his beginning work on *The Confessions*. The text of that as we have it was completed in 1770, though not published in Rousseau's lifetime, and the next major work, *Rousseau Judge of Jean-Jacques: Dialogues* was begun a couple of years later. The final significant autobiographical work, *The Reveries of a Solitary Walker*, also Rousseau's last work, was begun in 1776 and left unfinished at his death. It is these three works I shall be concentrating on in this chapter, giving central place to *The Confessions*, a work of enormous interest and power and one which is a real pleasure to read.

Rousseau's long-time publisher, Marc-Michel Rey, based in Amsterdam – where his house is today marked with a commemorative plaque – proposed to him in 1761 that he consider writing an autobiography. At first Rousseau did not warm to the idea, though he began to make some notes, to collect copies of letters and other materials that might prove useful. No doubt he drew on some of this when, in January 1762, he wrote four letters to Malesherbes, the Director of Publications, about himself and his situation. As glanced at previously in Chapter 2, Rousseau had become very anxious and distressed about delays in the printing of the text of *Émile* and he had begun to suspect hostile interference was holding up the process. He turned to Malesherbes for help and reassurance, which the latter was able to provide with great generosity and tact. By way of an expression of heartfelt gratitude, Rousseau wrote these letters in an attempt to explain the motives for his conduct and describing some of the principal determining events of his life (see also C11: 525 ff, OC I: 568 ff). These letters were not intended for publication but appeared, in an unauthorised version, in 1779. I shall look briefly at them again as a preamble to considering *The Confessions*.

In the first of them, Rousseau defends himself against the charge, levelled against him by many in the Paris salons and given a particular sting by some words of Diderot's (see C 9: 423 ff, OC I: 455 ff), that he is a misanthrope who seeks notoriety by affecting a love of the country and of solitude. Rousseau says that, in truth, what he hates is the falseness and artificiality of life in the city and that it his spirit of liberty and the desire to be able to speak and write openly without constraint that have led him to want to live in the serene surroundings of the countryside. There is no ostentatious motive in what he has done. The second letter recounts some of the events of Rousseau's life, and he gives in it his first account of the 'illumination' on his way to see Diderot, which changed the course of his life.

> I was on my way to see Diderot, then a prisoner at Vincennes. I had a copy of the *Mercure de France* in my pocket . . . My eyes lit on the question of the Academy of Dijon which occasioned my first piece of writing [the *Discourse on the Sciences and Arts*]. If anything was ever like a sudden inspiration it was the impulse that surged up in me as I read that. Suddenly I felt my mind dazzled by a thousand lights; crowds of lively ideas presented themselves at once, with a force and confusion that threw me into an inexpressible trouble; I felt my head seized with a vertigo like that of intoxication. A violent palpitation oppressed me . . . Oh, Sir, if ever I could have written even the quarter of what I saw and felt under that tree, with what clarity should I have revealed all the contradictions of the social system, with what force would I have exposed all the abuses of our institutions, in what simple terms would I have demonstrated that man is naturally good, and that it is through these institutions alone that men become bad . . . That is how, when I least thought of it, I became an author almost in spite of myself.
>
> (Hendel: 208–9, see also C 8: 327–9, OC I: 350–2)

In the Third Letter, Rousseau speaks of his present state of mind. He says it was only when he left Paris in 1756 to live at the Hermitage that he began to be able to experience true happiness, to take delight in the simple pleasures of existence and to enjoy his own lazy and dreamy nature. In such surroundings he can sense the presence of an infinite and benevolent creator. In the last of the letters, he sets out how it is, he thinks, he should be understood. His works are intended to benefit all human beings, not just a few, and that is why he avoids becoming caught up with intrigues and factions. Above all, he considers all people his equals; he hates injustice and inhumanity and, after his own fashion, has tried to fight against these. As noted, some of the episodes Rousseau speaks of in these letters are described again in The Confessions. But we also find Rousseau deploying accounts of his nature and motives which find a much expanded and elaborated form both in that, but especially in RJJ.

Work on C proceeded only intermittently up to 1764, but after that he made steady progress, working on Part I (Books 1–6) which goes up to 1741–2 during his stay in England in 1766 and bringing it more or less to completion by the spring of 1767. Part II (Books 7–12) was begun in 1769 and was completed by June 1770, around the time Rousseau returned to Paris for the last time. This brings the account up to 1765. He appears originally to have planned a third part, taking the story up to 1770, but this was abandoned not least because of a ban placed on readings from the earlier parts that he was giving to friends. Some of his erstwhile friends and supporters from whom he was now deeply estranged were fearful of what Rousseau would be saying about them and persuaded the authorities to prohibit these readings (since he was only allowed to reside in Paris on sufferance). I turn now to an account of this work.

THE CONFESSIONS

The Confessions is a massive work, well over a quarter of a million words in length, and I shall make no attempt to give a summary of it as a whole. I shall rather outline its overall content, and select a few passages to try to convey the brilliance of Rousseau's writing and something of the character of the narrative. I will conclude with some comments on how the work might be approached and interpreted. Right at the start, Rousseau says he intends to display 'a portrait in every way true to nature' (C I: 17, OC I: 5), and one of the many reasons for giving close attention to the work is to better understand what conception of 'nature' Rousseau is here deploying which he wishes to be true to. I shall return to this point, but we see straightaway the centrality of concerns in this work that also pervade his other writings.

Rousseau does not give titles to the twelve books of which C is composed; indeed, the divisions between the books often seem pretty arbitrary, some covering many years, some one or two only. However, following Peter France (1987), we can identify a reasonably straightforward shape of the work. Book 1 treats of Rousseau's childhood up to 1728 when he left Geneva. (The outline of Rousseau's life given in Chapter 2 above and the chronological table may usefully be referred to for more detail.) Books 2–4 cover his wandering years including his meeting with Madame de Warens, his conversion to Catholicism, his unhappy times in Turin and so on, up to 1732. Books 5 and 6 concern his settled life back with Madame de Warens, including the idyllic period at Les Charmettes. Displaced in her affections by Wintzenried, however, he resolved to set off for Paris armed with his scheme for a new musical notation, and the text of his play *Narcissus*: 'For I did not doubt that when I put my scheme before the Academy [of Sciences] it would cause a revolution' (C 6: 257, OC I: 272). At this point Part I of C concludes.

After a break in the composition of the text of two years, Rousseau begins Part II as follows:

> You have seen my peaceful youth flow by in a uniform and pleasant enough way, without great set-backs or remarkable spells of prosperity . . . What a different picture I shall soon have to fill in! After favouring my wishes for thirty years, for the next thirty fate opposed them; and from this continual opposition between my situation and my desires will be seen to arise great mistakes, incredible misfortunes, and every virtue that can do credit to adversity except strength of character.
>
> (C 7: 261, OC 1: 277)

Book 7 recounts the first fruits of his ambitions in Paris; and Book

8 his great success with his opera *The Village Soothsayer* in 1752. In Book 9 he tells of his retreat from Parisian life to the Hermitage, of his rupture with Madame d'Épinay and the estrangement from Diderot referred to in the discussion of the *Letters to Malesherbes* above. In Book 10, Rousseau, now living under the protection of the Duke and Duchess of Luxembourg at Montlouis, seems to recover his poise, but in Book 11 we learn of the disasters that overtook him following the publication of *Émile* and *The Social Contract*. The final book begins:

> Here begins the work of darkness in which I have been entombed for eight years past, without ever having been able, try as I might, to pierce its hideous obscurity. In the abyss of evil in which I am sunk I feel the weight of blows struck at me; I perceive the immediate instrument; but I can neither see the hand which directs it nor the means by which it works.
>
> (C 12: 544, C I: 589)

This book, which takes Rousseau's story up to his preparing to departure for England with David Hume at the end of 1765 can be called a story of exile. His writing at this time is marked by a strong edge of paranoia, as is plain from the passage cited. Thus, on the surface at any rate, the work is structured chronologically and leads us through those events of his life to which Rousseau attributes particular significance, with his own account of the sentiments, motives and meanings that these wear. We shall see, in a while, whether this overt structure discloses what is most enduring in the work.

As indicated, I want now to select just a few passages from the whole text which will, I hope, convey something of the character of the work. Book 1, recounting his childhood and youth, is the most polished of all the books and contains some quite beautiful descriptions of his early experiences and activities. One of these concerns Rousseau and his cousin planting a cutting from a willow, in order to emulate the tree-plantings of M. Lambercier, the pastor at Bossey with whom Jean-Jacques and Abraham, his cousin, were staying. In order to get water to their cutting, they devised a concealed trench through which water would run to their shoot from the supply that M. Lambercier provided for his own walnut tree. Rousseau writes:

> A few seconds after the first bucket was poured in we saw a trickle of water flow into our trench. At this sight our caution deserted us, and we set up such shouts of joy that M. Lambercier turned round; which was a pity since he had just been observing with delight how good the soil was around his tree and how greedily it absorbed the water. Shocked, however, to see it providing for two trenches, he also set up a shout. Then, taking a closer look he discovered our trick and sent straight for a mattock, which quickly knocked a few of our boards flying. 'An aqueduct! An aqueduct!' he cried, and rained down his merciless blows on every side. Each one of them pierced us to the heart. In a moment the boards, the runnel, the trench, and the willow were all destroyed, and the earth all around was ploughed up. But, in the course of all this frightful business, the only words uttered were his cries of 'An aqueduct! An aqueduct!' as he knocked everything to pieces.
>
> (C 1: 33, OC I: 23–4)

This passage captures very well the delight and excitement of the moment. Of more significance for his later life are the punishments Rousseau received from M. Lambercier's sister.

> Since Mlle. Lambercier treated us with a mother's love, she had also a mother's authority, which she exercised sometimes by inflicting on us such childish chastisements as we had earned . . . when in the end I was beaten I found the experience less dreadful in fact than in anticipation; and the very strange thing was that this punishment increased my affection for the inflicter . . . I had discovered in the shame and pain of the punishment an admixture of sensuality which had left me rather eager than otherwise for a repetition by the same hand . . . Who could have supposed that this

childish punishment, received at the age of eight at the hands of a woman of thirty, would determine my tastes and desires, my passions, my very self for the rest of my life, and that in a sense diametrically opposed to the one in which they should normally have developed.

(C 1: 25–6, OC I: 15)

And much more to the same effect. Rousseau wittily goes on:

To fall on my knees before a masterful mistress, to obey her commands, to have to beg for her forgiveness, have been to me the most delicate of pleasures; and the more my vivid imagination heated my blood the more like a spellbound lover I looked. As can be imagined, this way of making love does not lead to rapid progress, and is not very dangerous to the virtue of the desired object.

(C I: 28, OC I: 17; compare C 2: 78–9, C3: 90–91, C 6: 238–40 and C 7: 300–02 for more moments in Rousseau's chequered sexual history; OC I: 75–6, 88–9, 250–52, 320–22)

Other punishments, however, had perhaps even more fateful consequences. One of Mademoiselle Lambercier's combs had got broken, and suspicion had fallen on Rousseau. However, he inflexibly denied doing it and, in the text of C. continues to deny it. Rousseau writes:

Imagine a person timid and docile in ordinary life, but proud, fiery, and inflexible when roused, a child who has always been controlled by the voice of reason, always treated with kindness, fairness, and indulgence, a creature without a thought of injustice, now for the first time suffering a most grave one at the hands of the people he loves best and most deeply respects. Imagine the revolution in his ideas, the violent change of his feelings, the confusion in his heart and brain, in his small intellectual and moral being! . . . all I felt was the cruelty of an appalling punishment for a crime I had not committed. The physical pain was bad enough, but I hardly noticed

it; what I felt was indignation, rage, and despair . . . That first
meeting with violence and injustice has remained so deeply
engraved on my heart that any thought which recalls it summons
back this first emotion . . . There ended the serenity of my childish
life . . . even today I am conscious that memory of childhood's
delights stops short at that point.

(C 1: 29–30, C I: 19–20)

But Rousseau himself could be the perpetrator of injustice, as this
next story amply shows. Rousseau has been employed as a servant,
in Turin, by the Comtesse de Vercellis. When she dies, in the confusion of breaking up the household Rousseau steals a pink and silver
ribbon. It is soon found, but Rousseau claims that Marion, the cook
to Madame de Vercellis in her final illness, has given it to him:

She was sent for . . . When she came she was shown the ribbon. I
boldly accused her. She was confused, did not utter a word, and
threw a glance that would have disarmed the devil, but my cruel
heart resisted. In the end she firmly denied the theft. But she did not
get indignant. She merely turned to me, and begged me to
remember myself and not disgrace an innocent girl who had never
done me any harm. But, with infernal impudence, I repeated my
accusation, and declared to her face that she had given me the
ribbon . . . In the confusion of the moment they had not time to get
to the bottom of the business; and the Comte de la Roque, in
dismissing us both, contented himself with saying that the guilty
one's conscience would amply revenge the innocent. His prediction
was not wide of the mark. Not a day passes on which it is not
fulfilled.

(C 2: 87, OC I: 85)

Rousseau would appear to be sincere in his closing comment; he
returns to this episode in the Fourth Walk (Chapter) of *The Reveries*
some ten or so years later on. But, on the other hand, he is not
above finding some colour of excuse for what he did; fear of

disgrace, utter confusion, weakness and his tender age and so on, and within a page or two he is able to say: 'Poor Marion finds so many avengers in this world that, however great my offence against her may have been, I have little fear of carrying the sin on my conscience at death' (C 2: 89, OC I: 87). Rousseau settles the moral account rather too easily as well as congratulating himself that this is 'the sole offence I have committed'. A hasty impulse, induced by fear, may not make a bad man, but it scarcely leaves him in a position to be self-satisfied.

A more attractive Rousseau is visible in his self-mocking account of his passing himself off as a proficient musician and composer called Vaussore de Villeneuve offering a piece for a concert; this was in 1732:

> At last all was ready, I gave five or six premonitory taps on my conductor's desk with a handsome roll of paper. Attention! All was quiet. Gravely I began to beat time. They began. No, throughout all the history of French opera never was heard such a discordant row . . . The musicians were choking with laughter; the audience goggled their eyes . . . My wretched orchestra, who were out to amuse themselves, scraped loudly enough to pierce a deaf man's ear-drums. I had the audacity to go right on, sweating big drops, it is true, but kept there by shame.
>
> (C 4: 145–6, OC I: 149)

True, he gives himself consoling reflections about his later success with Le Devin just a few lines later, but the confession of this failure seems more candid.

From a hundred and one other moments worthy of note, I shall just bring forward four more. The first concerns another moment in Rousseau's sexual odyssey, his sexual initiation by Madame de Warens, his 'Maman':

> Mamma saw that to save me from the dangers of my youth it was time to treat me like a man, and this she did, but in the most

singular fashion that ever occurred to a woman in like
circumstances.

(This quotation and all those that follow
come from C 5: 186–90, OC I: 193–7)

She offers herself to Rousseau, but gives him eight days to think
about it:

> It might be supposed that these eight days dragged for me like so
> many centuries. On the contrary, I could have wished them
> centuries long. I do not know how to describe the state I was in; it
> was made up of fright mingled with impatience . . . How, by what
> miracle was it that in the flower of my youth I was so little eager for
> my first experience? How could I see the moment approaching with
> more pain than pleasure?

Finally, he comes up with the reason:

> The long habit of living with her on terms of innocence, far from
> weakening my feelings for her, had strengthened them, but at the
> same time it had given them a different turn, rendering them more
> affectionate, and more tender perhaps, but less sexual. By calling
> her Mamma and treating her with the familiarity of a son, I had
> grown to look on myself as such; and I think that is the real cause of
> my lack of eagerness to possess her.

And then to the eighth day:

> My heart fulfilled my pledges without any desire for the reward.
> I gained it nevertheless, and found myself for the first time in the
> arms of a woman, and of a woman I adored. Was I happy? No;
> I tasted the pleasure, but I knew not what invincible sadness
> poisoned its charm. I felt as if I had committed incest and, two or
> three times, as I clasped her rapturously in my arms I wet her
> bosom with my tears. As for her, she was neither sad nor excited;
> she was tranquil and caressing. As she was not at all sensual and

had not sought for gratification, she neither received sexual
pleasure nor knew the remorse that follows.

This is, by any standards, a remarkable account of a remarkable
event.

Notoriously, throughout his life Rousseau had great difficulty in
joining passionate romantic rapture with sexual and domestic
familiarity. In outlining his life above in Chapter 2, I wondered on
several occasions what Thérèse, his long-time companion and
finally his wife, made of his romantic follies and desperate attachments to other women, never mind the giving up of their children.
Here is Rousseau's account of their meeting; it is spring 1745 and
Rousseau is in lodgings in Paris:

> We had a new landlady who came from Orléans and, to look after
> the linen, she had taken a girl from her own town, of about twenty-
> two or twenty-three, who ate with us, as did our hostess. This girl,
> Thérèse Le Vasseur by name, was of a decent family . . . The first
> time that I saw this girl appear at table I was struck by her modest
> behaviour and, even more, by her bright and gentle looks, of which
> I had never seen the like before . . . They [the other lodgers] teased
> the girl, I sprang to her defence, and then the jokes were turned
> against me. If I had not felt any natural liking for the poor thing, pity
> and contrariness would have given me one . . . She was very shy,
> and so was I. Yet the intimacy which our common shyness seemed
> to preclude was very speedily formed . . . The sympathy of our
> hearts and the agreement of our dispositions had soon the usual
> result. She believed that she saw in me an honourable man, and she
> was not mistaken. I believed that I saw in her a girl with feelings, a
> simple girl without coquetry; and I was not mistaken either. I
> declared in advance that I would never abandon her, nor ever marry
> her. Love, esteem, and simple sincerity were the agents of my
> triumph; and since her heart was tender and virtuous, I did not need
> to be bold to be fortunate.
>
> (C 7: 309–311, OC I: 330–1)

A few lines later, he says: 'What I needed, in short, was a successor to Mamma' – but the Mamma of affection and familiarity, not rapture and ecstasy. And so it continued. When he and Thérèse went to live at the Hermitage in 1756, Rousseau confesses to unfulfilled longings:

My life with her [Thérèse] was unconstrained and, as you might say, subject to no conditions. Nevertheless I was never free from a secret heartache, whether I was with her or away from her.

(C 9: 395, OC I: 424)

His brooding continued:

How could it be that, with a naturally expansive nature for which to live was to love, I had not hitherto found a friend entirely my own, a true friend – I who felt so truly formed to be a friend? How could it be that with such inflammable feelings, with a heart entirely moulded for love, I had not at least once burned with love for a definite object? Devoured by a need to love that I had never been able to satisfy, I saw myself coming to the gates of old age, and dying without having lived.

(C 9: 396–7, C I: 426)

This comforting, self-pitying melancholy turned Rousseau's mind to his early affections, moments of intimacy and innocence with girls and 'I saw myself surrounded by a Seraglio of houris, by my old acquaintances a strong desire for whom was no new sensation to me. My blood caught fire, my head turned despite its grey hairs, and there was the grave citizen of Geneva, the austere Jean-Jacques at almost forty-five, suddenly become once more the love-sick swain' (ibid.).

Out of this 'intoxication' came the visions that provided the inspiration for *Julie, ou La Nouvelle Héloïse*:

The impossibility of attaining the real persons precipitated me into the land of chimeras; and seeing nothing that existed worthy of my exalted feelings, I fostered them in an ideal world which my creative imagination soon peopled with beings after my own heart . . . In my continual ecstasies I intoxicated myself with draughts of the most exquisite sentiments that have ever entered the heart of a man. Altogether ignoring the human race, I created for myself societies of perfect creatures celestial in their virtue and in their beauty, and of reliable, tender, and faithful friends such as I had never found here below . . .

(C9: 398, OC I: 427–8)

Rousseau forges ahead with the writing of the first part of Julie and then the incarnation of his heroine seemed to appear to him in the form of Sophie d'Houdetot, the sister-in-law of Madame d'Épinay (who was letting him use her cottage):

The return of spring had redoubled my amorous delirium, and in my erotic transports I had composed for the last parts of *Julie* several letters that betray the ecstatic state in which I wrote them . . . At precisely this same time I received a second unexpected visit from Madame d'Houdetot . . . she came to make a fresh visit to the Hermitage. On this occasion she came on horseback, in man's clothes. Although I am not very fond of such masquerades, the air of romance about this one charmed me, and this time it was love. As it was the first and only love in all my life, and as through its consequences it will ever remain a terrible and indelible memory to me, may I be forgiven for describing it in some detail.

(C 9: 408, OC I: 438–9)

'I saw my Julie in Madame d'Houdetot, and soon I saw only Madame d'Houdetot, but endowed with all the perfections with which I had just embellished the idol of my heart' (C9: 410, OC1: 440).

To follow the vicissitudes of Rousseau's passion would make a study all of its own, but to bring this dipping into the text to a close, I will just briefly turn to the consequences of his love that made it a 'terrible' memory to him. Not surprisingly, Madame d'Épinay and her friends, never mind Madame d'Houdetot's lover, Saint-Lambert, looked askance on Rousseau's extraordinary state, and his guilt, shame and sense of humiliation made him see their, no doubt anyway unfriendly, comments and attitudes as particularly poisonous and hurtful. A severe rupture was inevitable, and it was not long in coming, shot through with Rousseau's incipient paranoia:

> The secret accusations of treachery and ingratitude were spread more cautiously, and were for that reason even more effective. I knew that they charged me with heinous crimes, but I never could learn what they alleged them to be. All that I could deduce from public rumour was that they would be reduced to these four capital offences: (1) my retirement to the country; (2) my love for Madame d'Houdetot; (3) my refusal to accompany Madame d'Épinay to Geneva; (4) my leaving the Hermitage.
>
> (C 10: 456, OC I: 491)

Rousseau's suspicions particularly focused on Melchior Grimm, an intimate of Madame d'Épinay's and an urbane habitué of all those social circles from which Rousseau had removed himself:

> It was thanks to this superiority of his talents that, seeing the advantage which he could derive from our respective positions, he formed the plan of utterly destroying my reputation, and endowing me with an entirely opposite one, yet without compromising himself. His first move was to raise all around me an atmosphere of darkness which I should be unable to penetrate, in order to throw light on his manoeuvrings and unmask him . . . His great skill lies in his appearing to humour me while all the time maligning me, and thus giving his perfidy the appearance of generosity.
>
> (C 10: 457–8, OC I: 492–3)

The true accents of a persecution complex are very plain in this. The desperation in Rousseau's mind had its natural and inevitable effect; Sophie grew tired of his 'tempestuous correspondence' and after yet more twists and turns their intense relationship gradually faded away until it got to the point where, upon sending her copies of his works as they appeared, these 'still drew from her occasional letters and messages of slight importance but always polite'. So ends the grand passion of Rousseau's life, his 'first and only love'.

I hope these few extracts from Rousseau's text have conveyed something of the range, variety and vitality of his writing, its candour but also concealment, its insight but also its blindness. How then, overall, may one approach and assess this extraordinary work? On the first page Rousseau says this about his project:

> I have resolved on an enterprise which has no precedent, and which, once complete, will have no imitator. My purpose is to display to my kind a portrait in every way true to nature, and the man I shall portray will be myself . . . Let the last trump sound when it will, I shall come forward with this work in my hand, to present myself before my Sovereign Judge, and proclaim aloud: 'Here is what I have done, and if by chance I have used some immaterial embellishment it has been only to fill a void due to a defect of memory. I may have taken for fact what was no more than probability, but I have never put down as true what I knew to be false. I have displayed myself as I was, as vile and despicable when my behaviour was such, as good, generous and noble when I was so . . . So let the numberless legion of my fellow men gather round me, and hear my confessions. Let them groan at my depravities, and blush for my misdeeds. But let each one of them reveal his heart at the foot of Thy throne with equal sincerity, and may any man who dares, say, "I was a better man than he."
>
> (C 1: 17, OC I: 5)

A great number of Rousseau's registers are present in this passage; massive ambition, a sense of personal uniqueness; self-conceit; challenge and scorn of his fellows; exaltation of his own merits and so on. Because of the stress here on truthfulness, many critics, provoked perhaps by Rousseau's righteous tone, have looked for, and found, in the text many instances of falsification of kinds that reveal self-serving motives or an apparent inability to look unflattering facts in the face. And this despite the many episodes where, indeed, Rousseau displays his misdeeds – as we have seen. But is it as a more or less accurate narrative of his outward deeds and inner sentiments that the work is best understood? May we not rather see in it Rousseau's carving out a fresh form for self-understanding and assessing the meaning of a life to take? He shows, by his lengthy discussions of his feelings, the vagaries and inflections of his moods, in the dissection of his motives and so on the absolute centrality of the life of one's inner being to the substance and significance of a human existence, rather than that being consti-tuted by achievements, deeds and successes that make their mark in the world. One point of comparison here could be with Socrates, who disdained issues of status and worldly position in comparison with a life devoted to the pursuit of truth. The truth Rousseau seeks is, he says, 'truth to nature', but the work is as much an attempt to answer the question of what the nature and destiny of a man is as it is an attempt at telling the truth about that. The exaltation of the drama of the formation and unfolding of personality rather than a narrative of achievements was to be, and surely still is, hugely influential in the development of Romantic autobiography, about which I shall say more in the next chapter. Whatever one may finally make of it, The Confessions is one of the most absorbing and fascinating books ever written.

ROUSSEAU JUDGE OF JEAN-JACQUES: DIALOGUES

The text of The Confessions breaks off in late 1765, with Rousseau recounting how he left the island of Saint-Pierre to set off, he thought, for Berlin, but ended up going to Paris and then on to London in the company of David Hume (a sequence of events which he represents as the working out of yet another plot to ensnare him). Over the next five very troubled years, Rousseau worked on The Confessions, as described earlier, and brought to com-pletion his Dictionary of Music, published in 1767, finally settling in Paris in 1770. That year he drafted the Consideration on the Government of

Poland (discussed in Chapter 6, above), and alongside his botanising, music copying and preparation of his *Elementary Letters on Botany* he also began work, around 1772, on his next substantial work of self-explanation and justification, the remarkable *Rousseau Judge of Jean-Jacques: Dialogues*. I have already told the story of his attempt to place the manuscript of this in Notre-Dame but these events bear retelling. By January 1776, Rousseau had completed the work, but in a frenzy of mental distress, overwhelmed by a sense of persecution and rejection, he attempted to place a copy on the high altar, only to find the gates closed. He wandered the streets of Paris in despair, returning home late at night in a state of collapse. His disturbance still in full spate, he wrote a short note, 'To all Frenchmen who still love justice and truth', copies of which he thrust into the hands of passers-by and sent to various friends, still fighting with his inner demons and seeking some kind of relief and vindication. Not long after, the worst of his mania abated, and he began work on *The Reveries of a Solitary Walker*, to which I shall turn in a while.

RJJ is an extraordinary piece of writing, in which Rousseau – or rather a character called 'Rousseau' – appears as a participant in discussion with a Frenchman, a supposedly representative member of the public. One of the manuscripts gives the following table of contents. 'First Dialogue: Of the System of Conduct toward Jean-Jacques adopted by the administration with public approval. Second Dialogue: Of Jean-Jacques' character and habits. Third Dialogue: Of the Spirit of his Books and Conclusions'. Rousseau uses the dialogue form to develop a debate about his (Jean-Jacques) own character, motives, way of life and achievements between his alter ego 'Rousseau', the participant in the dialogues, and the Frenchman. 'Rousseau' begins with a recital of the innumerable calumnies and vilifications that are heaped upon Jean-Jacques. He aims gradually to reveal the truth about Jean-Jacques, a truth that will result from a visit paid to him by 'Rousseau' as described in the Second Dialogue, and from a careful and honest reading of his books as described in the Third Dialogue. This remarkable structural form gives the scope to view Jean-Jacques from three perspectives: as he is seen by others; as he is; and as he is present in his works, the views provided by the audience, the individual and the books.

The work is long and sometime laboured and repetitive, and I propose no close study of it here, but three themes in it stand out. First, and as glimpsed in the passages from C that I cited towards the end of the previous section, Rousseau devotes a good deal of space to considering the plots and deceits that are mounted against him by 'those gentlemen' unspecified who wished to profit from his humiliation and ignominy. The real motive for these plots is, he avers, the innocence and unaffected goodness that Jean-Jacques embodies and displays, which shames and angers those around him who are corrupted by a false sophistication, vanity and avarice which is shown up for what it is in comparison with this paragon. This, then, is the second broad theme: Jean-Jacques is at worst a weak creature, blown hither and thither by his feelings, scarcely a responsible being and certainly not the malign monster he is made out to be. Third, Rousseau insists on the coherence and consistency of Jean-Jacques' intellectual and moral enterprise in his diverse writings, again despite the many accusations that no one person could have produced original work of so many kinds, leading to suggestions of plagiarism.

I will illustrate these themes with some brief excerpts from the work, which will also convey something of its general tone and character. Starting with the last, Rousseau writes, through the voice of the Frenchman, as follows:

> In reading these books, it wasn't long before I felt I had been deceived about their contents, and that what I had been told were fatuous declamations, adorned with fine language but disconnected and full of contradictions, were things that were profoundly thought out, forming a coherent system which might not be true but which

offered nothing contradictory . . . in place of the bad intentions that had been attributed to him, I found only a doctrine that was as healthy as it was simple, which without Epicureanism and cant was directed only to the happiness of the human race.

(RJJ 3: 209, OC I: 930)

And what is this healthy and simple doctrine? It is this:

Following the thread of his meditations as best I could, I saw throughout the development of his great principle that nature made man happy and good, but that society depraves him and makes him miserable. The *Émile*, in particular – that book which is much read, little understood, and ill-appreciated – is nothing but a treatise on the original goodness of man, destined to show how vice and error, foreign to his constitution, enter it from outside and insensibly change him. In his first writings, he tries even more to destroy that magical illusion which gives us a stupid admiration for the instruments of our misfortunes and to correct that deceptive assessment that makes us honour pernicious talents and scorn useful virtues. Throughout he makes us see the human race as better, wiser, and happier in its primitive constitution.

(RJJ 3: 213, OC I: 934–5)

However,

Human nature does not go backward, and it is never possible to return to the times of innocence and equality once they have been left behind. This too is one of the principles on which he has most insisted. So that his object could not be to bring populous peoples or great States back to their first simplicity, but only to stop, if it were possible, the progress of those whose small size and situation have preserved from such a swift advance toward the perfection of society and the deterioration of the species . . . But despite these distinctions, so often and forcefully repeated, the bad faith of men of letters and the foolishness of *amour-propre* which persuades everyone that they are always the focus of attention even when they

aren't even being thought of, made the large nations apply to
themselves what had been intended only for small republics; and
people stubbornly insisted on seeing a promoter of upheavals and
disturbances in the one man in the world who maintains the truest
respect for the laws and national constitutions.

(Ibid.)

The curious mixture of self-aggrandisement, 'the one man in the
world . . .', antagonistic contempt for 'these gentlemen', 'men of
letters . . . always the focus of attention', and sound if somewhat
selective summary and assessment of Jean-Jacques' intellectual
project is thoroughly characteristic of the whole work.

In illustration of the second theme, Jean-Jacques the innocent
creature of feeling whose very simplicity is an unbearable reproach
to those who hate him, the following passage, representative of
many, will serve:

Nothing inspires as much courage as the testimony of an upright
heart, which draws from the purity of its intentions the audacity to
state aloud and without fear the judgments dictated solely by love of
justice and truth. But at the same time, nothing exposes someone
to so many dangers and risks coming from clever enemies as this
same audacity, which thrusts a passionate man into all the traps
they set for him, and surrendering him to an impetuosity without
rules, cause him to make a thousand mistakes contrary to
prudence, into which only a frank and generous soul falls but which
they know how to transform into so many atrocious crimes.
Ordinary men, incapable of lofty and noble feelings, never assume
feelings other than self-interested ones in those who become
impassioned; and unable to believe that love of justice and the
public good could arouse such zeal, they always invent personal
motives for them, similar to those they themselves conceal under
pompous names and without which they would never be seen
getting excited about anything.

(RJJ 2: 176, OC I: 887; these words are given to 'Rousseau')

And as for the plots and malign machinations against Jean-Jacques, here is a brief example from a long litany; the words this time are the Frenchman's:

> Above all . . . what is great, generous, admirable in our Gentlemen's plan . . . in preventing him from following his wishes and accomplishing his evil designs, they still seek to obtain the sweet things of life for him, so that he find what he needs everywhere and what he could misuse nowhere. They want him to be sated with the bread ignominy and the cup of disgrace. They even pretend to pay mocking, scoffing attention to him . . . which make[s] him even more ridiculous in the eyes of the populace. Finally, since he is so fond of distinctions, he has reason to be content: they are careful he does not lack for them, and he gets what he likes when he is pointed out everywhere . . . he is a Bear who must be chained for fear he will devour passersby. The poison of his pen is feared above all, and they spare no precaution to prevent him from emitting it. They leave him no means to defend his honour, because it would be useless to him, because on this pretext he would not fail to attack the honour of someone else . . . You can be sure that among the people who have been secured, the booksellers were not left out, especially those whom he used to frequent. One was even held for a long time at the Bastille on other pretexts, but in fact in order to indoctrinate him at greater leisure on the subject of J.J.
>
> (RJJ 1: 44–5, OC I: 716–7)

And a great deal more to the same effect. There is, quite patently, considerable disturbance of mind finding expression here, and the distress Rousseau was suffering must have been almost unbearable. Despite this being the pervasive tone of the work, there are – as we saw in the summary given by the Frenchman of Jean-Jacques' principal ideas – passages of real lucidity and penetration, including some fine elucidations of aspects of his conception of the nature of *amour-propre*, some of which I have drawn on earlier (see, for instance, RJJ 1: 9–10, 2: 112–3, OC I: 668–9, 805–6). But much else must be borne with to discover these valuable insights and it remains the case that this work of Rousseau's, fascinating though it is in conception, is one of the least read and probably justly so.

THE REVERIES OF THE SOLITARY WALKER

As referred to previously, the worst of Rousseau's mental distress abated in the summer of 1776. That autumn the bizarre accident in which he was knocked down by a Great Dane took place and this, in some inexplicable way, seems to have aided his recovery and the return of his freedom of mind. Rousseau gives a dramatic account of this accident in the Second Walk of the *Reveries* (RSW 2: 38, OC I: 1004–5); the ten sections of RSW are entitled *Promenades* – Walks rather than chapters – to capture the conception that what is recorded in *The Reveries* are miscellaneous memories, reflections, speculations that occupied Rousseau as he perambulated around Paris and its outskirts (see RSW 1: 32, OC I: 1000).

It was in the autumn of 1776 that he began *The Reveries*, his last major autobiographical work, indeed substantive work of any kind, but it remained uncompleted at his death in July 1778. The book begins with echoes of the distress of the preceding years:

> So now I am alone in the world, with no brother, neighbour or friend, nor any company left me but my own. The most sociable and loving of men has with one accord been cast out by all the rest. With all the ingenuity of hate they have sought out the cruellest torture for my sensitive soul, and have violently broken all the threads that bound me to them. I would have loved my fellow-men in spite of themselves. It was only by ceasing to be human that they could forfeit my affection. So now they are strangers and foreigners to me; they no longer exist for me, since such is their will. But I, detached as I am from them and from the whole world, what am I? This must now be the object of my inquiry.
>
> (RSW 1: 27, OC I: 995)

He goes on to speak of his resignation in the face of the world's contempt and rejection, and the peace of mind he has eventually won because he no longer hopes to be understood and esteemed by those around him. However, it is not wholly clear that the substance of the work bears out this claim. On the one hand he writes of preserving his reflections so that 'every time I read them they will recall my original pleasure. Thinking of the prize my heart deserved, I shall forget my misfortunes, my persecutors and my disgrace' (RSW 1: 32, OC I: 999–1000). But, on the other hand, in many of the walks he is still fiercely arguing his case against critics and detractors, so the wholly self-contained and self-addressed character claimed for the work is actually not that clear.

In the Second Walk, we have the story of Rousseau's accident. He gives a striking account of his state of mind on recovering consciousness:

> Night was coming on. I saw the sky, some stars, and a few leaves. The first sensation was a moment of delight. I was conscious of nothing else. In this instant I was being born again, and it seemed as if all I perceived was filled with my frail existence. Entirely taken up by the present, I could remember nothing; I had no distinct notion of myself as a person, nor had I the least idea of what had just happened to me . . . I felt throughout my whole being such a wonderful calm, that whenever I recall this feeling I can find nothing to compare with it in all the pleasures that stir our lives.
>
> (RSW 2: 39, OC I: 1005)

And he goes on to note the indecent haste with which rumours of his having been killed in the accident spread around Paris. The Third Walk concerns Rousseau's views about the purposes of his life and the nature of the maker of all things, saying as noted in Chapter 4: 'The result of my arduous research was more or less what I have written down in my "Profession of Faith of a Savoyard Priest", a work which has been ignobly prostituted and desecrated by the present generation, but which may one day effect a revolution in the minds of men' (RSW 3: 55, OC I: 1018). He goes on to

say: 'All the sharpest torments lose their sting if one can confidently
expect a glorious recompense, and the certainty of this recompense
was the principal fruit of my earlier meditations' (RSW 3: 57, OC I:
1020). And one can see in this that despite Rousseau's claim that he
is now indifferent to his fate in the world, he seeks consolation.
What he has been denied or deprived of as he sees it still shapes his
feelings and attitudes.

The Fourth Walk is an extended meditation on whether he has
been justified in choosing for his personal motto *Vitam impendere vero*
('Dedicate one's life to truth'). He refers once more to the 'terrible
lie' about the theft of the ribbon which we considered earlier in
this chapter, saying in his defence that he had no desire to harm the
girl but was overcome by invincible shame and timidity. Rousseau
seems to be broadly of the view that only deliberate falsehoods told
with the intent to harm count as a desertion of his motto, but he
introduces a number of complex distinctions which it would take us
too far afield to consider in detail. What, I think, is striking is that
whilst admitting that he has not wholly lived up to his 'proud
motto' his primary concern seems to be the self-debasement that
his weak lies has brought upon him. Whilst, no doubt, 'Truth is an
homage that the good man pays to his own dignity' (RSW 4: 80,
OC I: 1038), this to my mind is an odd note on which to end a
series of reflections prompted by the memory of an episode which
almost certainly did untold harm to the servant girl Marion. It
might have been more edifying to concentrate on her predicament
as opposed to his own loss of integrity.

The Fifth Walk treats of Rousseau's brief idyllic stay on the island
of Saint-Pierre in September 1765 after he had fled Môtiers. He
also speaks of this in Book 12 of C; it is worth comparing the
two accounts. It is memorable for Rousseau's evocation of the
extraordinary happiness he felt there however briefly:

> As evening approached, I came down from the heights of the island,
> and I liked then to go and sit on the shingle in some secluded spot

by the edge of the lake; there the noise of the waves and the
movement of the water, taking hold of my senses and driving all
other agitation from my soul, would plunge it into a delicious reverie
in which night often stole upon me unawares. The ebb and flow of
the water, its continuous yet undulating noise, kept lapping against
my ears and my eyes, taking the place of all the inward movements
which my reverie had calmed within me, and it was enough to make
me pleasurably aware of my existence, without troubling myself
with thought.

(RSW 5: 86–7, OC I: 1045)

Seldom has the tranquillising effect that absorption in the movement
of water – which many people experience – been so finely evoked.
But these days of peace and happiness are set in sharp contrast to the
concerns central to the Sixth Walk, in which Rousseau examines the
constraints of moral obligation. He complains that his kindly and
generous impulses are too often regarded by their recipients as 'no
more than an earnest of those that were still to come . . . and that
first freely chosen act of charity was transformed into an indefinite
right to anything else he might subsequently need . . . In this way
my dearest pleasures were transmuted into burdensome obligations' (RSW 6: 95, OC I: 1051–2). Whilst it is possible, and proper,
to see in this Rousseau's own peculiarly intense hatred of any kind
of constraint, he shows more generally in this subtle and penetrating
discussion just how too prominent a place being given to duty and
obligation in the shaping of people's conduct can destroy the very
things it was intended to maintain, the acts of help and support
people can offer one another. The critique of a coercive morality of
requirement and demand which we touched on in the discussion of
Émile is continued here.

The next Walk, the Seventh, treats of Rousseau's passion for
botany and of the particular significance of the pleasure in it when
it is not the result of mercantile or pharmacological interests. As
with his reveries by the lake, so too absorption in plants, trees,

herbs, and flowers stills the anxious and complaining spirit and gives it relief:

> Brought to life by nature and dressed in her wedding dress amidst the running waters and the song of the birds, earth in the harmony of her three kingdoms offers man a living, fascinating and enchanting spectacle, the only one of which his eyes and his heart can never grow weary.
>
> The more sensitive the soul of the observer, the greater the ecstasy aroused in him by this harmony. At such times his senses are possessed by a deep and delightful reverie, and in a state of blissful self-abandonment he loses himself in the immensity of this beautiful order, with which he feels himself at one.
>
> (RSW 7: 108, OC I: 1062)

But however much the little self may be stilled in such moments, Rousseau cannot, it seems, stop congratulating himself for being so different from other men in his capacity for such pleasures. This presence of the world of men in shaping Rousseau's thoughts – even when he says it has become nothing to him, as noted earlier – is even plainer in the Eighth Walk. In this he says: 'I remain upright because I cling to nothing and lean only on myself' (RSW 8: 126, OC I: 1077), and even sees that 'when I used to protest so fiercely against public opinion, I was still its slave without realising it' (ibid.). But yet, or so it seems to me, he is still burning with a desire to be understood and accepted and his stoic resignation is consolatory rather than elected as good in itself. This Walk does, however, contain some of Rousseau's sharpest observations on the character and role of *amour-propre* and usefully supplements the treatment he gives of that in DI and E, as discussed here in earlier chapters.

In the penultimate Walk, the Ninth, Rousseau reflects on his love for children despite having abandoned his own. As ever, he contrasts his own simple, innocent delights with the tainted and corrupt pleasures of the rich, but of course by presenting the matter thus he mars the very thing he seeks to exalt. Rousseau goes on to speak of buying some apples from a girl who has a stall at a fair so she can share them with some boys who otherwise could not have afforded them:

> Then I had one of the sweetest sights which the human heart can enjoy, that of seeing joy and youthful innocence all around me, for the spectators too had a part in the emotion that met their eyes and I, who shared in this joy at so little cost to myself, had the added pleasure of feeling that I was the author of it.
>
> When I compared this entertainment with those I had just left behind [an expensive party of Madame d'Épinay's], I had the satisfaction of feeling the difference which separates healthy tastes and natural pleasures from those that spring from opulence and are hardly more than pleasures of mockery and exclusive tastes founded on disdain.
>
> (RSW 9: 146, OC I: 1093)

Although there is deep truth in what Rousseau remarks on here (as he has, of course, in many other places too), there is a distressing self-conceit in it as well.

The final, uncompleted, Tenth Walk is only a two-and-a-half page fragment in which Rousseau begins to speak of his life with and feeling for Madame de Warens. How his reverie might have proceeded, we cannot tell; he has scarcely begun his account before it breaks off.

Rousseau began RSW by saying that the object of his inquiry was to answer the question: what am I? And the figure that emerges from these pages is very much one that exemplifies the 'great principle' I cited from RJJ earlier on – the figure of a man whom nature made happy and good but who was depraved and made miserable by society. Realising this, Rousseau withdraws from human contact and no longer in any way depends on the good opinion of others, becoming as self-sufficient and self-reliant as he possibly can. Or so he says. I have suggested, however, that his resignation is not as complete and final as he appears to think. In many ways his self-understanding and the direction of his feelings is governed by how, as he sees it, he is different from, and superior to, others (though in ways they would most likely not recognise). There are, despite this recurrent edge of self-aggrandisement, passages of great insight and beauty and this is, to my mind, one of Rousseau's most engaging books.

The three works we have looked at in this chapter comprise an extraordinary achievement, an exercise in self-disclosure and self-explanation without parallel. The Confessions is, in my opinion, the finest of the three, and a work of great interest; but the three together show a fertility of imagination, formal inventiveness, and boldness of design which would be sufficient to mark Rousseau out as a creative genius even had he not written all his other works.

FURTHER READING

Peter France, Rousseau: Confessions. Cambridge: Cambridge University Press, 1987. An accessible, brief introduction to The Confessions, its writing and character.

Ann Hartle, The Modern Self in Rousseau's Confessions: A Reply to St. Augustine. Notre Dame: Notre Dame University Press, 1983. Lays particular emphasis on the exploration of the nature of the self.

Christopher Kelly: Rousseau's Exemplary Life – The 'Confessions' as Political Philosophy. Ithaca, NY: Cornell University Press, 1987. A sensitive interpretation drawing on Rousseau's conceptions of exemplary lives.

James E. Jones: Rousseau's 'Dialogues': An Interpretive Essay. Geneva: Droz, 1991. A full commentary on RJJ.

Charles E. Butterworth, 'Interpretative Essay' in Jean-Jacques Rousseau, The Reveries of the Solitary Walker, tr. Charles E. Butterworth. Indianapolis, IN: Hackett Publishing Company, 1992. A scrupulous and detailed exposition and interpretation of the text.

Michael Davis, The Autobiography of Philosophy – Rousseau's The Reveries of the Solitary Walker. Lanham, MD: Rowman & Littlefield, 1999. An interpretation based in Heidegger's thinking.

Eight

Rousseau's Legacy and Influence

INTRODUCTION

The purpose of this chapter is to say something necessarily brief and highly selective about the influence that Rousseau and his writings have had upon subsequent philosophers, creative writers, upon social and political events and upon changes in sensibility, forms of self-understanding and visions of the good life. I shall be concentrating on his influence in Western Europe in the nearly three hundred years since his birth. That he has been, and remains, a profoundly influential figure is seldom disputed. Quite what form his influence has taken, and whether it has been for good or ill, is not so easily stated.

Early on in this book I quoted the following words of Kingsley Martin:

> Rousseau was a genius whose real influence cannot be traced with
> precision because it pervaded all the thought that followed him . . .
> he released imagination as well as sentimentalism; he increased
> men's desire for justice as well as confusing their minds, and he
> gave the poor hope even though the rich could make use of his
> arguments.
>
> (Martin: 219)

Allan Bloom gives a more explicit statement:

> Rousseau's presence is ubiquitous . . . The schools that succeed
> him are all isms, intellectual forces that inform powerful political or

social movements with more or less singleness of purpose. Rousseau resists such limitation . . . Therefore Rousseau did not produce an ism of his own, but he did provide the authentically modern perspective. His concern for a higher, nonmercenary morality is the foundation of Kant's idealism. His critique of modern economics and his questions about the legitimacy of private property are at the root of socialism, particularly Marxism. His emphasis on man's origins rather than his ends made anthropology a central discipline. And the history of the movement from the state of nature toward civil society came to seem more essential to man than his nature – hence historicism. The wounds inflicted on human nature by this process of socialization became the subject of a new psychology, especially as represented in Freud. The romantic love of the beautiful and the doubt that modern society is compatible with the sublime and pure in spirit gave justification to the cult of art for art's sake and to the life of the bohemian. The longing for rootedness and for community in its modern form is part of Rousseauian sensibility, and so is the love of nature and the hatred for nature's conquerors. All this and much more flows from this inexhaustible font. He possessed an unsurpassed intellectual clarity accompanied by a stirring and seductive rhetoric.

(Bloom, 'Rousseau's Critique of Liberal Constitutionalism': 145–6)

This is a formidable reckoning, and I shall not attempt to touch on all the themes Bloom brings forward. But I shall try to substantiate a little of what he says here by means of what may be thought of as a series of snapshots, in which we see Rousseau's presence in one or another intellectual or social scene. I begin, however, with the matter of Rousseau's place in relation to what are now seen as very large-scale changes in thinking that were taking place in the eighteenth century, his place in relation to the Enlightenment.

ROUSSEAU AND THE ENLIGHTENMENT

In different ways and at slightly different times, many nations and cultures experienced very significant changes in attitudes, in religious and scientific beliefs, in understandings of society, politics, the grounds of authority, etc. during the eighteenth century. These periods of change are usually referred to as the Enlightenment, sometimes qualified as the Scottish Enlightenment, the French Enlightenment and so on. Chadwick has written:

> The Enlightenment, by that name, was not a thing any English speaker knew during the earlier nineteenth century. It is a modern word. When English speakers first began to need a word to describe the climate of opinion in the age of the Encyclopedia, they used the German word *Aufklärung*, evidence enough that the notion had not yet reached the popular histories for schools. For three-quarters of the nineteenth century they did not think of the age as an enlightened age. Most of them thought of it with opprobrium as the age which ended in a nemesis of guillotine and terror.
>
> (Chadwick: 144)

A 'climate of opinion' is a vague and elusive phenomenon, but Rousseau is so commonly held to be a palmary figure of the French Enlightenment that his contribution to creating this climate needs to be considered. The leading figures of the French Enlightenment include Voltaire, Diderot, Condillac, d'Alembert – often referred to as *philosophes* – and Rousseau had dealings with all of them at various times in his life. Speaking in very broad and general terms, these thinkers saw themselves as engaged in clearing away mysteries, obfuscations, the clutter of outmoded ideas and institutions that impeded man's progress, prosperity and happiness. In place of the dead weight of this inheritance was to be put that which was transparent in its rational purpose and functioning, knowledge and institutions that were liberating to man's powers and forward-looking. In particular, the churches' – especially the Catholic Church's – control over learning, law, government and social and personal affairs generally was to be displaced. Universal secular reason, the methods and techniques central to natural science, was to acquire authority in their place; everything was to be investigated, explained, brought before the bar of rational scrutiny and evaluation and asked to prove its credentials. Famously, Kant wrote in his essay 'An Answer to the Question 'What is Enlightenment (*Aufklärung*)?':

> *Enlightenment is man's emergence from his self-incurred immaturity. Immaturity* is the inability to use one's understanding without the guidance of another. This immaturity is *self-incurred* if its cause is not lack of understanding, but lack of resolution and courage to use it without the guidance of another. The motto of Enlightenment is therefore: *Sapere Aude*! Have the courage to use your own understanding.
>
> (Kant: 54)

In general terms, then, the Enlightenment was a period in which dominant thinkers were committed to open, unimpeded inquiry, unchecked by dogma or any authority that could not itself undergo such inquiry. In principle anyone had the liberty to conduct such inquiries; no one was privileged, no one excluded from the onward march of critical investigation. Society's wise and learned men, whose opinions carried weight, ought to attain their position not by special dispensation or by subscription to some specific set of beliefs, but rather through the open and effective use of their talents. There is a strong egalitarian strand in Enlightenment thinking, and many of the ideas aired were very subversive of the established order even if few among the most prominent thinkers were advocates of any radical political action. The Encyclopedia, edited by Diderot and d'Alembert, to which frequent reference has been made in earlier chapters, and to which Chadwick alluded is usually treated as the most representative document of the Enlightenment, and its editors and contributors are among those most central to creating this 'climate of opinion'.

Where does Rousseau stand in relation to this constellation of ideas, attitudes and procedures of inquiry? As we considered in Chapter 3 above, his first mature work – *The Discourse on the Sciences and Arts* – took a very critical stance towards science and letters as contributing anything worthwhile to human well-being and improvement of life. He attacked those who propound clever and ingenious paradoxes that undermine the simple but life-saving beliefs of ordinary people. Yet at the time his essay was seen as itself largely an exercise in paradox and provocation, an exhibition of that free play of critical intelligence and wit that the *philosophes* themselves celebrated, rather than as a serious attack on them and their aspirations. Indeed, it could perhaps well be read as a call to greater and more honest dedication to the pursuit of truth, intended more to expose charlatans and pretenders than to undermine the cause of free inquiry itself.

However, in his later works, Rousseau's distance from some of the central elements of Enlightenment thinking became more pronounced and definite. Whilst, for instance, agreeing that reason is not capable of proving the existence of God, nor of sustaining religious conviction, he did not conclude that men were therefore better off without any religious belief at the centre of their lives; the want of that engendered only disabling scepticism or cynicism. Instead, Rousseau was guided by what 'in the sincerity of [his] heart' he cannot withhold assent from in regard to religious conviction; see the discussion of the *Creed* in Chapter 4 above. He came to feel that human affairs and the social order depended more on virtue and deep-rooted loyalties than on any knowledge of 'rational principles' of government or law. These last, he was wont to say, often do no more than provide excuses for the pursuit of narrow private interests. In these and other ways he became not just estranged from but hostile to the easy confidence that everything could be explained, everything could be governed through a set of explicit principles, and that society was changing in the direction of a better and happier future. He came increasingly to value a sense of mystery, humility and submission as truer to the deeper needs of the human spirit.

Vague and multi-stranded though conflicts between reason and faith, intellect and feeling, may be, Rousseau gave voice to some of those disquiets over the power and scope of science in relation to the nature and life of mankind that become quite extensive during the nineteenth century and occupied the attention of thinkers as diverse as Hegel and Matthew Arnold. What presents itself as 'enlightened' thinking even nowadays can sometimes be a set of ideas that are as restrictive and reductive as those it seeks to displace, and so far from offering a richer grasp of what we need to know and be in order to flourish often seems to diminish that.

So much on the one side. However, on another side Rousseau's contribution to Enlightenment thinking about the basis of political authority, the sources of sovereignty, is second to none. His overriding emphasis on the moral dignity proper to every single individual, his insistence that authority in the state lies in the general will of the people, clearly subverted existing hierarchies and systems of authority, in an irreversible way. But even in this Rousseau was concerned to limit an individualism that freedom from the existing bonds of society might encourage. He emphasises the need to develop and sustain the social spirit so that our fellow citizens' weal and woe are part of our own sense of well being if we are to have any kind of just and humane community. As with so many aspects of Rousseau's thinking, we find, Bloom emphasises, that his ideas do not fit neatly into one specific system or framework. We find him, rather, trying to recognise and respond to many diverse elements in our individual and social lives. Whilst he will no doubt always be thought of as a central figure in the Enlightenment, it can scarcely be said that his work is straightforwardly representative of that.

ROUSSEAU AND THE FRENCH REVOLUTION

Neither Martin nor Bloom refer directly in the passages cited to what is probably the best-known political event which is widely supposed to bear the stamp of Rousseau's influence, the French Revolution, which occurred eleven years after his death. That Rousseau was a very powerful influence on this seems almost too evident to need much discussion. His profound critique of inequalities of power, privilege and wealth; his insistence that sovereignty does not lie in some hereditary principle of kingship but with the general will of the people; his criticism of existing forms of government – all this and more seems so plainly in accord with the objectives of the Revolution that it would be unimaginable without his inspiration. Furthermore, clauses from the National Assembly's 'Declaration of the Rights of Man and of Citizens' look as if they could almost have been written by Rousseau. Clause I reads, in Thomas Paine's translation of 1791:

> Men are born, and always continue, free, and equal in respect of their rights. Civil distinctions, therefore, can be founded only on public utility.

And Clause VI goes thus:

> The law is an expression of the will of the community. All citizens have a right to concur, either personally, or by their representatives, in its formation. It should be the same to all, whether it protects or punishes . . .

Lastly, look at Clause X, with its echoes of Rousseau's discussion of the scope and limits of religious accountability:

> No man ought to be molested on account of his opinions, provided his avowal of them does not disturb the public order established by the law.

To this we may add that Robespierre claimed to have been inspired by Rousseau's writings from a very early age and that Rousseau's body was transferred to the Panthéon in 1794 as part of the reconstruction of a past deemed suitable for a new post-revolutionary France, copies of *The Social Contract* being carried in the procession accompanying his coffin. What more solid proof of the significance of Rousseau's work to the Revolution could be needed?

However, the matter has not been without controversy. Specifically, it has been argued, most notably in recent times by Joan McDonald in her book *Rousseau and the French Revolution* (1965), that *The Social Contract* was little known and read before 1789, basing her claim significantly upon the evidence of the numbers and size of editions of the work over the preceding twenty-five or so years. However, the cogency of her appraisal of the evidence has been decisively challenged by the work of R. A. Leigh in his *Unsolved Problems in the Bibliography of Rousseau* (1990), and in the light of his researches, which cover illicit editions also, a very different picture of the dissemination of Rousseau's work emerges, and one which allows the more ordinary view of this matter to be recovered.

But to hold that Rousseau had a central influence is not as such to determine quite how and why his work did so. And such matters will always be subject to debate and continuous argument. In my own estimation, greater weight should be attached to France's financial problems, the increased taxation demands and the highly opaque system of exemptions that went with this, and perhaps also to the seeming incongruity of France – the French king – giving support to the American side in the War of Independence – in which the rebels sought representation – while not apparently being willing to grant this to his own citizens. Rousseau's words no doubt provided a ready source to draw from to give voice to these discontents, and in that way led to their strengthening and wider dissemination. But I think it unlikely that his work had by itself sufficient potency to provoke discontent broad and deep enough to prompt revolutionary actions, and in any event it is very clear that attention to what he wrote was highly selective. There is something in the end inexplicable, I believe, about why a particular person and/or body of work should acquire this almost sacred power in a time of crisis. Having done so, further things will follow from it, but that is not to say it was anything more than a small part of a whole constellation of diverse causes generating the crisis in the first place. It should, for instance, be recalled that in the first years of the French Revolution there were no real calls for republicanism, and the dethroning and execution of Louis XVI were not the result of any press towards greater doctrinal consistency or completeness in relation to Rousseau's thinking. William Doyle writes: 'It is hard to imagine either Voltaire or Rousseau revelling in the events which, from only eleven years after their deaths, were often so glibly attributed to their influence. Robespierre, as proud a disciple as any of the Enlightenment, declared: "Political writers . . . had in no way foreseen this Revolution" '(Doyle: 74).

ROUSSEAU, KANT, HEGEL AND MARX

Significantly less indeterminate is the question of Rousseau's influence on Kant, the greatest German eighteenth-century philosopher and one of the most important philosophers of all time. I have referred on a number of occasions to Kant's work to illuminate Rousseau's thinking, and I chose one of Kant's famous remarks about Rousseau as an epigraph to this book. In one instance in Chapter 4, I cited Kant's remarks on a 'self-love that compares' in order to help understand Rousseau's conception of *amour-propre*; and in another to his discussion of men's self-interests neutralising each other, to throw light on the relation between the general will and the will of all, above in Chapter 5. It is true that in neither of these instances is explicit reference made to Rousseau's text, but there can be no serious doubt not only that his reflections were influenced by Rousseau's work but also that he was drawing overtly on it. Indeed, a good deal in Kant's political thinking about, for instance, the nature of a republic and the duties of citizens plainly bears the stamp of Rousseau's ideas, and I shall give an instance of this after having treated first of one other matter.

This concerns the impact Rousseau's thinking may have had on Kant's account of the categorical imperative as the supreme principle of morality and its connection with what Kant calls the dignity of human nature. This is a large and intricate set of issues, but even with a brief assessment we can I think note some important revealing connections here. The most famous formulation of the categorical imperative Kant gives is this: 'Act only on that maxim through which you can at the same time will that it should become a universal law' (Paton, *The Moral Law*: 88). From this alone one can draw little that might disclose any impact of Rousseau's ideas. But if (setting aside here all the questions about how these formulations relate to each other) we look at later formulations Kant gives to this supreme principle, then we can see how his thinking appears to contain Rousseauian elements. Thus in the so-called formula of the end in itself, Kant writes: 'Act in such a way that you always treat humanity, whether in your own person or in the person of any other, never simply as a means, but always at the same time as an end' (ibid.: 96). He explains this as imposing a limit on arbitrary treatment of others, and it makes them an object of reverence to each of us. In this we see, worked out in Kant's own theoretical system, the significance of mutual recognition and respect that Rousseau argued was essential to our moral being, our achieving standing with others in moral community, as most fully worked out in the arguments of *Émile*. But the plainest link seen in the 'Formula of the Kingdom of Ends', where by a 'Kingdom' Kant means a union of persons under common laws. And he goes on to say:

> A rational being belongs to the Kingdom of ends as a *member*, when, although he makes its universal laws, he is also himself subject to these laws. He belongs to it as its *head*, when as the maker of laws he is himself subject to the will of no other.
>
> (Paton: 101)

In this, we see a very close match with Rousseau's account of the dual position of members of the body politic in SC 1, 7 where, it will be remembered, he writes:

> Those who are associated in it [the body politic] take collectively the
> name of *people*, and severally are called *citizens*, as sharing in the
> Sovereign authority, and *subjects*, as being under the laws of the
> State.
>
> (SC I: 7, 192–3, OC III: 361–2)

What is at work here is Kant's excogitating as the basic principle of morality what Rousseau presents as the terms of republican citizenship. But Kant was quite clear about this, as is plain from other writings, and his debt to Rousseau is evident. In a striking passage, Kant writes as follows:

> it is possible to reconcile with each other and with reason the
> often misunderstood and apparently contradictory
> pronouncements of the celebrated *J.J. Rousseau*. In his essays *On
> the Influence of the Sciences* [the *Discourse on the Sciences and
> Arts*] and *On the Inequality of Man*, he shows quite correctly that
> there is an inevitable conflict between culture and the nature of
> the human race as a *physical* species each of whose individual
> members is meant to fulfil his destiny completely. But in his
> *Émile*, his *Social Contract*, and other writings, he attempts to solve
> the more difficult problem of what course culture should take in
> order to ensure the proper development, in keeping with their
> destiny, of man's capacities as a *moral* species, so that this
> [moral] destiny will no longer conflict with his character as a
> natural species.
>
> (*Conjectures on the Beginning of Human History*: 227–8)

and this, I suggest, presents very well what is at the core of Rousseau's project, even though he did not articulate it quite in these terms, at least not always.

One other area where we may see the impact of Rousseau's work on Kant concerns the 'moral proofs' of God's existence. This has been well discussed by O'Hagan, and needs only brief mention here (see O'Hagan: 269–70). In Chapter 4, I cited Rousseau's views, taken from the *Creed*, concerning the immateriality of the soul:

> If I had no proof of the immateriality of the soul other than the triumph of the wicked and the oppression of the just in this world, that alone would prevent me from doubting it. So shocking a dissonance in the universal harmony would make me seek to resolve it . . . When the union of body and soul is broken, I conceive that the former can be dissolved while the latter can be preserved.
>
> (E IV: 283, OC IV: 589–90)

This has close similarities to what Kant calls the 'postulates of pure practical reason', that are 'not theoretical dogmas but presuppositions of necessarily practical import . . . [that] justify speculative reason in holding to concepts even the possibility of which it could not otherwise venture to affirm'. And Kant identifies three postulates: immortality, freedom 'affirmatively regarded' and the existence of God, saying that 'The first derives from the practically necessary condition of a duration adequate to the perfect fulfilment of the moral law', which, in of course a different idiom, is extremely close to what Rousseau is saying (all quotations are from the *Critique of Practical Reason*, Book II, Chapter II, Section VI).

This argument concerns immortality of course, rather than the existence of God directly. But, as noted, Kant argues for a like basis for affirming God's existence, the need to have a 'coincidence of happiness with morality' which point is contained also in the passage from Rousseau cited. All three postulates Kant proposes are in place to prevent that 'shocking . . . dissonance in the universal harmony' that Rousseau speaks of.

Finally, no treatment, however slight, of Kant's responses to Rousseau would be complete without reference to the well known story that Kant, who was famous for the absolute regularity of his daily routines, deserted these because he became so completely absorbed in the reading of *Émile* that he was unaware of the passing of time. Unfortunately this agreeable anecdote appears to be untrue; it is likely that the story, if true at all, relates in fact to Kant's friend, the English merchant Joseph Green, who lived in Königsberg and was even more of a stickler for punctuality (see Kuehn: 154 ff and 458, note 153).

When we turn to the work of Hegel and Marx, where we might expect the impact of Rousseau's ideas to be very clear and pronounced – since they had so many like concerns – we find in fact that there is very little reference to or discussion of Rousseau, nor arguments that pretty plainly show the stamp of Rousseau's thinking. There is one well known passage in Hegel's *Philosophy of Right* that is worth attention however, albeit that, as I shall argue, it seems to reveal a quite striking mis or non-understanding of some of Rousseau's central notions. Hegel writes:

> Rousseau put forward the *will* as the principle of the state . . . But Rousseau considered the will only in the determinate form of the *individual* will (as Fichte subsequently also did) and regarded the universal will not as the will's rationality in and for itself, but only as the *common element* arising out of this individual will *as a conscious will*. The union of individuals within the state thus becomes a *contract*, which is accordingly based on their arbitrary will and opinions, and on their express consent given at their own discretion . . . Consequently, when these abstractions were invested with power, they afforded the tremendous spectacle, for the first time we know of in human history, of the overthrow of all existing and given conditions within an actual major state and the revision of its constitution from first principles and purely in terms of thought . . . they turned the attempt into the most terrible and drastic event. – In opposition to the principle of the individual will, we should remember the fundamental concept according to which the objective will is rational in itself, i.e. in its *concept*, whether or not it is recognised by individuals and willed by them at their discretion.
>
> (Hegel: *Elements of the Philosophy of Right*, Para. 258, p.277)

The most 'terrible and drastic event' Hegel is referring to here is the period of the Terror during the French Revolution.

Couched as this is in Hegel's complex conceptual idiom, his point is not instantaneously accessible, but it would appear that he has pretty thoroughly turned Rousseau's thinking on its head. For, through the concept of the general will, Rousseau is – as we have seen – precisely not relying on an individual's arbitrary will and opinions but seeking a rule for these that will address the common good of each and all. At most, Hegel could be speaking of the will of all, but Rousseau attaches virtually no real weight to this notion, and is rather looking for a notion of a union of wills addressed to the need for equal recognition and respect for all as the fundamental governing principle of law and justice. Certainly, Rousseau does not deploy the notions of an 'objective will ... rational in itself', but with the idea of the general will he is seeking for that which directs what each and all have good reason to seek in terms of their moral dignity and material well-being, which may have only a remote connection with what they would expressly consent to at their own discretion. Rousseau's discussions of the conflicts between particular wills and the general will, of forcing people to be free, of the role of a legislator – none of these would make sense if what Hegel said about him were correct. Quite how or why Hegel arrived at this (mis-) construction of Rousseau's ideas – which on this point are scarcely hard to notice even if hard to interpret exactly – is difficult to make out.

With regard to Marx, the case is in some ways even stranger, since there seems so much in common in their concerns with the overcoming of alienation, with relations of domination and servitude (enslavement), with the deformations produced in men and society by monopolistic appropriation of resources and much more. Engels said of the *Discourse on Inequality* that it 'includes a sequence of ideas which, in its dialectical detail, corresponds exactly ... with Marx's own masterpiece, *Capital*' (see Wokler, 'Rousseau and Marx': 220). But, as Wokler goes on to observe, if there was a great indebtedness on Marx's part to Rousseau it was not something of which he showed any awareness. This has not stopped – nor should it – commentators from tracing connections, but these tend more commonly to be in the form of trying to find proto-Marxian arguments and strategies in Rousseau rather than finding Marxian reliances on Rousseau. I myself suggested, when treating of the Discourse on Inequality, that Rousseau did not in fact give explanatory priority to the forces of production nor to economic factors generally but to the needs of amour-propre, in accounting for the emergence of social inequalities and the exploitation of the poor by the rich. But, for all that, there are striking points of comparison and contrast in their works, and study of these can be highly productive and interesting.

Before leaving this very selective account of Rousseau's impact or lack of it on some of the greatest German philosophers, it is pleasant to note these remarks of Arthur Schopenhauer, Hegel's arch-enemy, writing in his On the Basis of Morality:

> The foundation I have given to ethics certainly leaves me without a predecessor among the school philosophers . . . For many of them, the Stoics, for instance . . . positively reject and condemn compassion. On the other hand, my foundation is supported by the authority of J.-J. Rousseau, who was undoubtedly the greatest moralist of modern times. He is the profound judge of the human heart, who drew his wisdom not from books but from life, and intended his doctrine not for the professorial chair but for humanity. He is the enemy of all prejudice, the pupil of nature; he alone was endowed by nature with the gift of being able to moralise without being tedious, for he hit upon the truth and touched the heart.
>
> (Schopenhauer: 183)

ROUSSEAU AND ROMANTICISM

When considering above Rousseau's position in relation to the Enlightenment, I noted what an indeterminate notion 'the

Enlightenment' is. The same is certainly true of the notion of 'Romanticism' about which it has been observed that it has come to mean so many things that by itself it means nothing. However, just as Rousseau's name is inextricably linked with the Enlightenment, so it is also with the genesis of Romanticism, whatever quite that might be, so that it is necessary to consider what may be in view here. The subject is so vast, however, that, as indeed in the preceding sections, I shall do no more than pick up a few, but I hope telling, points.

S.S.B. Taylor has written as follows:

A working definition of French nineteenth-century romanticism would probably contain the following elements. It would see it as a reaction against the notion of a taste regulated by decorum or *bienséance* and as legitimising experience that had previously been seen as unseemly, taboo or of purely private interest. It abandoned the supposition that the ethos of art was by definition that of society and it legitimised the highly personal or individual as artistic material. In the process the stress previously laid on rational, lucid and representative statements in art was discarded and the irrational, the incoherent and even the deviant became acceptable, fertile sources of artistic experience. The artist turned his attention very markedly to the lower layers of consciousness and even to unconscious behaviour. He developed certain characteristic themes (nature, beauty, childhood, revolt, love, melancholia, *le mal du siècle*, nationhood, art for art's sake, the medieval, Homer, Shakespeare, etc.) but far more important than the theme was the role played by the imagination in transfiguring the object perceived and in stimulating a new level of artistic sensitivity and creative activity. In the process Art was transformed in its whole purpose from a social diversion into spiritual quest, and indeed into the highest vocation of man.

(Taylor: 4)

That such a conception of Romanticism is appropriate to central elements in Rousseau's achievement is quite evident. Specifically, The Confessions, particularly Part I of that, emerges, as the palmary document of the Romantic imagination. McFarland, in his book Romanticism and the Heritage of Rousseau (1995) writes that 'the Confessions manage[d] to shift the path of literature permanently into the mode of self-revelation . . .' (52). 'Rousseau's own true confessions not only turned literary attention from objectivity to the self', he goes on 'but recast the nature of that self'; instead of the heroic, Rousseau offers a self 'not merely ordinary and bumbling; it was discreditable as well' (55–6). Both the transformative power of imaginative subjectivity, but also one's self and the salient character of that self, are identified as central to Rousseau's creative original-ity. McFarland cites this striking comment of Hazlitt's comparing Rousseau and Wordsworth:

> Both create an interest out of nothing, or rather out of their own feelings; both weave numberless recollections into one sentiment; both wind their own being round whatever object occurs to them . . . Rousseau . . . interests you in certain objects by interesting you in himself: Mr. Wordsworth would persuade you that the most insignificant objects are interesting in themselves, because he is interested in them.
>
> (McFarland: 66)

In the light of this account of the character of the romantic imagin-ation, and the identification of The Confessions as the work which realises most vividly the power of the individual imagination and the centrality of the subject's own experience (compare C 10: 478–9, OC I: 516–7), it is almost impossible not to see a huge part of nineteenth- and twentieth-century poetry and literature – and, indeed, visual art – as fundamentally shaped by Rousseau's creative innovations, even where the writers themselves show no awareness of this. In McFarland's study to which I have been refer-ring, he goes on to consider Wordsworth, Coleridge and Shelley, among others, in their relations with Rousseau; the last was a particularly passionate admirer: 'Rousseau is indeed in my mind the greatest man the world has produced since Milton'. And we could also add Byron to this list of English writers hugely impressed and influenced by Rousseau. In France, Flaubert and Stendhal very clearly manifest the force of Rousseau's achievements; and in Germany, Goethe, Schiller, Hölderlin and many others were led by his example in diverse ways.

To explore any of these patterns of influence in depth would require extensive and detailed study quite beyond what may be pursued here. All I hope to have done is to note some well known connections in order to indicate the presiding place that Rousseau has in relation to the many facets of romanticism.

ROUSSEAU'S CONTEMPORARY PRESENCE: SOME EXAMPLES

In this concluding section, I shall pick out, more or less at random, some instances of contemporary work in which Rousseau's work has played a part, sometimes large, sometimes small. There is of course a huge Rousseau 'industry', as it is often disparagingly called, devoted to analysing and interpreting his ideas of which this book is an example, but that is not my concern here. Rather, I am interested in instances where a contemporary theoretician or creative writer had made explicit use of Rousseau's work in the development and explanation of his own ideas. It is neither scholarly interpretation, nor the uncertainties of 'influence', but the direct impact of Rousseau's ideas in current work that I want to touch on.

I begin with the work of John Rawls, probably the most significant political philosopher of the past thirty years. In his *A Theory of Justice* (1972), Rawls is guided by the idea 'that the principles of justice for the basic structure of society are the object of the original agreement. They are the principles that free and rational persons concerned to further their own interests would accept in an initial position of equality as defining the fundamental terms of their association' (Rawls: 11). What is this 'initial position' in which such persons are to accept these principles? Rawls goes on:

Among the essential features of this situation is that no one knows
his place in society, his class position or social status, nor does
anyone know his fortune in the distribution of natural assets and
abilities, his intelligence, strength and the like. I shall even assume
that the parties do not know their conceptions of the good or their
special psychological propensities. The principles of justice are
chosen behind a veil of ignorance. This ensures that no one is
advantaged or disadvantaged in the choice of principles by the
outcome of natural chance or the contingency of social
circumstances. Since all are similarly situated and no one is able to
design principles to favor his particular condition, the principles of
justice are the result of a fair agreement or bargain.

(Ibid.: 12)

The development and elaboration of these guiding ideas is a task that
occupies Rawls for a further six hundred pages. But we can clearly see
in these fundamental ideas and strategies the imprint of Rousseau.
Thus, when Rawls speaks of no one being 'able to design principles
to favor his particular condition' the likeness to what Rousseau says
in discussing the 'clauses' of the social contract, in Book I Chapter 6
of SC, is very striking. Rousseau, it will be recalled, says:

These clauses, properly understood, may be reduced to one – the
total alienation of each associate, together with all his rights, to the
whole community; for, in the first place, as each gives himself
absolutely, the conditions are the same for all; and, this being so, no
one has any interest in making them burdensome to others.

(SC I: 6, 191, OC III: 360–1)

Indeed, the 'veil of ignorance' procures much the same circum-
stance that 'total alienation' does in Rousseau's argument overall.

But, and this is the key point here, I am not here just picking up
on likenesses or hearing echoes. Rawls says explicitly that:

Since the original position can be given a Kantian interpretation,
this conception of justice does indeed have affinities with idealism.

> Kant sought to give a philosophical foundation to Rousseau's idea of
> the general will. The theory of justice in turn tries to present a
> natural procedural reading of Kant's conception of the kingdom of
> ends, and of the notions of autonomy and the categorical
> imperative.
>
> (Rawls: 264)

So the connection is made overtly, and indeed in a way that accords
with the account given of Kant's relation to Rousseau sketched
above in this Chapter. Elsewhere in his book, too, Rawls draws quite
extensively on the psychological and moral educational ideas of
Émile (see e.g. Rawls: 459, 463).

We may note two further uses of Rousseau's work in the related
fields of sociological interpretation and of cultural analysis. In
Richard Sennett's recent work *Respect* (2003), with its strikingly
Rousseauian subtitle: 'The Formation of Character in a World of
Inequality', he draws on the *Discourse on Inequality* at a number of
points. Specifically, in speaking of the 'seductions of inequality',
Sennett diagnoses the dynamics of envy in the drive to win the
esteem of others, using Rousseau's material directly. After citing
the passage in DI concerning people assembled to sing and dance
before each other discussed in Chapter 3 here, Sennett comments:

> There seems nothing exceptional in this passage until we compare
> it to Nietzsche's in *Beyond Good and Evil*: 'We have to force morals to
> bow down before hierarchy'. Nietzsche's counsel is just to be strong,
> to take pride in yourself. For Rousseau, the superior is not
> indifferent to the weak: their envy confirms he has something of
> value. How can he elicit it?
>
> (Sennett: 90–1)

And he rightly points out that 'the weak' are complicit in the processes that result in their inferiority; everyone is apt to wish to hold
a superior position themselves, and thus willingly sustains the pattern of relations and interactions that generates this differentiation

of persons, and which we discussed at length in Chapter 3. Sennett goes on: 'His [Rousseau's] essay concludes on a note of pessimism, however, just because he feared the dynamics of seduction to be more powerful than those of self-respect. Other people have been taken too seriously, oneself not enough' (ibid.: 93). I do not necessarily accept the account of Rousseau given by Sennett, but that is not here to the point.

We find a related use of Rousseau's material being made by Francis Fukuyama in his best-selling *The End of History and the Last Man* (1992). He wrote:

Rousseau in the *Second Discourse* points out that true human needs are actually very few in number . . . All other human wants are not essential to happiness, but arise out of man's ability to compare himself to his neighbours and feel himself deprived if he does not have what they have. The wants created by modern consumerism arise, in other words, from man's vanity, or what Rousseau calls his *amour-propre*. The problem is that these new wants, created by man himself in historical time, are infinitely elastic and incapable of being fundamentally satisfied.

(Fukuyama: 83)

The insatiable appetites that are necessary to 'modern consumerism' are, indeed, given a profound diagnosis by Rousseau, as is here noted. Fukuyama goes on to give a very central place to the 'desire for recognition' which he rightly also connects with Rousseau's theory of *amour-propre* though not quite along the lines argued for in this book, as well as with the more well-known theories of Hegel on this.

Moving beyond the use made of Rousseau's theoretical works, I shall end by referring to the presence of *The Confessions* in the work of two contemporary novelists. One of the most intriguing, witty and entertaining books of recent years to make use of Rousseau's writings is Andrew Crumey's *Mr Mee* (2000). The novel takes its rise, in part, from two figures who make a brief and enigmatic appearance in Book 10 of Rousseau's *Confessions*, M. Ferrand and M. Minard (see C10: 467–9, OC I: 504–6); but also C11: 526–7, OC I: 570–1). Rousseau came to know these men at Mont-Louis, where they too had lodgings, and he played chess with them. In time he came to suspect that the 'old women', as Thérèse called them, were interfering with his papers, and he broke off further contact. Crumey brings this episode vividly to life with high humour; and running in parallel with this we have the story of the elderly Mr Mee's discovery of the power of the internet, his search there for a non-existent encyclopedia, his uncovering of internet pornography and subsequent sexual adventures. And this in turn interlocks with a university teacher's failed attempts to seduce one of his students. The novel is intricate and many-layered, but very amusing and shows how, in highly idiosyncratic ways, Rousseau's work is still capable of spurring creative imagination.

Another novel which draws its inspiration also from *The Confessions* is William Boyd's *The New Confessions* (1987). This concerns the life of John James Todd, the son of an Edinburgh surgeon, born just before the end of the nineteenth century. The hero is captured during the First World War, where a sympathetic guard brings him pages torn from a copy of *The Confessions* day by day, and John James is completely entranced by this. After the war, he makes a highly successful film of *Julie*, and also Part I of the *Confessions* but only after great difficulties. His planned further films based on the *Confessions* are never completed and in ways that partially parallel Rousseau's own life, he behaves absurdly in love, suffers persecution and ostracism and succumbs to periods of acute paranoia.

Here is what Boyd says about John James's first reading of The *Confessions*:

I was seized and captivated by this extraordinary autobiography – so intensely I could have been reading about myself. Read it, buy it, and you will see what I mean. I knew nothing of Rousseau, nothing of his life, his work, his ideas, and precious little about eighteenth century

Europe, but the voice was so fresh, the candour so moving and unusual, it made no difference. Here was the story of the first truly honest man. The first modern man. Here was the life of the individual spirit recounted in all its nobility and squalor for the first time in the history of the human race. When I set the dogeared stack of pages down at the end of my seven-week, fervid read I wept. Then I started reading it again. This man spoke for all of us suffering mortals, our vanities, our hopes, our moments of greatness and our base corrupted natures.

(Boyd: 197)

It seems suitable to end on this note.

FURTHER READING

Norman Hampson, The Enlightenment. Harmondsworth: Penguin, 1968. An impressive and accessible historical overview.

Mark Hulliung, The Autocritique of Enlightenment: Rousseau and the Philosophers. Cambridge, MA: Harvard University Press, 1994. A subtle treatment of the tensions between Rousseau and the leading philosophes and their ideas.

Joan McDonald, Rousseau and the French Revolution 1762–1791. London: Athlone Press, 1965. Argues that Rousseau's influence has been exaggerated.

Carol Blum, Rousseau and the Republic of Virtue: The Language of Politics in the French Revolution. Ithaca: Cornell University Press, 1986. A wide-ranging treatment, quite critical of Rousseau at certain points.

Ernst Cassirer, Rousseau, Kant and Goethe. Princeton: Princeton University Press, 1945, 1970. A classic essay on Kant's relations to Rousseau.

Thomas McFarland, Romanticism and The Heritage of Rousseau. Oxford: Clarendon Press, 1995. A very learned and subtle treatment of Rousseau's work and influence.

Irving Babbitt, Rousseau and Romanticism. New Brunswick: Transaction Publishers 1919, 1991. A classic essay, very critical of Rousseau's influence undermining classical and Christian world views.

Rousseau does not make use of a large range of technical terms, and for this reason this glossary is brief and intended only for quick reference. The notions signified by the terms listed are all discussed at length in the main text.

amour de soi (love of self)   A natural desire for one's own well being, possessed by all animate creatures. In man it may have both an instinctive and a reflective form.

amour-propre (self love)   A desire to enjoy consideration from, the favour and good regards of, others as one's due. Often takes on a competitive character. The interpretation of this is controversial as is the translation of the word, which is often left untranslated.

citizen   A fully participating member of the sovereign body (q.v.) of the state, in Rousseau's account of that.

corporate will   The desire of a subgroup within the state for their sectional or factional advantage.

general will   The will of the whole body of the citizens in declaring law to themselves for their common good. A controversial notion.

government   A body with functions delegated by the sovereign (q.v.) concerned with the application of law to individuals and the maintenance of law.

legislator   A quasi-divine 'superior intelligence' guiding the people to devise appropriate laws for themselves.

liberty (natural) The scope to do what one wants, as and when one wants, without reference to or control by anyone else.

liberty (civil) Natural liberty circumscribed by law, by the direction of the general will.

liberty (moral) The scope to do what is in accord with one's rights and responsibilities as a moral being interacting with other moral beings. A controversial notion.

nature, natural Terms of multiple signification, covering for instance, what is untouched by artifice, but also what conduces to the realisation of a creature's (man's) proper potential.

perfectibility The human capability to learn from experience and to adapt behaviour in the light of this the better to secure one's own good.

prince An alternative name Rousseau gives to the government (as a body).

sovereign(ty) The source of ultimate authority in the state, and of the laws. The sovereign body for Rousseau comprises all adult members of the state. As participating in sovereign functions they are called citizens (q.v.).

Bibliography

PRIMARY TEXTS IN FRENCH

J.-J. Rousseau, *Oeuvres Complètes*, Volume I, eds. B. Gagnebin and M. Raymond (Paris: Éditions Gallimard, 1959). Contains: *The Confessions; Rousseau Judge of Jean-Jacques: Dialogues; The Reveries of the Solitary Walker.*

J.-J. Rousseau, *Oeuvres Complètes*, Volume II, eds. B. Gagnebin and M. Raymond (Paris: Éditions Gallimard, 1964). Contains: *Julie, or La Nouvelle Héloïse; Narcissus.*

J.-J. Rousseau, *Oeuvres Complètes*, Volume III, eds. B. Gagnebin and M. Raymond (Paris: Éditions Gallimard, 1964). Contains: *Discourse on the Sciences and Arts; Discourse on the Origin of Inequality; Discourse on Political Economy; The Social Contract; Project for a Constitution for Corsica; Considerations on the Government of Poland; Letters from the Mountain.*

J.-J. Rousseau, *Oeuvres Complètes*, Volume IV, eds. B. Gagnebin and M. Raymond (Paris: Éditions Gallimard, 1969). Contains: *Émile; Émile and Sophie; Letter to Christophe de Beaumont; Writings on Botany.*

J.-J. Rousseau, *Oeuvres Complètes*, Volume V, eds. B. Gagnebin and M. Raymond (Paris: Éditions Gallimard, 1995). Contains: *Letter to d'Alembert on the Theatre; Dictionary of Music; Letter on French Music; Essay on the Origin of Languages; Project for a New Musical Notation.*

J.-J. Rousseau, *Correspondance Complète de Jean-Jacques Rousseau*, ed. R.A. Leigh, 52 volumes (Geneva: Institut et Musée Voltaire, and Banbury, UK: The Voltaire Foundation, 1965–98).

ENGLISH TRANSLATIONS

The list below includes those used in the text and other helpful sources, taking Rousseau's works in date order.

Discourse on the Sciences and Arts, in Jean-Jacques Rousseau: *The Social Contract and Discourses*, tr. and introduced by G.D.H. Cole, revised and augmented by J.H. Brumfitt and

J.C. Hall, updated by P.D. Jimack (London: Dent Everyman, 1993). Abbreviated as Cole *et al*.

Discourse on the Origin of Inequality, in Cole *et al*. There is also a translation by Maurice Cranston: *A Discourse on Inequality* (Harmondsworth: Penguin, 1964).

Essay on the Origin of Languages, tr. J.H. Moran and A. Gode in *On the Origin of Language* (Chicago: University of Chicago Press, 1966). Also in *The Discourses and Other Early Political Writings*, tr. and ed. Victor Gourevitch (Cambridge: Cambridge University Press, 1997).

Discourse on Political Economy, in Cole *et al*.

Letter to M. d'Alembert on the Theatre, in *Politics and the Arts*, tr. and introduced by Allan Bloom (Ithaca, NY: Cornell University Press, 1960).

Julie, or the New Heloise, tr. and annotated by P. Stewart and J. Vaché. *Collected Writings of Rousseau*, Vol. 6, series editors R.D. Masters and C. Kelly. (Dartmouth College: Hanover NH and London, University Press of New England, 1997). There is also an abridged text, tr. Judith H. McDowell (University Park, PA: Pennsylvania State University Press, 1968).

Letters to Malesherbes, in *Citizen of Geneva* – Selections from the Letters of Jean-Jacques Rousseau, tr. C.W. Hendel (New York: Oxford University Press, 1937).

Emile, or On Education, tr. and introduced by Allan Bloom (New York: Basic Books, 1979; London: Penguin, 1991).

The Social Contract, in Cole *et al*. There is also a translation by Maurice Cranston: *The Social Contract* (Harmondsworth: Penguin, 1968).

Letter to Christophe de Beaumont, selections in *The Indispensable Rousseau* compiled by J.H. Mason (London: Quartet, 1979).

Project for a Constitution for Corsica, in *Rousseau: Political Writings*, tr. and ed. F. Watkins (Edinburgh: Nelson, 1953).

The Confessions, tr. and introduced by J.M. Cohen (Harmondsworth: Penguin, 1953).

Considerations on the Government of Poland, in *Rousseau: The Social Contract and Other Later Political Writings*, tr. Victor Gourevitch (Cambridge: Cambridge University Press, 1997).

Rousseau Judge of Jean-Jacques: Dialogues, tr. J.R. Bush, C. Kelly and R.D. Masters, *Collected Writings of Rousseau*, Vol. 1, series editors R.D. Masters and C. Kelly (Dartmouth College, Hanover NH and London: University Press of New England, 1990).

Reveries of the Solitary Walker, tr. and introduced by Peter France (Harmondsworth: Penguin, 1979). There is also a translation, with interpretative essay, by Charles Butterworth (Indianapolis, IN: Hackett, 1992).

Botanical Letters etc., in *Botany, A Study of Pure Curiosity*, tr. K. Ottevanger (London: Michael Joseph, 1979).

Additionally, the following translations and editions merit mention:

The Indispensable Rousseau compiled by J.H. Mason (London, Quartet, 1979). A very helpful selection drawn from whole range of Rousseau's works.

The Discourses and Other Early Political Writings, tr. and ed. Victor Gourevitch (Cambridge: Cambridge University Press, 1997). Contains the first two *Discourses* together with replies to critics; Preface to *Narcissus*; *Letter to Voltaire on Providence*; *Essay on the Origin of Languages*.

The Social Contract and Other Later Political Writings, tr. and ed. Victor Gourevitch (Cambridge: Cambridge University Press, 1997). Contains: *Discourse on Political Economy; The Social Contract; Considerations on the Government of Poland*.

Collected Writings of Rousseau, eds. R.D. Masters and C. Kelly (Dartmouth College, Hanover NH and London: University Press of New England). Starting with a translation of *Rousseau Judge of Jean-Jacques: Dialogues* in 1990, this continuing edition will comprise the most comprehensive and authoritative translation of Rousseau's works into English.

GENERAL BIBLIOGRAPHY

This includes the items cited as further reading; other works referred to in the text; collections of essays on Rousseau; some important and useful books on Rousseau not otherwise referred to; a selection of important books in French on Rousseau. This is a necessarily only small selection from a huge body of secondary literature on or related to Rousseau's life and works.

Babbitt, Irving, *Rousseau and Romanticism*. New Brunswick, NJ: Transaction Publishers, 1991 (1919).

Baczko, Bronislaw, *Rousseau, Solitude et Communauté*, tr. from the Polish by C. Brendhel-Lamhout. Paris: Mouton, 1974 (1970).

Barnard, F.M., *Self-Direction and Political Legitimacy: Rousseau and Herder*. Oxford: Clarendon Press, 1988.

Bertram, Christopher, *Rousseau and the Social Contract*. London: Routledge, 2004.

Bloom, Allan, 'Introduction' to *Émile*, tr. Allan Bloom. New York: Basic Books, 1979; London: Penguin 1991.

—— 'Introduction' to *Politics and the Arts*, Rousseau's Letter to d'Alembert on the Theatre, tr. Allan Bloom. Ithaca, NY: Cornell University Press, 1960.

—— 'Jean-Jacques Rousseau' in *History of Political Philosophy*, eds. L. Strauss and J. Cropsey. Chicago: University of Chicago Press, 1987 (third edition).

—— 'Rousseau's Critique of Liberal Constitutionalism', in *The Legacy of Rousseau*, eds. C. Orwin and N. Tarcov. Chicago: University of Chicago Press, 1997.

Blum, Carol, *Rousseau and the Republic of Virtue: The Language of Politics in the French Revolution*. Ithaca, NY: Cornell University Press, 1986.

Boyd, William, *The New Confessions*. London: Penguin, 1988.

Broome, J.H., *Rousseau: A Study of His Thought*. London: Arnold, 1963.

Burgelin, Pierre, *La Philosophie de l'existence de J.-J. Rousseau*. Paris: Presses Universitaires de France, 1977.

Butterworth, Charles E., 'Interpretative Essay' in *The Reveries of the Solitary Walker*, tr. C.E. Butterworth. Indianapolis, IN: Hackett, 1992.

Cameron, David, *The Social Thought of Rousseau and Burke*. London: Weidenfeld, 1973.

Canovan, M., 'Rousseau's Two Concepts of Citizenship' in *Women in Western Political Thought*, eds. E. Kennedy and S. Mendus. Brighton: Wheatsheaf, 1987.

Cassier, Ernst, *Rousseau, Kant and Goethe*, tr. J. Gutmann, O. Kristeller, J.H. Randall. Princeton: Princeton University Press, 1970 (1945).

—— *The Question of Jean-Jacques Rousseau*, tr. P. Gay. New Haven, CT: Yale University Press (second edition) 1989 (1954).

Cell, Howard and MacAdam James, *Rousseau's Response to Hobbes*. New York: Peter Lang, 1988.

Chadwick, Owen, *The Secularization of the European Mind in the Nineteenth Century*. Cambridge: Cambridge University Press, 1975.

Chapman, John W., *Rousseau: Totalitarian or Liberal?* New York: AMS Press, 1956.

Charvet, John, *The Social Problem in the Philosophy of Rousseau*. Cambridge: Cambridge University Press, 1974.

Cobban, Alfred, *Rousseau and the Modern State*. London: George Allen & Unwin, 1964.

Cohler, Anne, *Rousseau and Nationalism*. New York: Basic Books, 1970.

Colletti, Lucio, *From Rousseau to Lenin*, tr. J. Merrington and J. White. London: New Left Books, 1972.

Cooper, Laurence D., *Rousseau, Nature, and the Problem of the Good Life*. University Park, PA: Pennsylvania State University Press, 1999.

Cranston, Maurice, *Jean-Jacques: The Early Life and Work of Jean-Jacques Rousseau, 1712–1754*. London: Allen Lane, 1983.

—— *The Noble Savage: Jean-Jacques Rousseau, 1754–1762*. London: Allen Lane, 1991.

—— *The Solitary Self: Jean-Jacques Rousseau in Exile and Adversity*. London: Allen Lane, 1997.

—— 'Introduction' to Jean-Jacques Rousseau, *A Discourse on Inequality*. Harmondsworth: Penguin, 1984.

Cranston, Maurice and Peters, Richards S., *Hobbes and Rousseau: A Collection of Critical Essays*. New York: Anchor, 1972.

Crocker, Lester, *Jean-Jacques Rousseau: The Quest (1712–58)*, New York: Macmillan, 1968.

—— *Jean-Jacques Rousseau: The Prophetic Voice (1758–78)*. New York: Macmillan, 1973.

Crumey, Andrew, *Mr Mee*. London: Picador, 2000.

Darnton, Robert, *The Great Cat Massacre*. London: Penguin, 1985.

Davis, Michael, *The Autobiography of Philosophy: Rousseau's The Reveries of the Solitary Walker*. Lanham, MD: Rowman & Littlefield, 1999.

de Man, Paul, *Blindness and Insight*, second edn. London: Methuen, 1983.

della Volpe, Galvano, *Rousseau and Marx*, tr. J. Fraser. London: Lawrence & Wishart, 1978.

Dent, N.J.H., *Rousseau*. Oxford: Basil Blackwell, 1988.

—— *A Rousseau Dictionary*. Oxford: Blackwell Publishers, 1992.

Derathé, Robert, *Le Rationalisme de J.-J. Rousseau*. Paris: Presses Universitaires de France, 1948.

—— *Jean-Jacques Rousseau et la Science Politique de son temps*. Paris: Vrin, 1988 (1950).

Doyle, William, *The French Revolution* – A Very Short Introduction. Oxford: Oxford University Press, 2001.

France, Peter, *Rousseau: Confessions*. Cambridge: Cambridge University Press, 1987.

Fukuyama, Francis, *The End of History and the Last Man*. London: Penguin, 1992.

Garrard, Graeme, *Rousseau's Counter-Enlightenment*. Albany, NY: State University of New York Press, 2003.

Gay, Peter, 'Reading about Rousseau' in Peter Gay, *The Party of Humanity*. London: Weidenfeld, 1964.

Gildin, Hilail, *Rousseau's Social Contract: The Design of the Argument*, Chicago: University of Chicago Press, 1983.

Goldschmidt, Victor, *Anthropologie et politique: les principes du système de Rousseau*. Paris: Vrin, 1983.

Gray, John, *Enlightenment's Wake*. London: Routledge, 1995.

Grimsley, Ronald, *Rousseau and the Religious Quest*. Oxford: Clarendon Press, 1968.

—— *Jean-Jacques Rousseau: A Study in Self-Awareness*, Cardiff: University of Wales Press, 1961.

—— *The Philosophy of Rousseau*. Oxford: Oxford University Press, 1973.

Guéhenno, Jean, *Jean-Jacques Rousseau*, tr. J. and D. Weightman, 2 vols. London: Routledge, 1966.

Hall, J.C., *Rousseau: An Introduction to his Political Philosophy*, London: Macmillan, 1973.

Hampson, Norman, *The Enlightenment*. Harmondsworth: Penguin, 1968.

Hartle, Ann, *The Modern Self in Rousseau's Confessions: A Reply to St. Augustine*. Notre Dame: University of Notre Dame Press, 1983.

Harvey, S., Hobson, M., Kelley, D.J., Taylor, S.S.B, *Reappraisals of Rousseau*. Manchester: Manchester University Press, 1980.

Hegel, G.W.F., *Elements of the Philosophy of Right*, ed. A.W. Wood, tr. H.B. Nesbit. Cambridge: Cambridge University Press, 1991 (1821).

Hendel, C.W., *Citizen of Geneva*: Selections from the Letters of Jean-Jacques Rousseau, New York: Oxford University Press, 1937.

—— *Jean-Jacques Rousseau: Moralist*, 2 vols. Indianapolis, IN: Bobbs-Merrill, 1934.

Horowitz, Asher, *Rousseau, Nature, and History*. Toronto: University of Toronto Press, 1987.

Hulliung, Mark, *The Autocritique of Enlightenment: Rousseau and the Philosophes*. Cambridge, MA: Harvard University Press, 1994.

Hume, David, 'Account of the controversy between Hume and Rousseau' (*The Concise Account*) in *Philosophical Works*, David Hume, Vol. 1. Edinburgh: William Tate, 1826 (1766).

Huizinga, J.H., *The Making of a Saint*. London: Hamish Hamilton, 1976.

Jones, Colin, *The Great Nation*. London: Allen Lane, Penguin Press, 2002.

Jones, J.E., *Rousseau's 'Dialogues': An Interpretive Essay*. Geneva: Droz, 1991.

Kant, I., *Religion Within the Limits of Reason Alone*, tr. T.M. Greene and H.H. Hudson. New York: Harper & Row, 1960 (1794).

—— *Perpetual Peace*, in *Kant: Political Writings*, ed. H. Reiss, tr. H.B. Nisbet. Cambridge: Cambridge University Press, 1991 (1796).

—— 'An Answer to the Question "What is Enlightenment?" ' in *Kant: Political Writings*, ed. H. Reiss, tr. H.B. Nisbet. Cambridge: Cambridge University Press, 1991 (1784).

—— *Groundwork of the Metaphysic of Morals*, tr. H.J. Paton under the title: *The Moral Law*. London: Hutchinson, 1961 (1785).

—— 'Conjectures on the Beginning of Human History' in *Kant: Political Writings*, (1786).

—— *Critique of Practical Reason*, tr. L.W. Beck. New York: Library of Liberal Arts, 1993 (1788).

Kelly, Christopher, *Rousseau's Exemplary Life – The 'Confessions' as Political Philosophy*. Ithaca, NY: Cornell University Press, 1987.

Kuehn, Manfred, *Kant – A Biography*. Cambridge: Cambridge University Press, 2001.

Launay, M., *Jean-Jacques Rousseau: Écrivain Politique*. (1712–1762), second edn, Geneva: Slatkine, 1989.

Leigh, R.A. (ed.), *Rousseau After 200 Years*. Cambridge: Cambridge University Press, 1982.

Leigh, R.A., *Unsolved Problems in the Bibliography of J.-J. Rousseau*. Cambridge: Cambridge University Press, 1990.

Levine, Andrew, *The Politics of Autonomy*. Amhurst, MA: University of Massachusetts Press, 1976.

Locke, John, *Some Thoughts Concerning Education*, eds. J.W. Yolton and J.S. Yolton. Oxford: Clarendon Press, 1989 (1695).

Lovejoy, A.O., 'Rousseau's Supposed Primitivism' in A.O. Lovejoy, *Essays on the History of Ideas*. Baltimore, MD: Johns Hopkins Press, 1948.

Martin, Kingsley, *French Liberal Thought in the Eighteenth Century*. London: Phoenix House, 1962.

Masters, R.D., *The Political Philosophy of Rousseau*. Princeton: Princeton University Press, 1968.

McDonald, Joan, *Rousseau and the French Revolution 1762–1791*. London: Athlone Press, 1965.

McFarland, Thomas, *Romanticism and the Heritage of Rousseau*. Oxford: Clarendon Press, 1995.

Melzer, A.M., *The Natural Goodness of Man*. Chicago: University of Chicago Press, 1990.

Miller, James, *Rousseau: Dreamer of Democracy*. New Haven, CT: Yale University Press, 1884.

Morgenstern, Mira, *Rousseau and the Politics of Ambiguity: Self, Culture, and Society*. University Park, PA: Pennsylvania State University Press, 1996.

Noone, J.B., *Rousseau's Social Contract*. London: Prior, 1980.

O'Hagan, Timothy (ed.), *Jean-Jacques Rousseau and the Sources of the Self*. Aldershot: Avebury, 1997.

O'Hagan, Timothy, *Rousseau*. London: Routledge, 1999.

Okin, S.M., *Women in Western Political Thought*. London: Virago, 1980.

Orwin, C. and Tarcov, N. (eds.), *The Legacy of Rousseau*. Chicago: University of Chicago Press, 1997.

Paton, H.J., *The Moral Law*, translation of I. Kant: *Groundwork of the Metaphysic of Morals*. London: Hutchinson, 1961.

Plattner, Marc, *Rousseau's State of Nature: An Interpretation of the Discourse on Inequality*. DeKalb, IL: Northern Illinois University Press, 1997.

Polin, R., *La Politique de la Solitude*: Paris, Sirey, 1971.

Porter, Roy, *Enlightenment*. London, Penguin, 2001.

Rawls, John, *A Theory of Justice*. Oxford: Oxford University Press, 1972.

Riley, Patrick, *The General Will before Rousseau*. Princeton: Princeton University Press, 1986.

Riley, Patrick (ed.), *The Cambridge Companion to Rousseau*. Cambridge: Cambridge University Press, 2001.

Roche, Kennedy F., *Rousseau: Stoic and Romantic*. London: Methuen, 1974.

Roosevelt, Grace G., *Reading Rousseau in the Nuclear Age*. Philadelphia: Temple University Press, 1990.

Rosenblatt, Helena, *Rousseau and Geneva*. Cambridge: Cambridge University Press, 1997.

Schopenhauer, A., *On the Basis of Morality*, tr. E.F.J. Payne. Indianapolis, IN: Library of Liberal Arts, 1965 (1841).

Schwartz, Joel, *The Sexual Politics of Jean-Jacques Rousseau*. Chicago: University of Chicago Press, 1984.

Sennett, Richard, *Respect: The Formation of Character in an Age of Inequality*. London: Allen Lane, 2003.

Shklar, Judith N., *Men and Citizens: A Study of Rousseau's Social Theory*. Cambridge: Cambridge University Press, 1985 (1969).

Starobinski, Jean, *Jean-Jacques Rousseau: Transparency and Obstruction*, tr. A. Goldhammer. Chicago: University of Chicago Press, 1988 (1971).

Strong, Tracy B., *Jean-Jacques Rousseau: The Politics of the Ordinary*, Thousand Oaks, CA: Sage, 1994.

Talmon, J.L., *The Origins of Totalitarian Democracy*. Harmondsworth: Penguin, 1986 (1952).

Taylor, S.S.B., 'Rousseau's Romanticism' in S. Harvey et al. (eds.), *Reappraisals of Rousseau*. Manchester: Manchester University Press, 1980.

Trachtenberg, Zev M., *Making Citizens: Rousseau's Political Theory of Culture*. London: Routledge, 1993.

Viroli, Maurizio, *Jean-Jacques Rousseau and the 'Well-Ordered Society'*, tr. D. Hanson. Cambridge: Cambridge University Press, 1988.

Waltz, Kenneth N., *Man, the State and War*. New York: Columbia University Press, 2001 (1959).

Williams, Huntington, *Rousseau and Romantic Autobiography*. Oxford: Oxford University Press, 1983.

Wokler, Robert, 'The *Discours sur les sciences et les arts*, and its offspring: Rousseau in reply to his critics', in S. Harvey et al. (eds.), *Reappraisals of Rousseau*. Manchester: Manchester University Press, 1980.

—— 'Rousseau and Marx' in D. Miller and L. Siedentop (eds.), *The Nature of Political Theory*. Oxford: Clarendon Press, 1983.

—— *Rousseau on Society, Politics, Music and Language: An Historical Interpretation of his Early Writings*. New York: Garland, 1987.

—— *Rousseau – A Very Short Introduction*. Oxford: Oxford University Press, 2001.

Wokler, Robert (ed.), *Rousseau and Liberty*. Manchester: Manchester University Press, 1995.

Wright, E.H., *The Meaning of Rousseau*. London: Oxford University Press, 1929.

Understanding the Political Philosophers
From Ancient to Modern Times

Alan Howarth, London Metropolitan University, UK

'I would certainly recommend this as a first political philosophy book to any student and, indeed, as a refreshingly unpretentious read for a wider audience.'

– Tim Hayward, Times Higher Educational Supplement

234x156: 320pp
Hb: 0-415-27590-3
Pb: 0-415-27591-1

Feminism and Modern Philosophy

Andrea Nye, University of Wisconsin, USA

Feminism and Modern Philosophy introduces students to the main thinkers and themes of modern philosophy from different feminist perspectives, and highlights the role of gender in studying classic philosophical texts. It reveals new insights into the lives and works of major figures such as Jean-Jacques Rousseau and David Hume, and is crucial to an appreciation of the advent of feminist philosophy.

234x156: 168pp
Hb: 0-415-26654-8
Pb: 0-415-26655-6

Routledge Philosophy GuideBook to Rousseau and the *Social Contract*

Christopher Bertram, University of Bristol, UK

Rousseau and the Social Contract introduces and assesses:

- Rousseau's life and the background of the *Social Contract*
- The ideas and arguments of the *Social Contract*
- Rousseau's continuing importance to politics and philosophy

198x129: 224pp
Hb: 0-415-20198-5
Pb: 0-415-20199-3

Political Philosophy

Dudley Knowles, University of Glasgow, UK

'Throughout there is a masterly grasp of common-sense moral and political thinking which is never at the mercy of the wide range of approaches presented, and never falls into unnecessary abstraction which makes the book a firmly reliable source for undergraduate understanding of the subject.'
– *Philosophical Books*

216x138: 408pp
Hb: 1-85728-760-6
Pb: 1-85728-550-6